Storytelling for l

STORYTELLING FOR LAWYERS

PHILIP N. MEYER

OXFORD
UNIVERSITY PRESS

OXFORD
UNIVERSITY PRESS

Oxford University Press is a department of the University of Oxford.
It furthers the University's objective of excellence in research, scholarship,
and education by publishing worldwide.

Oxford   New York
Auckland   Cape Town   Dar es Salaam   Hong Kong   Karachi
Kuala Lumpur   Madrid   Melbourne   Mexico City   Nairobi
New Delhi   Shanghai   Taipei   Toronto

With offices in
Argentina   Austria   Brazil   Chile   Czech Republic   France   Greece
Guatemala   Hungary   Italy   Japan   Poland   Portugal   Singapore
South Korea   Switzerland   Thailand   Turkey   Ukraine   Vietnam

Oxford is a registered trademark of Oxford University Press
in the UK and certain other countries.

Published in the United States of America by
Oxford University Press
198 Madison Avenue, New York, NY 10016

CIP data is on file at the Library of Congress.

ISBN 978-0-19-539663-8 (paperback)
ISBN 978-0-19-539662-1 (hardback)

10
Printed in Canada

For Anthony G. Amsterdam,
with gratitude and admiration.

For my family, with love.

Contents

Acknowledgment

FROM 2003 THROUGH 2008 I collaborated with Anthony G. Amsterdam preparing instructional materials for the Narrative Persuasion Institute. In this book I draw on these materials. I am grateful to Tony for his encouragement and support enabling me to write this book.

Storytelling for Lawyers

I

Introduction

Somewhere along the way one discovers that what one has to tell is not nearly so telling as the telling itself.

—HENRY MILLER, "REFLECTIONS ON WRITING," in THE WISDOM OF THE HEART

A good story and a well-formed argument are different natural kinds.... It has been claimed that one is a refinement or abstraction from the other. But this must be either false or true in only the most unenlightening way. They function differently... and the structure of a well-formed logical argument differs radically from that of a well-wrought story.

—JEROME BRUNER, ACTUAL MINDS, POSSIBLE WORLDS

I. Lawyers Are Storytellers

Some years ago I practiced law. Most of my time was spent telling stories. I spoke to insurance adjusters and parole officers, to attorneys representing clients with adversarial interests, to government bureaucrats. And of course, I told stories in court. Typically, I told simple plot-driven, fact-based narratives. Of course, I tried to make my stories factually meticulous and accurate. But I constantly ordered and reordered events as I reconstructed the past to serve my clients' purposes. Usually, I depicted my clients sympathetically, even when I did not believe this was their true "character." When it served my purposes, I made the plots of my stories vivid and compelling. Sometimes, however, I flattened or obscured events, or sped up narrative time, or softened reality with intentional shifts from one genre into another. Other times, I slowed down time, focused on specific sequences of crucial images, or employed forms that heightened the impact of a story.

I learned to watch and listen to how my audience listened to me, and I would respond to their concerns, reshaping my stories to fit the shape of their imaginings. I recall the novelist John Irving instructing students at the Iowa Writers' Workshop that effective storytelling requires "ruthlessness" and commitment to constructing a coherent and seamless world. It is apparent to me that successful lawyers are at ease with their storytelling roles of depicting "The World According To" in the battle of competing stories inside and outside the courtroom. And I now believe that many of the lessons I learned from creative writers of fiction and nonfiction are as important to successful law practice as any doctrine.

Make no mistake about it—lawyers are storytellers. It is how we make our livings. In law practice effective storytelling is often outcome-determinative; sometimes it is literally a matter of life or death. Of course, storytelling practice in law is also unlike the work of other popular storytellers. Lawyers are ethical and truthful storytellers; imagination is informed, shaped, and limited by evidence. The lawyers' voice and persona are different; the rules of, and constraints upon, formal legal storytelling are explicit and unlike those of other popular storytellers. Further, lawyers often do not tell complete stories, typically leaving it to others (judges, juries, decision makers) to complete the tales and inscribe codas of meaning. Nevertheless, as lawyers we have much to learn from studying the craft of storytelling and applying these lessons to our legal practice. As professional storytellers we can do our jobs better the more consciously we deploy the tools of the storyteller's craft.

II. Legal Arguments Are Stories in Disguise

All arguments, at any level or in any type of practice, are built upon arrangements of the facts of a particular case. These facts are shaped into stories carefully fitted with legal rules and precedent. It is impossible to make *any* legal argument without telling *some* stories about the facts and about the law.

Unlike an analytical argument, the structure and internal components of a "story" are never pointed out or made explicit to a listener or reader. The "verisimilitude"—or lifelikeness—crucial to effective storytelling demands that the audience not be distracted by, or even be aware of, the technical craft that shapes the material, lest the storyteller risk breaking the story's "spell" over its audience.

Nevertheless, as storytellers have understood for millennia, there *is* a powerful and well-defined narrative architecture or structure in stories. There are clear principles that inform storytelling practice. This is no less true for the types of stories that lawyers tell. As Henry Miller observes, and as any effective litigation attorney knows, the truth of a story is in its telling. Likewise, a story's form is inseparable from its content; the two are inextricable.

But how does a lawyer tell a "good"—effective, purposeful and persuasive, compelling and factually meticulous, and truthful—story? What theory, techniques, and craft are helpful to legal storytellers? What, for example, are the components of an effective plot? How does a story turn on a narrative theme, and how does a theme inform a litigator's theory of the case? What are the commonly recurring plots (the stock stories) employed in various types of law practice? What are relevant genres? Who are the characters in legal stories? How are these characters cast into specific roles? And how is character best depicted and developed? What is narrative time and how is it artfully and strategically employed and manipulated? Why does setting matter profoundly in some types of legal storytelling and not at all in others? What stylistic lessons might lawyers learn from other masterful popular storytellers, including novelists, journalists, and moviemakers?

Unfortunately, the standard law school curriculum directs little, if any, systematic attention to developing storytelling skills; indeed, doctrinal legal education devalues the complex stories at the heart of the law and the storytelling skills crucial for practice. Perhaps, in part, this is based on a shared misbelief that these skills are intuitive or cannot be taught. Perhaps, in part, it is believed that lawyers learn about storytelling through their practices simply because we do so much of it.

Strangely, in a profession where storytelling skills matter profoundly, lawyers typically do their work without ever reflecting systematically on the nature of their craft. It is the simple premise of this book that lawyers, law students, and academic generalists may benefit from this exploration. This book provides a guide for the journey. It is not, however, a storytelling cookbook; there are no easy-to-follow recipes for effective legal storytelling. Instead, the text identifies and foregrounds the components of a story and visits principles of storytelling craft useful to lawyers.

III. The Parts of a Story

Although there are no simple recipes or paint-by-the-numbers formulae for effective storytelling, there are discrete elements or components of all stories. For example, journalists learn to address the Five Ws in constructing stories: Where? Who? What? When? Why?

Narrative theorists have devoted entire academic careers to distilling and separating the components or dimensions of a story and comprehending their interrelationships—how these components fit together seamlessly, and how adjusting or fine-tuning one aspect of a story inevitably affects all other aspects as well. One of the most distinguished theorists, Kenneth Burke, formulated the "Pentad"—a five-part analysis of the human drama as it is reconfigured in narrative (or story). Tracking the journalist's Five Ws, Burke identified "Five Key Terms of Dramatism."[1]

My colleague Anthony Amsterdam, in turn, reformulated Burke's Pentad as a tool relevant to formulating and constructing legal stories, as follows:

1. Scene
2. Cast and Character
3. Plot
4. Time Frame
5. Human Plight

This roster also identifies the primary divisions of this book. Of course, these components are twisted together and interlocking, the DNA of a story that reveals the nature of the story and of the world itself. Nevertheless, it is useful to canvass these components individually throughout the process of constructing a story.

This book begins with the component of plot because it is typically the most important component of legal stories. Legal stories, especially in litigation, are plot-driven and protagonist-centered stories. Other aspects of the story take a backseat to plotting. The second and third chapters of the book focus on plotting and provide close analysis of a plot-driven legal story as a primary illustration: Gerry Spence's closing argument at trial on behalf of plaintiff Karen Silkwood. Chapters 4 and 5 are about character construction in legal storytelling practice. The legal story analyzed as a primary example here is Jeremiah P. Donovan's remarkably engaging and theatrical "character-based" closing argument on behalf of the reputed mobster Louis "Louie" Failla. This legal story is a complex and subtle tragicomedy; at the core is Donovan's depiction and development of Failla's complex character. Chapter 6 addresses the importance of discrete and selected aspects of the stylistic component of legal storytelling including voice, perspective, rhythms of language, and use of scenes and summaries. Chapter 7 explores the creation and depiction of the settings and stages on which legal stories unfold; it examines how the scope and boundaries of the "world of the story" are, in many cases, strategically crucial to legal storytelling. Finally, chapter 8 focuses on the topic of narrative time and how the inexorable progression of linear and forward-moving time is inevitably reshaped and transformed in a story. Although narrative time appears to mimic real time, it seldom, if ever, does so.

IV. Movies and Closing Arguments

Many of the popular culture examples of stories employed in this book are drawn from movies. This may be, partially, because in my day job, in addition to teaching traditional doctrinal subjects (criminal law and torts), I teach law and film and law and popular culture, and have written extensively about these subjects. Consequently, I turn instinctively to popular film for illustrations of stories relevant to lawyers, even though many of these films are not about legal subjects.

Furthermore, in our predominantly visual popular culture, movies are typically more familiar than literature. Teaching law students and practitioners over the past twenty years, I have discovered a heightened visual literacy exists in our media-obsessed popular culture. But the reasons for choosing these visual texts as primary examples in this book are deeper.

First, the stories that lawyers tell, especially trial stories, exist within a wide range of popular storytelling practices. Advertising, popular songs, television programming, YouTube videos, novels, memoirs, and creative nonfiction influence and, in turn are influenced by, other popular stories and storytelling practices. The stories and storytelling practices that are most influential upon legal storytellers are visual storytelling practices, especially those in the cinema, and especially the linear, protagonist-centered, theme-based, hard reductionist stories of Hollywood entertainment films. These stories influence and inform courtroom storytelling including the substance, style, structure, and content of trial work. In many ways, the trial practitioner intuitively draws upon the content and form of popular film to connect with his audience, just as moviemakers draw upon the drama of the law, the theme and value of justice, and the subject of the trial in so many recent popular movies.

Second, the work and professional role of the trial lawyer is specifically akin to that of the movie director. Effective litigators, like Hollywood directors and screenwriters, typically storyboard evidence into clear and purposeful plots. Experienced trial lawyers, like Gerry Spence and Jeremiah P. Donovan, whose closing arguments are analyzed in this book, are especially adept at converting evidence introduced at trial into well-shaped and carefully constructed stories. The narrative story structure frames how jurors process and interpret evidence and provides the basis for juror deliberations and verdicts. Jurors passively watch and witness the drama of the trial as it unfolds in the courtroom theater, almost as if sitting in the darkness at the movies; their attention, expectations, and story consciousness are often shaped and prefigured by Hollywood cine-myths.

Finally, the nature of the trial itself is changing rapidly. Many of these changes are caused by the use of new technologies, especially aural and visual "paratexts" at trials, including computer simulations, visual aids, video and audio evidence, and other often professionally produced storytelling enhancements and devices. The impact of this technology is profound and often transformative. There has been a reinvention of the ways stories are told, and this affects the stories themselves. As in Spence's and Donovan's closing arguments, evidence is often presented orally or visually. These are present-tense voices and images, rather than past-tense testimonial evidence. Like a director in the movies, the artful legal storyteller weaves together these materials; in this weaving, there is often a radical reinvention in the content and form of trial storytelling. Additionally, lawyers' work is the subject of numerous television programs and films.

As a result of these changes in courtroom storytelling practices, and in jurors' expectations about lawyers and legal storytelling, a phenomenon has emerged: jurors seem to make sense out of evidence in deliberations by referring to other imagistic stories, primarily drawn from television and popular entertainment films. No longer does popular culture merely present images of the law; popular culture embodies and creates the law.

Sophisticated and shrewd trial lawyers—like Spence and Donovan—are aware of the interpenetration of law practice and popular culture. As a result, stories told at trial and in oral argument—like Spence's civil closing argument on behalf of Karen Silkwood, or Donovan's closing argument on behalf of the criminal defendant Louie Failla—are, curiously, a form of entertainment. Stories are packaged in theories and imaginative forms that capture the imagination of jurors and embody other popular stories, often borrowed from the plots of Hollywood movies.

Storytelling for Lawyers uses movies as examples of compelling popular stories, employs narrative theory to understand how these stories are artfully constructed, and maps insights from analyses onto the domain of legal stories, including the masterful closing arguments by Spence and Donovan. It is my intention that this book may provide a narrative primer and suggest a model for strategies that will assist lawyers in developing their own legal storytelling practices.

2

Plotting I

THE BASICS

[Plot is] the intelligible whole that governs a succession of events in any story.... A story is made out of events to the extent that plot makes the events into a story.
—PAUL RICOEUR, "NARRATIVE TIME"

If you listen to the way people tell stories, you will hear that they tell them cinematically.
—DAVID MAMET, ON DIRECTING FILM

If you're ever in doubt about how to end your story, think in terms of an "up" ending. There are better ways to end your screenplay than have your character caught, shot, captured, die, or be murdered.
—SYD FIELD, SCREENPLAY: THE FOUNDATIONS OF SCREENWRITING

I. What Is Plot?

Peter Brooks, a leading American narrative theorist, tells an anecdote about a brilliant graduate student in his advanced narrative theory seminar. According to Brooks, this young woman was so imbued with narrative prescience that she could accurately predict the plot trajectories of novels, anticipating the endings, by a close reading of the opening pages. That is, she could decode the plot structure embedded within the story from the outset of the telling. The point of the anecdote is that, as Michael Roemer suggests, stories are already over before they begin and, especially in law, are written to justify a predetermined or desired outcome.

I have had similar experiences while teaching torts and criminal law courses. First-year law students in torts and criminal law inevitably observe that they can predict the outcome of a case by a close reading of the beginning of the opinion where the court tells the factual story framing the legal analysis that follows.

Here, for example, are the opening paragraphs from *Coblyn v. Kennedy*,[1] an intentional torts case taught early in the first semester. There are two related legal issues in the case. The first issue is whether, as a matter of law, the plaintiff can recover for the tort of false imprisonment. The story the court tells, like most judicial storytelling, is designed to appear plotless, merely a chronology or recitation of the facts determined at trial. The story is told exclusively from the perspective of the plaintiff. The court frames the plot narrowly to fit the legal issue: defendant contends that, as a matter of law, "no unlawful restraint [was] imposed by force or threat upon the plaintiff's freedom of movement." The court retells this portion of the story and embeds a plot within its telling:

> We state the pertinent evidence most favorable to the plaintiff. On March 5, 1965, the plaintiff went to Kennedy's, Inc. (Kennedy's), a store in Boston. He was seventy years of age and about five feet four inches in height. He was wearing a woolen shirt, which was "open at the neck," a topcoat and a hat. "Around his neck" he wore an ascot which he had "purchased previously at Filenes." He proceeded to the second floor of Kennedy's to purchase a sport coat. He removed his hat, topcoat and ascot, putting the ascot in his pocket. After purchasing a sport coat and leaving it for alterations, he put on his hat and coat and walked downstairs. Just prior to exiting through the outside door of the store, he stopped, took the ascot out of his pocket, put it around his neck, and knotted it. The knot was visible "above the lapels of his shirt." The only stop that the plaintiff made on the first floor was immediately in front of the exit in order to put on his ascot.
>
> Just as the plaintiff stepped out of the door, the defendant Goss, an employee, "loomed up" in front of him with his hand up and said: "Stop. Where did you get that scarf?" The plaintiff responded, "Why?" Goss firmly grasped the plaintiff's arm and said: "You better go back and see the manager." Another employee was standing next to

him. Eight or ten other people were standing around and were staring at the plaintiff. The plaintiff then said, "Yes, I'll go back in the store" and proceeded to do so. As he and Goss went upstairs to the second floor, the plaintiff paused twice because of chest and back pains. After reaching the second floor, the salesman from whom he had purchased the coat recognized him and asked what the trouble was. The plaintiff then asked: "Why [did] these two gentlemen stop me?" The salesman confirmed that the plaintiff had purchased a sport coat and that the ascot belonged to him.[2]

The salesman became alarmed by the plaintiff's appearance and the store nurse was called. She brought the plaintiff into the nurse's room and gave him a soda mint tablet. As a direct result of the emotional upset caused by the incident, the plaintiff was hospitalized and treated for a "myocardial infarct."

There is a second legal issue analyzed in the opinion: whether plaintiff's detention was permissible under a statute that permits the store owner to detain a customer who is suspected of shoplifting for a reasonable time, and in a reasonable manner, provided there are reasonable grounds for the detention. The court, however, chooses strategically not to tell this part of the story; it concludes that it does not have to do so because, based on its initial telling of the story, there were "no reasonable grounds for believing that the plaintiff was committing larceny and, therefore, he should not have been detained at all."[3] It adds that the "physical restraint in a public place imposed upon the plaintiff, an elderly man, who had exhibited no aggressive intention to depart, could be said to constitute an unreasonable method by which to effect a detention."[4] Then the court analyzes the law of reasonable suspicion at some length and finally, in my opinion, does the right thing by providing a just and correct legal outcome, affirming the verdict of the trial court for the plaintiff.

My point is twofold: first, my first-semester students, not yet jaded by law school, are correct when they say that they can predict the outcome from reading the initial summary of the facts. Like Brooks's prescient graduate student, the students intuitively realize that the opening or beginning of the opinion determines the trajectory of the plot for both the factual and legal stories that follow. It also anticipates the ending and outcome of the case. Second, even where the legal storyteller is an appellate judge who is purportedly retelling a story "objectively," merely presenting the facts in a simple linear chronology, she inevitably constructs the trajectory of a purposeful plot to reach a predetermined outcome. In doing so, the judge affirms the value of justice, inscribing legal meaning upon the case and providing closure to the story.

Plotting is important in all legal storytelling. It is crucial in legal advocacy that can best be understood as the battle of competing stories in the courtroom. But what concepts or applied narrative theory might be useful as tools for reflective lawyer-storytellers engaged in this battle?

A. Basic Terms and Concepts

1. What Is Plot?

Law stories, like all stories, are the creations of an unseen intelligence that selects, shapes, and transforms raw material into *events* and then arranges these events into the ordered *sequence* of a story. This sequence of events, or plot, provides meaning to the human affairs depicted in the story.

These events do not come ready-made like prenumbered pieces or the links to be inserted into a preconfigured chain. The nature of the plot itself determines what kind of actions can serve as events in the story and enter the plot itself. Events that fit one plot will not fit another and must be excluded. This relationship creates a curious dynamic—the plot controls events but, in turn, is shaped by the events it controls. The meaning of the whole is always a product of the parts yet, simultaneously, the parts derive their meaning from the whole. The plot and event create one another; there is a symbiotic interdependency between the two. This relationship may seem circular or even obscure, and more will be said about it throughout this book. For now, I observe that:

- Only some kind of events fit into any particular type of plot; and
- When the story begins, the reader must be clued into what type of story it is going to be.

2. Narrative Profluence and Causation

"The king died and then the queen died" is merely a chronological listing of two unrelated occurrences. But add a mere two words: "the king died and then the queen died *of grief.*" These two events are not yet a plot, but the events are pushed together and connected. The reader or listener is drawn into what is—apparently—the beginning of a story. The audience (listener or reader) attempts to put one and one together and may speculate how the king died or whether the queen's love of the king caused her to take her own life. How can a mere two words accomplish so much? It is because these two words attach the events causally and establish a forward movement or narrative propulsion, without providing a complete explanation of the relationship between events. Thus, the audience must fill in the gap and determine the causal relationship, and to do so compels asking, "What happens next?"

In film, and also in the artful cinematic storytelling practices of contemporary legal storytellers, the events and the interconnections between events are often not fully described or made explicit. Instead, events are depicted in scenes that are placed into sequences. This montage artfully suggests the movement of a profluent plot.

Profluence is the purposeful forward movement between the events in the plot of a story. Teachers of creative writing, including the novelist John Gardner, observe that the profluence in a plot provides a forward narrative momentum that is much more than mere inertia.

Plots in law stories, strongly akin to popular commercial entertainment films, have clear narrative trajectories and dynamic internal movement. The audience for legal stories—especially those told by advocates in litigation, whether to a jury or a skeptical trial or appellate judge—is seldom an especially tolerant or patient audience. As a result, the plots of stories told in courtrooms and in legal briefs are typically straightforward and often compressed, more akin to the narrative structure of popular films than to that of literary novels. Legal stories are built upon strongly profluent plots.

3. Story Logic

Peter Brooks, the narrative theorist, makes the useful observation that the dictionary definitions of the various meanings of "plot" share a conceptual sense of restraint and closed-ended shape. Consider these definitions:

1. A small piece or measured area of land;
2. A ground plan or diagram;
3. A series of events outlining the action of a narrative or drama; and
4. A clandestine plan or scheme.

Each of these alternatives is characterized by "the idea of boundedness, demarcation, the drawing of lines to mark off and order."[5] Inherently, there are parameters and constraints shaping the plot and compelling the outcome of a complex story. One obvious constraint on the trajectory of the plot of any well-wrought story, especially the plot of a legal story, is the ending—the point of the story—which gives the story closure and meaning. *Story logic* has to do with the fitness of outcomes. From the very first word in a story, or image in a movie, every movement of plot works in anticipation of its ending. This is why, as a practical matter, storytellers are often taught to know their ending and to structure the plot by working backward from the ending and desired outcome.

The sequence of events, especially the final ending and resolution of the plot, provides *meaning to the human affairs* depicted in the story. Put another way, a plot makes the whole of the story much greater than the sum of its parts, supplying a trajectory and implying a reason for its telling. The plot builds upon early events and heads toward some culmination—an ending that events anticipate. In this movement, the storyteller makes an implicit promise that the plot will reveal meaning and an understanding of the human affairs within the story.

B. An "Austere" Definition of Plot

From a young age, children are taught that every story needs a beginning, a middle, and an end. David Lodge economically defines these terms: "a beginning is what requires nothing to precede it, and an end is what requires nothing to follow it, and a middle needs something both before and after it."[6] Anthony G. Amsterdam and Jerome Bruner provide a richer definition, a unitary framework that applies to legal storytelling:

The unfolding of the plot requires (implicitly or explicitly):

1) an initial *steady state* grounded in the legitimate ordinariness of things,
2) that gets disrupted by a *trouble* consisting of circumstances attributable to human agency or susceptible to change by human intervention,
3) in turn evoking *efforts* at redress or transformation, which succeed or fail,
4) so that the old steady state is *restored* or a new (*transformed*) steady state is created,
5) and the story concludes by drawing the then-and-there of the tale that has been told into the here-and-now of the telling through some *coda*—say, for example, Aesop's characteristic *moral of the story.*

That is the bare bones of it.[7]

Here, it is instructive to apply this definition to better understand the movement (the narrative "profluence") in the plot of a one-paragraph short story by Leonard Michaels as analyzed by David Lodge:

> The Hand
> I smacked my little boy. My anger was powerful. Like justice. Then I discovered no feeling in my hand. I said, "Listen, I want to explain the complexities to you." I spoke with seriousness and care, particularly of fathers. He asked, when I finished, if I wanted him to forgive me. I said yes. He said no. Like trumps.[8]

"The Hand" is a short and self-contained story, yet the plot is rich and complex. *The Hand*'s "power-to-weight ratio" is high, and there is no excess in the story (it is a narrative koan of sorts).

Confidently anticipating the modern reader's awareness of plot structure, Michaels creates a profluent plot; the story provides a subtle and complex meaning to the human affairs depicted within it, and the ending is more than merely a termination point or cessation of activities. Michaels achieves this effect by trusting that the reader will read the words slowly and carefully, grafting them onto an internal narrative framing (along the lines of the plot structure that Amsterdam and Bruner describe) that enables the reader to fill in any gaps in the narrative logic with meaning.

An initial steady state grounded in the legitimate ordinariness of things.

What is the *initial steady state* in "The Hand?" It is implicit. It is in the order of a presumed domestic tranquility that precedes the commencement of the action. It is, for this reader, a framing image of a family where, presumably, the father has power and authority and the atmosphere is one of domestic order. The reader constructs for herself the *anterior steady state:* the "calm before the storm."

That gets disrupted by trouble consisting of circumstances attributable to human agency or susceptible to change by human intervention.

The *trouble* arrives in the very first sentence when the narrator smacks his little boy. The trouble here is clearly attributable to the *human agency*—the actions and will—of the father. The rhetorical point of the story is to explore whether the course of *events* will be *susceptible to change by human intervention*; that is, whether the father can do anything about it once he has struck his little boy or whether the forces that he unleashes are beyond his control.

Trouble (or *conflict*) often takes many forms depending, in part, on the story's *genre*. The trouble may be external—the villain in black in a melodrama—or it may be internal—a flaw within the character of the protagonist that calls forth her fate from within a tragedy. In my reading, the trouble in "The Hand" is both internal (within the narrator) and external (the actions of "the hand" are, simultaneously, beyond the control of the narrator-protagonist). The narrator then attempts to describe (if not understand) his emotional state and identify the nature of the trouble: "My anger was powerful. Like justice."

In turn evoking efforts at redress or transformation, which succeed or fail.

The plot moves into the second part of the story. There is a deepening *conflict*: the tension between father and son intensifies within the father when he struggles with "the hand." The father now discovers that he has "no feeling" in his hand. Lodge observes that the hand is "both a synecdoche and metaphor for the 'unfeeling' parent."[9]

Here, the first-person narrator *evokes efforts at redress*, struggling to return to the initial (anterior) *steady state* while the son and, perhaps the autonomous "hand," push the narrative toward a transformative ending.

"Listen, I want to explain the complexities to you," the father says, apparently to the son. Lodge notes Michaels's selection of the adult word "complexities" and how the father speaks with "seriousness and care, particularly of fathers."[10] There is an irony in the father's choice of adult words, especially since he has "no feeling" in the hand that seems to operate independently of his own free will.

But it is the son, seemingly, who better grasps the situation and asks, after the father finishes speaking, "if I wanted him to forgive me." Thus, the son attempts a reversal,[11] struggling to establish a *transformed steady state* embodied in a redistribution of power between the father and son.

So that the old steady state is restored or a new (transformed) steady state is created.

And then there is the *climax*: "I said yes. He said no." There is no clear return to the "anterior" steady state of the prior relationship between father and son. Nor is there progression toward a new (*transformed*) steady state. Instead, there is an uncomfortable disequilibrium. Michaels plays against the reader's expectations of how the climax typically resolves narrative movement in a profluent plot: the situation is left "up in the air."

> *And the story concludes by drawing the then-and-there of the tale that has been told into the here-and-now of the telling through some coda—say, for example, Aesop's characteristic moral of the story.*

The coda acknowledges the situation at the end of the story, as the father stands in a curious external relationship with his son, and in his interior struggle with "the hand" as well; both are captured in a two-word observation borrowed from a card game signifying the particular characteristics of the standoff: "like trumps."

And, as Amsterdam and Bruner observe, "that is the bare bones of it."[12]

C. Theme and Theory of the Case

The next building block in plot construction (and, simultaneously, a primary constraint upon plot construction) is the narrative theme. Simply put, the theme is the controlling idea or core insight of a story. It is the fundamental understanding or "truth" about the meaning of the human affairs that the story's carefully sequenced events convey. As John Gardner observes, "theme…is not imposed on the story but evoked from within it—initially an intuitive but finally an intellectual act on the part of the writer."[13] Plots are shaped around core narrative themes that, in turn, determine the functional choices the storyteller makes in selecting, shaping, and sequencing the events into a story.

The dictionary first defines theme as "a subject on which a person speaks, writes, or thinks; a topic of discussion or composition."[14] It is reminiscent of the composition teacher asking her student to reduce an essay to a single clarifying phrase that articulates the subject. There is a second dictionary definition: a theme is "a subject which provokes a person to act; a cause *of* or *for* action or feeling."[15] This gets more to the bottom of it; this definition moves toward describing the interior dimensions of a narrative *theme* and how it works on the listener or reader. The theme provides a unique and unstated quality that sparks in the audience a sense that the story will develop in a certain way. The telling confirms that the movements of plot follow a thematic spine so that the sequence of events conveys a purposeful manifestation of this theme. May there be more than one theme in a story? Yes. How many? It depends on the genre of the story and the internal story logic. Legal stories, too, may have multiple narrative themes, though typically there are seldom more than two. And, perhaps at least in this way, compressed law stories are more akin structurally to popular entertainment films than to novels, which often develop multiple themes simultaneously.[16]

Finally, there is a third dictionary definition of theme: "the principal melody or plainsong in a contrapuntal piece; a prominent or frequently recurring melody or a group of notes in a composition."[17] That is, the story theme announces itself over and over; it is often strongly intimated, although it is seldom, if ever, explicit. In movies, the visual imagery and the music (including the lyrics within the music) suggest the theme by incorporating a "recurring melody." Recurring visual images and shots of settings further suggest the *thematic* core of the story. Although there is seldom visual imagery or literal "music" in law stories (certainly not in legal briefs and seldom at trial or in oral trial or appellate arguments), nevertheless, effective lawyers display the theme by using certain readily identifiable recurring techniques in both their literal voice (in speech) and their stylistic voice in writing.

While the theme is seldom made explicit, and only gradually dawns on the audience over time, the effective legal storyteller is always aware of the theme. As John Gardner advises young storytellers, the (legal) storyteller "sharpens and clarifies his ideas, or finds out exactly what it is that he must say, testing his beliefs against reality as the story represents it, by examining every element of the story for its possible implications with regard to his theme."[18]

Narrative theme is distinct from, yet related to, the litigator's concept of the *theory of the case*. The core distinction is, perhaps, that in the theory of the case facts are structured to fit and match the elements of legal rules; the facts are presented in such a way that they invoke specifically (rather than evoke metaphorically) the normative principles and legal rules on which the litigator must rely to win. The issue-focused theory of the case identifies crucial and disputable factual propositions that the trier of fact must find to be true or untrue. These propositions determine whether each element of the legal rule is established, and ultimately whether the attorney's client will leave the courtroom satisfied or disappointed. To fit the legal theory of the case, the attorney whittles the facts down to essentials, pulls them apart, and makes them subservient to the overriding legal principles and explicit elements of legal rules. The theory of the case is always explicit; the narrative theme is seldom, if ever, explicit.

Take, as a brief example, Johnnie Cochran's storytelling in the O. J. Simpson closing argument. His theory of the case is simple: incompetent and corrupt police investigators botched the investigation and, perhaps, planted evidence at the crime scene to convict Simpson. The state's evidence simply does not prove Simpson's guilt beyond a reasonable doubt; thus, Simpson cannot be convicted of murder.

Cochran's successful story is, as is often the case in criminal trials and criminal appellate briefs, based on the narrative theme of betrayal by all-powerful state actors. Simpson has been betrayed by the system, by corrupt police investigators, by a "rush to judgment" as to Simpson's guilt, and by a racist police department that must be stopped by the heroic jury. Cochran's argument is ultimately about justice and injustice (e. g., betrayal and tyranny):

> Things happen for a reason in your life. Maybe there is a reason why you were selected. There is something in your character that helps you understand this is wrong. Maybe you are the right people at the right time at the right place to say, "no more, we are not going to have this. ["] What they've done to our client is wrong. O. J. Simpson... is entitled to an acquittal. You can't trust the message.[19]

D. Genre and Melodrama

In a pure legal argument—if, indeed, one exists, as if legal arguments are somehow akin to mathematical formulae or scientific proofs—the specific propositions that lead to a result can supposedly be independently verified, and the structure of the logic is made explicit within the argument itself.

This is not so in plotting a story. Stories do not conform to uniform and explicit externalized rules of narrative logic. But there *are* multiple models and templates of plots embedded in the expectations of the audience. Legal storytellers intuitively and, indeed, often explicitly, draw on these embedded narratives and narrative framing.

For example, the reader's or listener's expectations about what is a proper outcome from action constrain or shape the story. These narrative expectations may, in turn, vary according to the genre of the story, establishing certain expectations that the storyteller then typically may not transgress.

One genre of storytelling that often predominates in litigation is melodrama. Melodrama, as explained by narrative theorists, is not limited to the exaggerations of character and situations depicted in afternoon soap operas or in middle-brow cinematic tearjerkers. It is more broadly yet, simultaneously, more precisely defined by narrative theorists. The influential literary scholar Northrop Frye observes:

> In melodrama two themes are important: the triumph of moral virtue over villainy, and the consequent idealizing of the moral views assumed to be held by the audience. In the melodrama of the brutal thriller we come as close as it is normally possible for art to come to the pure self-righteousness of the lynching mob.[20]

The genre of melodrama presents the battle between good and evil reduced to its simplest form, where the hero-protagonist battles to the death against the swarthy, evil, black-caped villain, the antagonistic force against whom the hero's worth is measured. The pleasures of pure melodrama are equally straightforward: we root for the hero to triumph in the end against the evil villain. But the protagonist-hero must go through much "trouble" and conflict (against internal and external forces antagonistic to his will) in order to prevail if his victory is to have meaning, and for the story to be compelling to its audience. Melodrama is a particularly effective genre for certain types of combative legal storytelling.

For example, plaintiffs' torts cases are typically tried and argued as melodrama; the jury is implored to conceptualize the plaintiff as the hero struggling to overcome the forces of antagonism overwhelmingly aligned against her. Alternatively, the storyteller portrays the plaintiff as the victim who must be redeemed (in a wrongful death case) or rescued (in a personal injury case) by the heroic jury in its verdict against the defendant, sometimes punishing the wrongdoer (with punitive damages) and enabling justice to prevail. Curiously, the most critical character in the melodrama may not always be the hero-protagonist, but rather the villain-antagonist, because it is only against the antagonistic force of the villain that the worth of the hero (both the plaintiff and the jury) is truly measured.

Michael Roemer observes that melodrama "shows us as we are supposed to be and wish to see ourselves"; it "permits us at once to believe in evil and to exorcise it by projecting it onto another—one who is *un*like us: the outsider or stranger."[21] Thus, as Alfred Hitchcock observes, "The more successful the villain, the more powerful the story."[22] Of course, there is much more to it than this, as we will see as we explore this genre.

II. Plot Structure in Two Movies

Now let's apply some of this basic vocabulary to analyzing the plot structure of two popular movies: the classic 1952 Western *High Noon* and a box office blockbuster of the 1970s, Spielberg's *Jaws*. I choose these movies for several reasons: first, I assume that readers are already familiar with these plots, especially the more recent *Jaws*—both are part of our common cultural heritage. Both are melodramas of different sorts that fit under the rubric of this genre. Both plots emphasize the external conflict and the battle between the virtuous and heroic protagonist against an apparent and well-defined villain; we know what the outcome of the battle will be from the beginning, although we do not know, exactly, how the heroic protagonist will accomplish the task, or the strength of the forces of opposition that the hero will encounter and must overcome along the way. Second, these movies are narrative templates in theme and genre for the complex closing arguments by Gerry Spence and Jeremiah Donovan analyzed in subsequent chapters of this book.

Spence converts evidence into a story that is, by design, part monster thriller and part classical Western with a primary theme of heroic salvation of a community in a wild and still lawless western territory on the edge of civilization. Donovan's closing argument is a complex character-based betrayal story, akin to *High Noon*'s secondary theme, about an ambivalent protagonist who struggles against inner demons and internal conflicts, as well as against the will of a powerful and vicious villain.

A. Genre and Theme

Let's begin with *Jaws*. There is nothing subtle or complex about this movie. The genre is pure melodrama. The structural form is provided by a linear, forward-moving narrative that conforms to the viewer's expectations. The antagonist is a readily identifiable and fearful "otherworldly" force that grows progressively more destructive as it tests the mettle of the heroes' strengths, talents, and abilities. Just as in any Marvel Comics fable, epic tale,[23] or legend, the heroes are tested as they take their brave stands to prove themselves, save the community, and show that goodness triumphs over evil. In the struggle of a melodrama like *Jaws*, the heroes are stand-ins for our better selves, and they prove their merit and embody our virtues of strength, courage, honor, and self-sacrifice, put on display in combat.[24]

Jaws also works *intertextually*:[25] its theme interacts with, and is evocative of, other stories in a subgenre already familiar to the viewer: Anglo-American epic sea stories. As Michael Roemer observes, *Jaws* is a "positivist retelling of *Moby Dick*" with its "problem of Ahab and the whale (the idea of an indifferent and malevolent universe)."[26] Spielberg's *Jaws* pares the literary elements (including any thematic complexity and internal conflict within characters) down to the external bones of melodramatic plotting, providing characters with just enough whispers of individuation in the "backstory" to allow the audience to identify with the dedicated and rational scientist, the family man and former tough-guy New York cop, and the "mythic" seafaring captain borrowed from another time. The plot is constructed so that "the evil here is entirely in the monster, and the valiant captain saves his community without having to sacrifice himself."[27]

The theme in *Jaws* is remarkably straightforward. It is about the battle of good against evil, with good ultimately winning out over evil just when the world seems on the edge of destruction. The plot affirms our notions of how the world works,[28] with a proper balance restored by the timely intervention of three self-sacrificing heroes who overcome differences of background and strategy to prevail in the end.

The genre of *High Noon* is the familiar Western, with its characteristic theme being the ravaging of a vulnerable community by evil antagonists. In the Western's familiar *stock story*, the heroic protagonist, who is also often an outsider and drifter himself, comes into the community to stand up against the outlaw bad guys, save the town from anarchy and destruction, and teach the townsfolk the crucial lesson that courage and self-sacrifice are the costs of survival in this dangerous and lawless territory. Screenwriter Carl Foreman and director Fred Zinnemann retain many of the conventions of this Western melodrama genre in *High Noon*, but they intentionally deepen the stock story in many ways, transforming the theme and implicating other genres.

The plot of *High Noon*, like *Jaws*, can be readily boiled down into a few sentences: Marshal Will Kane is retiring and hanging up his guns after marrying his beautiful, young Quaker bride, Amy. He receives word that the villainous outlaw Frank Miller, whom Kane sent away for murder, has been released from prison and is returning on the noon train. Despite the admonitions of the townspeople and the pleas of Amy, Kane decides not to flee but to stand up to Miller and his outlaw band. He is, seemingly, abandoned by all and must stand up against the outlaws alone.

Of course, this plot summary doesn't do justice to the movie. *High Noon* is a subtle and complex story. Unlike *Jaws*, *High Noon* emphasizes character and character development in the complex psychological relationships and struggles of the various characters in anticipation of Frank Miller's arrival. There is the internal psychological struggle within the protagonist, Will Kane, who must choose between fulfilling his manly destiny and duty as gunfighter-marshal and respecting the deeply held pacifist beliefs of his Quaker bride. Kane's internal struggle is further complicated by the intimation that there are nonheroic reasons for fighting Miller's gang: jealousy over the Latina temptress who was the lover of both Kane and Miller, competition between the middle-aged Kane with the younger former deputy to protect his former paramour, and desire to prove his mettle ("a man's gotta do what a man's gotta do").

The other primary characters are equally complex. Kane's pacifist Quaker wife, Amy, and his former mistress are all multilayered, intensely individualized characters, compounded of desires, ideals, loyalties, aspirations, and loathings. The townspeople and other secondary characters (such as the mayor and the young deputy) are vividly portrayed and distinct as well. Only the villainous outlaws have the characteristic simplicity of the melodrama genre. Unlike *Jaws*, where the story is about how the heroes battle against the shark, the plot in *High Noon* focuses on how the complex characters respond internally, and with each other, to the forces of antagonism bearing down upon them.

Thus, the primary themes of *High Noon* are loyalty and betrayal. Under the pressure imposed by the impending arrival of the outlaw gang, characters reveal themselves, are betrayed by one another and the community, and in turn betray themselves. Only at the climax do the principals (Kane, Amy, and Helen Ramirez) seem to redeem their integrity—Kane and Amy by standing up to the outlaw gang to save the community that refuses to save itself, and the Latina temptress by finally leaving Kane and the corrupt town to save herself, not because she is afraid but because she no longer belongs in the community, just as she no longer belongs to Kane.

In *High Noon*, the plot assumes a tragic dimension when, at the coda revealing the meaning of the tale, the hero-protagonist throws down his badge at the feet of the townspeople who have betrayed him, signaling the loss of the value of community and the meaning of law. Kane and Amy leave in disgust, with scorn for the townspeople. Fortunately for the viewer, Kane still has the solace of Amy and maintains his own integrity, as well as the sympathy of the audience.

B. Basic Plot Structure in *High Noon* and *Jaws*
(Applying the Amsterdam-Bruner Model)

An initial steady state grounded in the legitimate ordinariness of things.

Both movies begin with the anticipatory "calm before the storm": the normative "steady state." *Jaws* opens with images of the carefree vacationers frolicking innocently (and vulnerably) at a firelit beach party; it is a luminous, moonlit summer evening on Amity Island, a vacationer's paradise. In *High Noon* the steady state is equally idyllic. The older, beloved, and heroic marshal is finally receiving his just deserts and moral reward; having driven the evil outlaws from the community, he is marrying the incandescently gorgeous Amy. Amid the well-wishes of the community, the marshal hangs up his guns, retires his badge in anticipation of the arrival of his replacement, and prepares to depart on his honeymoon.

That gets disrupted by a trouble consisting of circumstances attributable to human agency or susceptible to change by human intervention.

The trouble in both movies arrives early, the initiating action (the inciting incident) launching the trajectory of the plot.[29] In *Jaws,* it takes the form of a man-eating rogue shark. In *High Noon*, trouble arrives with the announcement that members of the Miller gang are gathering and that Frank Miller, the villain, has been released from prison. This is a somewhat more sophisticated introduction of the trouble. The arrival is signaled through action (the members of the gang gather on the outskirts of town), revisited through imagery (train tracks, clocks ticking down to Frank Miller's arrival at high noon), and even signaled through an explicit musical presentation and foregrounding of the theme (the core story-song), all maintaining the tension of the conflict between the outlaw gang (the villain) and Marshal Kane (the protagonist) throughout the progressive movements and the internal psychological complications of the narrative.

Whether nonhuman or human, the trouble must be susceptible to change by human intervention, creating the *struggle* with the malevolent forces of antagonism and evil in such a way that the audience can side with the protagonist and participate in the deepening conflict. In the movies—just as we will see in legal storytelling—it is important to make the first act short, clarifying the theme and clearly breaking the anterior steady state to reveal the nature of the trouble and the identity of the antagonist.

In turn evoking efforts at redress or transformation, which [lead to a struggle, in which the efforts] succeed or fail.

In theater, it is commonly observed that the middle of the story is the most difficult part to construct. The progressive *complications* caused by the antagonist (or forces of antagonism) intensify while the protagonist attempts to reestablish the stability of the anterior steady state or press on toward a new and redefined narrative order. The two movements can be separate: for example, the trouble gets progressively uglier, deeper, or harder to overcome or builds to a cataclysmic climax before the hero finally intervenes. There are other possible patterns: for example, the hero (or other forces) can appear to intervene and superficially and momentarily still the trouble. This, however, is merely a false and premature ending; the victories are illusory, often part of the villain's plan until the villain arises renewed, reinvigorated for battle. At this point the "true" confrontation or struggle between good and evil begins.

In *Jaws* the sequence of events after the arrival of the trouble is extremely purposeful, linear, and forward moving. There are few of the stops and starts characteristic of other genres, other than slowing the pace down momentarily to allow the viewer to catch a breath before the next attack, the next battle, all building toward the final confrontation. Battles between the fishermen and the shark are punctuated by shark attacks and superficial psychological adjustments between the various players along the way. There are, as is typical in melodrama, false and "premature" endings (when, for example, another shark is captured and mistaken as the evil culprit). But these digressions are merely preparatory interlineations, biding time, allowing for the tension to build before returning to the waters for the next round of action scenes that are at the core of the film.

The shark becomes progressively bolder and more relentless, demonstrating the enormity of its evil, and adhering to Hitchcock's maxim. The villainous shark—Jaws—invades a sheltered beach pond and seizes a helpless swimmer; it destroys a boat and kills another victim. It embodies the forcefulness of unstoppable natural forces of disaster packaged into the form of an archetypal villain. As the community veers psychologically from denial to panic, all that is apparent is that the community cannot protect itself; it is up to the heroes to intervene. The two heroes in *Jaws*, an intellectual oceanographer (played with self-deprecating humor by Richard Dreyfuss) and a former New York

City cop (Roy Scheider) enlist the aid of a mythic ancient mariner (portrayed with a mock Shakespearean theatricality by Robert Shaw). The three head out fully loaded with mythic and modern weapons to take on their superhuman prey, to meet on the ocean, a setting far beyond the zone of human habitation. It is a primal scene, in a liminal space, beyond the realm of civilization. The ensuing battle to the death (the climax) takes up the last third of the movie. The outcome of the battle, which is never in doubt, enables the audience to vicariously participate in the ultimate combat, with the shared understanding that such guiltless enjoyment is the pleasure of the genre where the characters (like the villains) are not all quite human.

In *High Noon,* the breaking of the steady state, initiated by the arrival of the Miller gang, creates a different and more complex narrative structure, progressively introducing new dimensions to the basic problem that needs resolution before the story can end. The plot focuses on the interplay between the various "complex" characters, positioning these characters in relation to the hero and the villain and in relation to one another.

The *progressive complications* of the plot emerge as the clock ticks down toward noon. It is just after 10:30 when the film begins; Miller will arrive at 12:00 to exact his revenge on Kane and, perhaps, the town as well. The film is cleverly shot in a "real" narrative time, with one minute of screen time equaling one minute of story time. As Miller's arrival looms, Marshal Kane first thinks about leaving with his new Quaker bride, adhering to his promise to her to give up the gun. He can't betray himself, however; he returns to town. The story is about the meaning of loyalty and an exploration of the psychology of betrayal. Within this unifying theme the various subplots fit together:

1. Kane's new Quaker bride, Amy, is torn between her love for her new husband and her loyalty to her Quaker pacifist beliefs grounded in her experience of the death of her father and brother in a gunfight years ago.
2. Kane's young deputy, Harvey, betrays Kane and refuses to join him in the fight against the Miller gang, not because he is afraid, but because Kane has betrayed him professionally by refusing to appoint him as the new marshal because he is young and inexperienced.
3. Kane's former mistress has taken up with Harvey, her new protector against her former lover Miller. Perhaps this is more an act of revenge against Kane, whom she still loves, but who betrayed her when he chose his new, very blond, and upper-class Quaker wife (the incongruously East Coast ingénue Grace Kelly), who is less than half his age.

Each of these complex subplots resolves neatly with these important secondary characters making a fateful decision at the moment of crisis: Amy forsakes her pacifist beliefs and chooses to stay loyally by Kane's side, taking up the gun and killing one of the gang herself. Helen Ramirez chooses to be loyal to herself. No longer Kane's lover and no longer in need of a protector from Miller, she recognizes that she no longer has a stake in the community and willfully departs on the same train that brings Miller. Harvey, for his part, tries unsuccessfully to obtain Kane's position as the sheriff and Helen's protector. Equally unable to compel Kane to leave town, Harvey ultimately sells out Kane, refusing to risk his life and join in the battle against the Miller gang.

Meanwhile, the townspeople, one by one and group by group, betray Kane and themselves, refusing to come to his aid to save the community from the ravages of the antagonist. Their abandonment of Kane anticipates the climax of the film by leaving Kane to face the Miller gang single-handedly. This theme of betrayal fits well within the form of the melodrama; it explores the capitulation of good to evil. It is self-betrayal on a grander scale; the community compromises integrity in the face of evil based on self-deception repackaged as rationality.

So that the old steady state is restored or a new (transformed) steady state is created.

In *Jaws* the climax is dramatic, but purely physical. The characters remain static and unchanged, and the anterior steady state of calm on the island is restored. Transcendent evil has been defeated by goodness and virtue. The dawn breaks on Amity Island, and crowds of bathers will soon be returning to the waters.

In *High Noon* the outcome is much different. The plot pushes forward to a new and transformed steady state. The bad guys have been defeated in the climax; good is victorious over evil. Kane enjoys the sweet reward of Amy's love and his own honor reclaimed. Kane has saved the community and will ride off into the sunset, just as Western heroes traditionally do. But there is no simple resolution. Kane cannot go back into the past; he cannot ignore the hypocrisy and cowardice of the townspeople. The ending is transformative.

And the story concludes by drawing the then-and-there of the tale that has been told into the here-and-now of the telling through some coda—say, for example, Aesop's characteristic moral of the story.

In *Jaws*, there is a slight wisp of irony underlying the restorative ending and the innocence of the bathers returning to the waters; it is as if nothing has transpired in the plot, there are no lessons to be learned, and the past is already eliminated. The sharkfest is already banished from collective memory.

In *High Noon* the coda placed upon the transformative ending is far more complex. The town is joyful at Kane's victory as they come out of hiding. But when Kane quickly and joylessly departs he flings his star—the marshal's badge, signifying justice and law and order—down upon the ground, where he has just left the bodies of Frank Miller and the Miller gang, in disgust. He boards the buckboard with Amy and wordlessly leaves town. The audience is left to ponder the meaning of the coda's final images. Certainly, the ending signifies that a transformation has taken place and that Kane will never return to this community in the Old West ever again.

3

Plotting II

PLOT STRUCTURE IN A CLOSING ARGUMENT
TO A JURY IN A COMPLEX TORTS CASE

*Give me the story—please, the story. If I can finally under-
stand the case in simple terms, I can, in turn, tell the same
story to the jury and make them understand it as well. I go
about my life confused most of the time, but when I get
something clear I can usually communicate it. Getting it
clear is not the work of huge minds, which are often baffled
by themselves, but the labor of ordinary minds that understand [the] simplest of stories. . . . [M]ost of all, lawyers
must be storytellers. That is what the art of advocacy comes
down to—the telling of the true story of one's case.*

—GERRY SPENCE

*It appears that the evidence is weighed in the context of a good
story, and not the other way around. . . . The evidence sends me
looking for a good story with which to support it, but the evidence does not create the story on its own.*

—GERRY SPENCE

LET'S USE THE concepts underlying the plotting of movie melodramas to analyze plotting in renowned lawyer Gerry Spence's heartfelt closing argument on
behalf of Karen Silkwood in *The Estate of Karen Silkwood v. Kerr-McGee.*[1] We

will then compare the narrative structure of Spence's argument in *Silkwood* with the plots in the two movies previously analyzed.

Initially, the story told in the closing argument does not look or feel like the plotting in the two movies. Obviously, Spence's medium consists of spoken words, not film images. And unlike the unitary, linear, and highly profluent plots in *Jaws* and *High Noon*, the *Silkwood* argument encompasses analogies, aphorisms, and ministories, all knitted together with the law. The storytelling, at least when read on the page, initially appears somewhat redundant or copious at times; it lacks the sleek narrative design and constantly forward-moving profluence of the two movies. Also, like every litigation story, there is no closure or final ending; Spence leaves this figuratively in the jury's hands, employing final anecdotes to prefigure the proposed ending while empowering the jury to deliver justice. Throughout the argument, Spence shifts away (zigzags) from the story to fulfill the legal obligations of the argument (i.e., to prove his legal theory of the case). He is also limited by legal constraints (i.e., evidentiary relevance) and obligations (i.e., to include and address all crucial evidence, to respond to the defendant's theory and story, to confine his narrative to the evidence introduced at trial and inferences from this evidence in telling a meticulous and truthful story).

Structurally, Spence's closing argument is unlike *Jaws* and *High Noon* in another way. Unlike the two movies, Spence presents two discrete closing arguments—an opening and a rebuttal—each approximately two hours in length (roughly equivalent to the running time of a typical Hollywood movie). Of equal importance, there are two discrete plots intertwined within these arguments: the past-tense story of what happened to Silkwood as Spence revisits the evidence, and also Spence's retelling of the present-tense story of the trial itself. The careful layering and interconnection of these two stories—the first, a traditional Western melodrama with the added complement of a villainous corporate beast who gradually comes alive and emerges from beneath rural mud springs, the second, a mythic courtroom quest for justice in the Silkwood case—is subtle and complex.

The myth here, the Quest of the Jury for Justice, is possibly as important as the melodrama. How so? Unlike fictional movies, legal stories are calls to action, especially when told to juries by plaintiffs in torts cases and by criminal defendants. A successful Hollywood movie must draw the audience in, inducing viewers to identify with certain "sympathetic" characters, and in doing so to become what has been termed a "side participant" in the action. But the audience isn't implicitly or explicitly asked to do anything. Spence's closing argument, however, must do much more than this. A legal argument converting evidence into story is, in the technical terms of language theory and philosophy, an "illocutionary act," and a successful one is a "perlocutionary act." The legal story asks the audience to do something, and if successful, persuades them to do it. Spence's closing argument in *Silkwood* is this type of story, and his storytelling requires this dual, or double-stranded, narrative (the complementary strands of melodrama and myth) to achieve its purposes.

Finally, unlike most Hollywood movies—although some fictional movies do employ the technique of limited narrative "voice-overs"—Spence repeatedly steps outside the story he is telling to provide a first-person commentary on the plots of the stories that he is telling. He describes how the events he depicts strike him morally and emotionally; in this way he steps into the jury box and becomes one of the jurors. And his commentary marks important plot points and transitions in the two two-hour closing arguments delivered without notes. It explicitly ties together various strands of the dual plots, and facilitates a clear plot structure so that neither the jury nor Spence become confused or lose their places in the plot structure of such a complex narrative; he serves as a guide so that the jury is not diverted into unintended mud springs of Spence's own making.

Nevertheless, despite these differences, the story that Spence weaves in *Silkwood* is, like *Jaws* and *High Noon*, a heroic melodrama. *Silkwood* is strongly akin thematically, in genre, and in important aspects of narrative structure to its cinematic counterparts. The plot could have been manufactured in Hollywood and, indeed, its basic structure transferred quite well to the screen when *Silkwood*, the Academy Award–winning movie, was produced.[2]

I. The "Backstory"

Karen Silkwood worked as a lab analyst at Kerr-McGee's Cimarron plant, located near Crescent, Oklahoma.[3] Silkwood's job was to grind and polish plutonium pins used in manufacturing fuel rods for nuclear power plants. She performed her tasks in a glove box designed to seal the worker from the plutonium inside. In addition to her position as a lab analyst, Silkwood also served as a union representative. She had filed complaints on behalf of the workers with the union and the Atomic Energy Commission (AEC) pertaining to safety violations and hazards at the plant and, at the request of the AEC, had undertaken a covert investigation, accumulating records and documenting Kerr-McGee's violations of regulations and reporting of safety infractions.

On consecutive days in 1974, Silkwood was contaminated by radioactive materials at work and, after testing positive upon completing her shift at the plant, was scrubbed and decontaminated. Kerr-McGee then sent a team to test Silkwood's apartment for radioactive contamination, and high levels of contamination were discovered. Silkwood was sent to Los Alamos Scientific Laboratory, where her lungs tested positive for radioactive contamination. On the day after her return from Los Alamos, she had arranged to meet with a reporter from The *New York Times* to provide the data she had collected about the dangers of working at the Kerr-McGee plant, and about how safety and quality-control records pertaining to the manufacturing of the fuel rods had been falsified. Silkwood died in a mysterious one-car accident on the way to the meeting. The reporter and a union representative went to the car the next day, but they found no records or materials. Silkwood's apartment was quickly quarantined, and all of her personal property inside was buried in a nuclear waste site.

After Silkwood's death, Silkwood's father tried unsuccessfully to obtain $5,000 for the value of her personal property from Kerr-McGee. Kerr-McGee refused to settle. He then contacted Spence, who sued Kerr-McGee on behalf of Silkwood's children and family for $10,505,000: $500,000 for Karen's physical and mental pain and suffering as a result of the contamination, $10,000,000 in punitive damages, and $5,000 for the loss of Karen's personal property. Spence later increased the request for punitive damages to $70 million.

The trial began in March 1979. It took eleven weeks. There were no clear answers as to how Silkwood was contaminated, what materials she was going to provide regarding Kerr-McGee's falsification of documents, and the causes of Silkwood's suffering and tragedy. Nevertheless, basing its decision on a theory of strict liability, and supplementing it with an award of punitive damages, the jury returned a verdict for $10,505,000. Kerr-McGee appealed the punitive damages award of $10,000,000. The parties eventually settled punitive damages at $1.38 million.

II. *Annotated Excerpts from Gerry Spence's Closing Argument on Behalf of Karen Silkwood*

A. Setting the Stage

Just as *Jaws* and *High Noon* have characteristic visual styles well suited to their subjects, themes, and narrative structures, Gerry Spence chose to deliver his

closing argument in a particular style equally well suited to the subject matter. It is instructive to listen to a tape of Spence reading the text of the closing
argument as if he were acting on a stage: he speaks in a deep and resonant
voice and at a much more deliberate and slower pace than normal conversa-
tional speech, allowing his words to have a luxuriousness and seeming moral
authority as he moves through the peaks and valleys of evidence and imagery,
gradually building to a crescendo:

> Thank you, Your Honor. Well, here we are. Every good closing argu-
> ment has to start with "Ladies and Gentlemen of the Jury," so let me
> start that way with you. I actually thought we were going to grow old
> together.... We've spent a season here together. I haven't been home to
> Jackson for two and a half months. And, although I'm a full-fledged
> Oklahoman now,... I'm homesick. And I'm sure you're homesick, too.
> I'm sure this has been a tough one on you.... [W]e made it through
> this matter together, and I'm pretty proud of that.[4]

Spence then affirms the specialness and importance of the jury in this particular case and the importance of the moment to him as well, contemplating
with awe the heroic task that lies ahead of them both:

> It's the longest case in Oklahoma history, they tell me. And, before the
> case is over, you will know, as you probably already know, that this is
> probably the most important case, as well.... [A]nd it's the most impor-
> tant case of my career. I'm standing here talking to you now about the
> most important things I have ever said in my life. And, I have a sense
> that I have spent a lifetime, fifty years, to be exact, preparing somehow
> for this moment with you.[5]

This is a shrewd version of a classic lawyer's proem, a set piece, used rhetorically to "secure the good will of the audience by making the speaker appear
to be a worthy person...and, at the same time, by appealing to values the
audience and speaker share."[6] In other arguments Spence employs similar set
pieces.[7] It is crucial to empower and affirm the importance of the jury (especially in plaintiff's torts and criminal defense cases). Spence reestablishes his
relationship with the jury after a long and grueling trial, speaking to them
directly for the first time since the voir dire many weeks earlier. He speaks as
if he were with them in the jury box as a witness to the making of history and
as if he appreciates their struggle to make meaning out of the evidence, and

their personal sacrifice. He also presents himself as a willing guide for them on their own heroic quest toward justice and toward writing the correct ending of Silkwood's story.

B. Theory of the Case and Narrative Theme

Closing arguments, like popular entertainment films, often begin with a strong narrative "hook" to capture the imaginative attention of the jury. After multiple "false starts,"[8] Spence presents the plaintiff's legal "theory of the case"; he spins the law into a careful anecdote. The plaintiff's legal theory was strict liability, which meant that Spence had to convince the jury only that Silkwood was contaminated by the plutonium that Kerr-McGee produced. The judge has bought Spence's legal theory, and it will be presented in instructions (and a verdict form) given to the jury: legally, Karen Silkwood's estate does not have to prove how she became contaminated, only that she was contaminated by the plutonium produced by Kerr-McGee; the only "story" that will relieve the defendant of liability is if Silkwood intentionally removed the plutonium from the plant and contaminated herself (even a story of Silkwood's own negligence at the plant contaminating herself with plutonium will not suffice).

Nevertheless, it is a legal issue that is potentially complex and confusing for the jury, as the judge's jury instructions include burdens of proof, elemental statements of the law regarding strict liability, and even a multipart verdict form. But Spence's narrative "hook" translates this legal complexity into a simple anecdote, a straightforward ministory that fits neatly within the larger story of the case:

> Well, we talked about "strict liability" at the outset, and you'll hear the court tell you about "strict liability," and it simply means: "If the lion got away, Kerr-McGee has to pay." It's that simple—that's the law. You remember what I told you in the opening statement about strict liability? It came out of the Old English common law. Some guy brought an old lion on his ground, and he put it in a cage—and lions are dangerous—and through no negligence of his own—through no fault of his own, the lion got away. Nobody knew how—like in this case, "nobody knew how." And, the lion went out and he ate up some people—and they sued the man. And they said, you know: "Pay. It was your lion, and he got away." And the man says: "But I did everything in my power—I had a good cage—had a good lock on the door—I did everything that

I could—I had security—I had trained people watching the lion—and it isn't my fault that he got away." Why should you punish him? They said: "We have to punish him—we have to punish you—you have to pay." You have to pay because it was your lion—unless the person who was hurt let the lion out himself. That's the only defense in this case: unless in this case Karen Silkwood was the one who intentionally took the plutonium out, and "let the lion out," that is the only defense, and that is why we have heard so much about it.

Strict liability: "If the lion gets away, Kerr-McGee has to pay," unless Karen Silkwood let the lion loose. What do we have to prove? Strict liability. Now, can you see what that is? The lion gets away. We have to do that. It's already admitted. It's admitted in the evidence. They admit it was their plutonium. They admit it's in Karen Silkwood's apartment. It got away. And, we have to prove Karen Silkwood was damaged. That's all we have to prove.[9]

In contrast, the defendant must provide an affirmative defense and prove by a preponderance of the evidence that Karen Silkwood intentionally took the plutonium from the plant to her home and poisoned herself. Rather than front-loading the legal explanation or filling the space with an abstract argument explaining how Kerr-McGee has failed to meet its burden, Spence employs a second parallel ministory to characterize the evidence presented by defendant's attorneys at trial and, more important, to provide a narrative framework for the defendant's theory of the case: he employs the fitting and bucolic analogy of "the mud springs." First, Spence reminds jurors that Kerr-McGee has only one legal defense, that Karen Silkwood took the plutonium from the plant and poisoned herself; this is "the only possible defense that Kerr-McGee has."[10] Spence then warns the jurors that the defendant will attempt to lure them into the "mud springs" and admonishes them not to be deceived:

[I]f you want to clear up the water, you've got to get the hogs out of the spring. And, if you can't get the hogs out of the spring, I guarantee you can't clear up the water.... And the thing that I say to you is "keep out of the mud springs" in your deliberations. You are not scientists—I'm not a scientist—my only power is my common sense. Keep out of the mud springs. You'll be invited there [by the defendant, in closing argument]. Use your common sense. You'll be invited to do number-crunching of your own [by the defendant]. You'll be invited to play word games [by the defendant]. You'll be invited to get into all kinds of irrelevancies. And I only say to you that you have one hope— don't get into mud springs—keep your common sense, and take it with you into the jury room.[11]

Throughout his closing argument Spence refers numerous times to these two ministries as a legal shorthand: the anecdote of the lion who got away (embodying Spence's legal theory of strict liability) and the analogy of the mud springs (a reference to the defendant's strategy of obfuscation). Spence reflects upon this strategy: "In preparing the Silkwood case I outlined the story, but on the opposite page in the notebook I wrote out a few words, a slogan of sorts, that stood for my entire argument, my [legal] *theme*: '*If the lion gets away, Kerr-McGee has to pay*'. I played and replayed that [legal] theme like the recurring refrain in a song."[12]

This shorthand provides a rhyming aphorism that sticks in the mind like Johnny Cochran's equally melodic hook, "If the glove doesn't fit, you must acquit." It enables Spence to dispense quickly with the issue of liability and focus primarily on the issue of punitive damages: how Kerr-McGee should be punished for allowing the "lion to get away." In doing so, Spence strategically claims melodrama as the proper genre for the competing storytelling, challenging the defense to the difficult task of reversing the polarities of the story and convincing the jury that Karen Silkwood is the deceitful antagonist who poisoned herself, while Kerr-McGee is the virtuous protagonist. That is, if melodrama is the only way to understand what happened, then either Silkwood is the hero and Kerr-McGee is the villain, or it's the other way around. And if it's the former, then Silkwood wins on liability and the only question that remains is how much to punish Kerr-McGee for its actions so that it will change its evil ways. Thus, Spence's task is not only to tell the story persuasively as melodrama but to tell it so persuasively that melodrama becomes the only way to think about the case. Otherwise, Spence could construct his melodrama and Kerr-McGee could tell a competing story in another genre or simply attempt to disrupt the mapping of melodrama onto the facts by making the characters and actions more ambiguous. Hence, Spence's careful admonition to the jurors to beware of the mud springs.

Spence's core narrative is a simple and traditional Western melodrama. In this story, Karen Silkwood possesses the internal psychology characteristic of hero-protagonists in prototypical Westerns: she is a loner-outsider, possesses impressive integrity, and sacrifices self-interest and autonomy for the greater community. According to the screenwriting guru Syd Field, the archetypal Western hero is portrayed as "fighting against the injustices of the system; he is a true individual, true to himself and his ideals, unbending in spirit, unyielding in the belief of spirit."[13] These heroes, because of their strength, individuality, and spirituality, are readily misunderstood by the community.

According to Field, the character of the Western hero in the classical Western melodrama is defined by two specific challenges:

> One is the physical challenge, which requires the hero to perform a courageous act during battle, like saving a life, or an entire village.... The other heroic challenge is the spiritual challenge, an adventure during which the hero experiences the transformation of consciousness and becomes "realized," then returns with the ancient and profound message that has echoes through time, like "see God in each other."[14]

These are the precise challenges that Silkwood meets in Spence's closing argument. First, there is the physical challenge of her battle with Kerr-McGee to save the community (even if it ultimately results in her own self-sacrifice and death). Second, Spence's Silkwood undergoes a transformation of consciousness in herself and returns to reveal to the community her message of discovery. In answer to one of the riddles he poses about Silkwood for the jury to solve, "Who was she?," Spence suggests this answer: "I say she was a prophet."[15]

Perhaps the greatest narrative and structural challenge for Spence, however, is to make Kerr-McGee—the corporation—into the all-powerful villain demanded by melodrama. Remember that in melodrama, the virtue of the hero—and the effectiveness of the story—can be measured only against the strength of the antagonistic force. So to elevate to heroic status not only Silkwood but also the jury (who must write the final chapter and ending to the story) and Spence himself (possibly akin to the three nautical heroes in *Jaws*), Kerr-McGee must come alive as an effective and singular melodramatic villain. Spence must coalesce all of the forces of antagonism aligned against Silkwood into an organic and clearly visualized entity. Kerr-McGee must become The Beast, and The Beast must come alive to enlist the empathy of the jury, inspiring a desire to complete the story with a powerful and transformative ending, and to provide a meaningful coda to the tale. The genre of melodrama demands villainy, and Spence's initial task is to fashion the defendant into this role.

C. The Steady State and the Arrival of the Trouble

Spence finally opens his story with a depiction of an anterior steady state that is unlike the anterior steady state depicted in *Jaws* (the summer on the idyllic Amity with the swimmers at play) or in *High Noon* (the wedding ceremony of Amy and Kane after Kane has cleaned up the town, with the grateful towns-people in attendance). Spence's storytelling anticipates narrative expectations of the juror audience in the late 1970s. His opening subtly references two compelling and profoundly relevant cultural events that took place during the second and third weeks of the Silkwood trial and that had been covered extensively in the news and popular media: the release of the movie *The China Syndrome*, about a devastating nuclear power accident, and the real-world accident at Three Mile Island that the movie seemed to presciently anticipate.

The setting of the core past-tense story is Crescent, Oklahoma. When the story begins the trouble has already arrived. Spence could have begun differently, but instead he opens his story at a moment when the powerful villain already holds the upper hand and the innocent community is in its vice-like grip:

> It was a time of infamy, and a time of deceit, corporate dishonesty. A time when men used men like disposable commodities—like so much expendable property. It was a time when corporations fooled the public, were more concerned with public image than with the truth.
>
> It was a time when the government held hands with these giants, and played footsie with their greatest scientists. At the disposal of the corporation, to testify, to strike down the claims of people, and it was too late. It was a sad time, the era between '70 and '79—they called it the Cimarron Syndrome.[16]

The form or genre of the story is prefigured in this darkly atmospheric and self-consciously literary opening: the opening suggests that this story is about good versus evil, about the monstrous corporation working against the community. The evil corporation will call forth the arrival of a heroic individual (Silkwood) who is willing to stand up to corporate greed and institutional corruption and ultimately sacrifice herself for the good of her community. This opening is also literary in that it locates the case in a specific historic context and claims a profound importance for the case and the argument. That is, this case is not a torts lawsuit about the wrongful death of an individual plaintiff; it is about a crucial historical moment that might mark the transition from one dark period to the hopeful possibility of something else. Spence's opening anticipates the narrative expectations of his juror audience in the late 1970s, after the deceits of the Vietnam War, after the corruptions of Watergate, and amid the greedy abuses of corporate and institutional power of the private sector of the day (the "Cimarron Syndrome").

This opening is a narrative "marker" defining a steady state. And it is a clear marker to which Spence will return at the close, emphasizing it in his dark vision of what the future narrative landscape might look like if the jury fails to act heroically and hold Kerr-McGee accountable. This dark noir-like opening is self-consciously literary and dramatic. Spence's challenge is not just to the jury: his closing argument must now live up to this opening; he is obliged to deliver a story with a worthy hero and a villain to match, and he must now connect the personal story of Karen Silkwood with corruption on a historical stage that, perhaps, the narrowness of the legal issues at trial may not suggest and the rules of evidence may not allow.

Although there are other places where Spence could begin his story, he chooses this one. He observes in his advice to advocates, "A story may start anywhere—each story has an infinite number of possible beginnings."[17] To this he adds, "Each of these beginnings can lead to a finite number of middles, but each of these middles must lead to one, and only one, end."[18] Spence ends his rebuttal argument, his portion of the storytelling, eventually winding his way back to this dark place, the anterior steady state, foreshadowing in a dream what the future might look like if the jury does not act heroically and provide a transformative ending, by inscribing a new meaning and coda on the tale. It suggests an outcome if the jury, instead of following the jurors' oath to the grail of justice, becomes "lost in the mud springs" along the way: stuck, unable to move, like cows sinking into traps, manipulated and led away from his truthful story by defendant's arguments and innuendo (a talking Beast who only has learned to speak the language of money).

D. Another Story within a Story: The Jury and "The Quest of the Hero"

As I observed earlier, there is a second crucial story, and another narrative axis, embedded within Spence's closing argument, typical of plaintiffs' closing arguments in torts cases (and also of many defendants' closing arguments in criminal cases).[19] That is, the story is not just a past-tense melodrama about what happened to Karen Silkwood; it is simultaneously a present-tense story about the trial itself, the quest for truth, culminating in an affirmation of the value of justice at stake in the case. The trial leading up to the jury deliberations provides an incomplete narrative, a work-in-progress: a story told without an ending. At the core of this story is the decision makers' heroic quest for justice. It will be for the jury to discover truth, complete the story, and inscribe meaning on the tale. To discover this meaning and to do what is right, and to fulfill the commands of their heroic oath, the jurors must go out in search of the truth. Spence explicitly recognizes this mythic and heroic quest and suggests that the jury must solve three compelling and difficult riddles and return from the darkness and confusion of the evidence with the grail of justice.

And so Spence evokes the mythic "call to the hero" in his argument: "What is the $70 million claim about?...I don't want to see workers in America cheated out of their lives. I'm going to talk to you about that a lot. It hurts me. It hurts me. I don't want to see people deprived of the truth—the cover-ups. It's ugly. I want to stop it."[20] This begins the jury's quest for justice, commanding jurors to solve the puzzle of the case and to prevent the villain from prevailing in the end. Spence breaks from his story to explain:

> What is this case not about? The case is not about being against the nuclear industry.... But it is about the power of truth, that you have to use in this case somehow, because it has been revealed to you now— you know it—and if there is only one thing that can come from this case...and that if this case makes it so expensive to lie, and to cover up, and to cheat, and to not tell the truth, and to play numbers games, that it makes it so expensive for industry—this industry—to do that, that the biggest bargain in life, the biggest bargain for those companies is the truth.[21]

Spence then cleverly interweaves these two discrete narratives: the present-tense mythic story of the trial with the past-tense melodramatic story about what happened to Karen Silkwood. Again, there is an artful zigzagging pattern established between past and present (akin to his zigzagging between theme and theory of the case). Structurally, Spence somehow must move smoothly in time, transitioning between past- and present-tense events as he revisits evidence at trial, without confusing the jury and, simultaneously, he must allow sufficient space and room to empower the jury to do its narrative task. This is a difficult feat; Spence must not confuse the jury as to which narrative he is referring to, or have gaps of narrative "holes" in his story logic, or otherwise cause the jurors to lose their place in the story. Simultaneously, Spence cannot foreground or reveal explicitly his narrative design.

In commenting on plot structure at the core of legal argumentation and suggesting how to convert argument into story, Spence observes that "a story is more magnetizing to the listener who feels his/her active participation will be necessary for the story to achieve its proper ending"; he notes that "[a]nywhere along the way, however, it is possible to lose even the most sympathetic listener if the teller veers off the course of beginning/middle/end."[22] Of course, this storytelling must also be truthful and meticulous in that it is: (1) consistent with the evidence and without internal contradictions (internal narrative logic); (2) plausible in terms of the jurors' experience and how it fits with jurors' knowledge about what happens in the "real world" ("instantiation"); and (3) comprehensive, matching to and fitting with the evidence and the law.[23] But it must also, paraphrasing Jerome Bruner, facilitate and compel jurors to go "beyond the information given,"[24] suggesting to the jurors (or decision makers) how to retrieve a deeper meaning to the human affairs depicted in the story while avoiding confusion and creating a "mud springs" of its own along the way, so that the singular powerful and transformative ending to Silkwood's story is apparent to the jury in their deliberations.

Specifically, to do this, at the end of his rebuttal closing argument, Spence will ask the jurors to assume the heroic mantle of their oath by contemplating and solving three essential riddles necessary to discover the truth of what happened to Silkwood and then to determine what the proper ending of the story should be. Finally, employing a familiar set piece that he has used in other arguments, Spence will implore the jury to write the ending and take the action necessary to complete the story. It is too late to save Silkwood's life, but it is not too late to give her life meaning, and it is not too late to rescue the young and innocent workers at the plant and save the community still held hostage by the evil Kerr-McGee. Although the ending is left up to the jury, at the finale of his rebuttal closing argument Spence suggests the answers to these riddles of how the jury must act to fulfill their heroic oath.

1. "[W]hat is this case about?"[25] Spence's suggested answer: "[I]t is about the power of truth, that you have to use in this case somehow, because it has been revealed to you now—you know it."[26]
2. "Who is Karen Silkwood?"[27] and "What was she trying to tell the world?"[28] Spence's suggested answer: "[A] brave, ordinary woman who did care. And she risked her life, and she lost it. And she had something to tell the world, and she tried to tell the world. What was it that Karen Silkwood had to tell

the world? That has been left to us to say now. It is for you, the jury, to say it for her."[29]

3. "How does this all tie in?" Rephrased more concretely: "Did she know too much?…Who contaminated her?…How much did she know?"[30] Spence's suggested answer: "She knew enough to bring this whole mess to an end."[31]

E. Progressive Complications: The Nature of the Trouble

Prior to casting the heroine, Silkwood, onstage, Spence revisits patiently the evidence introduced at trial presented, primarily, by the various employees of defendant Kerr-McGee. He divides these witnesses into two discrete and identifiable groups: the members of the villainous outlaw band (representatives or "agents" of the archenemy Kerr-McGee) and the often sympathetic yet confused "townspeople" (the workers at the plant; members of a disempowered community of victims who will, like Silkwood, soon become the victims of the predatory and evil corporation).

First, however, Spence must give life to the villainous corporate defendant and make it into a singular and powerful entity, the initiator of the melodrama, seemingly in control of all that takes place afterward. As Hitchcock suggests, the effective depiction of the villain is crucial to the success of a melodrama. That is, "the more successful the villain, the more powerful the story."[32] And yet this strategy poses a narrative problem for Spence. The corporation Kerr-McGee is not only nonhuman, it is not "alive"; it is, in Spence's own words, like "some weird invisible extraterrestrial lifeless glob."[33] Nevertheless, this problem also provides an imaginative opportunity for Spence, who observes, "Although corporations are not alive, they [nevertheless] possess a life of their own."[34]

Like Spielberg in *Jaws*, Spence must successfully provide a character-based identity to the defendant through careful attribution of the human qualities of motivation, intentionality, and an increasing purposefulness. Spence's version of Kerr-McGee is of a rapaciously greedy and devouring entity that values money and profits far more than it does the lives of its workers. In suggesting how to develop arguments against corporations, Spence cites Charles Reich's description of a corporation: "The corporation is an immensely powerful machine, ordered, legalistic, rational, yet utterly out of human control, wholly and perfectly indifferent to any human value."[35] Like the shark in *Jaws*, whose appetite is whetted initially by the taste of blood, Spence's Kerr-McGee grows ever bolder and darker and more powerful as his story progresses: the corporation becomes progressively more venal, greedy, and devouring, preferring these profits over the lives of its workers and then finally, Spence intimates, intentionally undertaking or at least encouraging the murder of Silkwood (although Spence tells the jury that he is not allowed to speculate on this matter).

At the end of his rebuttal argument, Spence suggests that allowing Kerr-McGee to go unpunished and unrepentant will result in far more than simply unfairness and injustice to Silkwood. If Kerr-McGee is not stopped, Spence visualizes in his final dream sequence a dark vision of corporatist tyranny throughout the land and the destruction of endless young lives by plutonium poisoning and cancer. The filmmaker and literary theorist Michael Roemer observes:

> Popular story shows us as we are supposed to be and wish to see ourselves. Like the community itself, it represses what tragedy includes. By projecting evil onto the other, it purges us of our dark and dirty secrets, frees us up from self-division, and fosters *communitas* by giving us someone to hate and fear. Yet *unlike* Positivism, it retains its belief in the power of evil. Indeed, without a destructive threat—whether it be divine or human—there is no story.[36]

Here, for example, is how Spence initially attributes the ability to "speak the language of money" to the corporate defendant Kerr-McGee in his closing argument:

> You know, I was amazed to hear that Kerr-McGee has eleven thousand employees—eleven thousand employees. That's more than most of the towns in the state that I live in—that it is in thirty-five states—well, I guarantee that corporation does not speak "South," it doesn't speak "Okie," it doesn't speak "Western," it doesn't speak "New York." And it is in five states—or in five countries. It doesn't speak any foreign language. It speaks one language universally. It speaks the language of money. That is the only language that it speaks—the only language that it understands—and that is why the case becomes what it is. That's why we have to talk back to that corporation in money.[37]

Of course, it is then crucial for the jury to speak in the language that the defendant understands, and in such a forceful way that the corporation will change its behavior. Subsequently, Spence zigzags back to his legal theory of punitive damages, as if a law professor speaking to first-year students, providing a simplified understanding of utilitarian and retributionist rationales for such punishment:

> I want to quote an instruction that you will hear. It is the basis of punitive damages—that's the $70 million to punish. Punitive. To exemplify. Exemplary. So that the rest of the uranium plutonium, and the nuclear industries in this country, will have to tell the truth. The basis of punitive and exemplary damages rests on the principle that they are allowed as punishment of the offender for the general benefit of society, both as a restraint upon the transgressor—restraint upon the transgressor— that is, against Kerr-McGee, so they won't do it anymore, and a meaningful warning and example—to deter the commission of like offenses in the future.[38]

F. "The Setup": The Villainous Outlaw Gang versus the Townspeople

Spence carefully, but selectively, revisits crucial excerpts of the testimony of the various witnesses. The witnesses are divided into two oppositional groups: there are the defendant's witnesses—agents of the evil corporation, subsumed by the will of the greedy and devouring corporate monolith, hungry only for money, who devalue the lives of the workers, leaving a wake of destruction by plutonium and the cancers that will follow. And there are also the defendant's experts, also paid employees, testifying to draw the jurors into the mud springs. On the other side are the plaintiff's witnesses: innocents, victims, members of a community without a voice or purpose. And these witnesses are complemented by the chorus of plaintiff's experts, wise old men and helpers, who explain what the outcome will be for the community.

In revisiting the testimony, the order of the voices within the closing argument is not in the sequence of the chronology of presentation at trial. Rather, the voices are cast in counterpoint to one another. Further, in terms of evidentiary rules and legal relevance, it is interesting that many of these witnesses were even allowed to testify since the issues at trial were extremely limited and narrowed by the plaintiff's own legal theory (product liability and strict liability) and the judge's own charge: Kerr-McGee had to prove by a preponderance of the evidence (as an affirmative defense) that Karen Silkwood intentionally removed the plutonium from the Kerr-McGee plant that caused her contamination. Therefore, the legal issues pertained to the events that occurred during the nine days Silkwood was contaminated and, most simply put, how she was contaminated. Nevertheless, over the objection of counsel, the judge admitted evidence pertaining to operations at the Kerr-McGee plant over a six-year period, although Silkwood only worked at the plant for two years, and about events occurring in areas of the plant where Silkwood never worked and did not have access to.[39] It is almost as if expansive principles of narrative logic and Spence's narrative theme trumped the plaintiff's own theory of the case and somehow compelled the trial court judge to afford Spence wide latitude in introducing evidence to shape and frame his story on a grander stage than the rules of evidence would seemingly allow.

Here, for example, is how Spence revisits the testimony and juxtaposes contrasting depictions of the testimony of several witnesses. First, Mr. Utnage (outlaw villain), then "Young Apperson" (community member):

Mr. Utnage

I want to talk about the design of that plant very quickly. It was designed by Mr. Utnage. He never designed any kind of a plant.... And I confronted him with scores of problems—you remember those 574 reports of contaminations—they were that thick [*indicating*], in two volumes.... I asked him about a leak detection system. "We do not need a leak detection system," he said. "What do we need a leak detection system for? We can see it. We can see it." Here is the man who told you that as long as you can't see it, you're safe. And we know that the amount of plutonium, a half a gram of plutonium, will contaminate the whole state of Oklahoma, and you can't see it. They let it flop down into the rooms, and Jim Smith said one time it was in the room a foot thick on the floor. Do you remember the testimony? He said he designed a safe plant. And he believed the company lie that plutonium does not cause cancer. He sat there on that stand under his oath and looked at every one of you under his oath, and he said that plutonium has never been known to cause cancer. Well, now, either he lied, or he bought the company lie and didn't know. But he was the man who designed the plant. You wouldn't have to design a very good plant if you didn't think plutonium caused cancer, it wouldn't bother you. You wouldn't work very hard. There wouldn't be much to worry about. Like mayonnaise.[40]

"Young Apperson"
[D]o you remember young Apperson sitting there [*indicating*]? You remember his open face—I liked him a lot—an open, honest boy—blond, curly hair—you remember him, two and a half months ago? He said, "Thirty percent of the pipes weren't welded when I came, when the plant was opened. Thirty percent of the pipes were welded after the plant was in operation, and I was there and I saw those old welds." And he wasn't a certified welder himself, and he was teaching people in an hour or two to be welders themselves—not a certified welder on the job. "There was things leaking everywhere," he said. You remember how he was describing how he was there welding the pipe and they jerked the oxygen out, and he had to gasp for air—the contamination—to survive the moment? Jim Smith talked about the valves breaking up from the acid. So much for the design of the plant.[41]

Each description of character and recitation of testimony is discrete, shaped in relationship to the other pieces of testimony, elliptical pieces, part of a careful overall arrangement. These are all parallel constructions. Each begins with a visualization or imagistic depiction of character, then a summary of testimony, ending with Spence's rhetorical flourish and an almost unnoticeably ironic commentary as Spence moves outside the images and sits alongside the jury observing the witness and providing a throwaway comment. For example, Spence observes that Mr. Utnage's indifference to and ignorance of the notion that loose plutonium causes cancer is "like mayonnaise." Or after recounting testimony by young Apperson, who sees the "things leaking everywhere," Spence observes ironically, "[s]o much for the design of the plant."

This elongated initial movement provides the "setup" for the confrontation between the melodramatic hero (Silkwood) and the archetypal villain (Kerr-McGee and its evil minions) to save the townspeople and the community from destruction. This slow initial movement frames the clearly marked pattern of the classic heroic rescue narrative also presented in *High Noon* and *Jaws*. Unlike the heroes in those films, however, Spence's Silkwood will never do successful combat in a final climactic battle; she will merely provide her warnings of the future and die in the process of attempting to rescue the community. It is then for the jury to intervene and complete the hero's journey by writing the proper ending to the unfinished story.

Finally, after proceeding through much additional testimony and evidence, Spence signals his transition to the next stage of the plot (the dramatic confrontation). Again, Spence keeps the pieces (the sequence of the plot) discrete, suggesting the relationship between narrative sections not through a clear and explicit linear chronology, but as if by principles of cinematic montage. For example, he reintroduces snippets of testimony from another witness, "Hammock, the highway patrolman" (formerly a Kerr-McGee employee), to whom Kerr-McGee allegedly shipped defective fuel rods that, in Hammock's words, "had a bad weld, or too large a weld sealing in the plutonium pellets."[42] And then he jumps back into the jury box, as if sitting next to the jurors. "It just turns my guts," Spence observes, as if psychologically he cannot refrain from doing so, "[t]hey were shipping defective pins to a breeder reactor knowing they were defective, to Washington where the people—the State of Washington—where the people are going to somehow be subjected to the first breeder reactor in this country."[43]

Spence comments forcefully to the jurors in the first person, marking that this preliminary piece of his argument is near completion and that he will finally be moving on to the next stage in his story structure. He is now a moral commentator and guide for the jury upon what he has presented so far:

> I couldn't get over it—I couldn't sleep—I couldn't believe what I had heard. I don't know how it affected you. Maybe you get so numb after a while—I guess people just stand and say, "exposure, exposure, exposure, exposure, exposure—cancer, cancer, cancer, cancer, cancer, cancer, cancer, cancer, cancer, cancer, cancer, cancer, cancer, cancer, cancer, cancer, cancer," until you don't hear it anymore. Maybe that is what happens to us. I tell you, if it is throbbing in your breast—if cancer is eating at your guts, or it's eating at your lungs, or it's gnawing away at your gonads, and you're losing your life, and your manhood, and your womanhood, and your child, or your children, it then has meaning— they are not just words. You multiply it by hundreds of workers, and thousands of workers, that is why this case is the most important case, maybe, in the history of man. That is why I'm so glad you're on this jury, and that we are a part of this thing together.[44]

G. The Arrival of the Prophet

Finally, the heroine Silkwood is cast back onstage. "How does this all tie in with Karen Silkwood?" Spence asks.[45] After yet another digression, or zigzag, back to his legal theory of damages, "if the lion gets away, they have to pay," Spence reintroduces the protagonist Karen Silkwood, characterized as a moral and religious person, a union organizer, deeply concerned about her fellow workers, who has been silenced and slandered by Kerr-McGee at trial. As with his initial setup, Spence is extremely patient and deliberate in developing Silkwood's character as a heroic protagonist, in opposition to the image of Silkwood presented by defendant's witnesses. Spence goes far back in time and begins his depiction of Silkwood as a child:

> Who is Karen Silkwood? Who was she? Well, it's a fear that sometimes the whole truth doesn't get to you. What would have happened in your mind about Karen Silkwood if all you ever heard was [*Kerr-McGee supervisor*] Longaker, who was full of his own vindictiveness against her? You would have believed, by his statements: "Karen Silkwood was [an] uncouth, moody, unreliable, vindictive, sloppy woman, a miserable hate monger, and tried to get even with the company by intentionally contaminating herself—that is what she was, she was an unmitigated moody bitch," to put it plainly. Is that who she really was? You know yourself, and you know your friends, and you know me by where we come from. She was a happy child, a good child, she was correctly reared by the church, and she had her life in the church, and she loved church, and she was a scholarship student, and she was a chemistry major. She was bright, she could understand. But, more than anything else, she cared. At that corporation plant there was somebody who cared, and it was Karen Silkwood. Somebody who cared a lot about others.[46]

Here, Spence resurrects Karen Silkwood and brings her actual voice into the courtroom—through edited audiotape segments—so that the jury can hear her and put an identity to answer the question of who she was (whose version of Silkwood is to be believed). These excerpts are parallel (almost identical) in length to the excerpts from the various witnesses' testimony that Spence previously quoted to the jury. Each is a parallel yet elliptical piece of an organized ensemble or arrangement of voices of the community, with Silkwood now placed at the center. At the end of each edited taped excerpt, Spence repeats her final phrase in her own voice for emphasis, providing a final rhythmic "beat" before moving on. These pieces are carefully arranged, akin to a tightly ordered sequence of building-block scenes in the storyboard constructed for a movie.

> [Spence] You know, I got this here so that you could hear her voice once more. This is the voice when she was talking to [*union representative*] Steve Wodka. She never knew it would be played in a

courtroom with her bones rotting in the grave. But her voice is still quite alive. Now you judge for yourself who Karen was. [*Reporter's note: The following portion of a cassette, Plaintiff's Exhibit 31, played in open court.*]

Karen Silkwood [her voice]

And, I've got one here that we're still passing all welds no matter what the pictures look like. We either grind down too far—and I've got a weld I would love for you to see just how far they ground it down till we lost the weld trying to get rid of the voids and inclusions and the cracks. And, I kept it.

[Spence repeats] "And I kept it."[47]

Spence similarly frames other taped excerpts:

[Spence] And I had Wally get this other part so that you could hear it. [*Reporter's note: The following portion of a cassette, Plaintiff's Exhibit 31, played in open court.*]

Karen Silkwood [her voice]

Ah, in the laboratory we've got eighteen- and nineteen-year-old boys, you know, twenty and twenty-one, I mean, and they didn't have the schooling so they don't understand what radiation is. They don't understand, Steve, they don't understand.

[Spence repeats] They don't understand, Steve, they don't understand.[48]

And then, Spence answers his own rhetorical question as to who *he* thinks Silkwood is, identifying her as "a prophet":

Who was she? I say she was a prophet, an ordinary woman who cared, and could understand, doesn't have to be anything other than an ordinary woman who cared and understood in order to be a prophet. I don't mean that she's anything, you know, biblical—I mean, she was an ordinary person who cared, and she prophesied it this way: "If there is something going on"—this was an actual quote—"If there is some-thing going on, we're going to be susceptible to cancer, and we are not going to know about it for years." She says this to you, ladies and gen-tlemen: "Something has to be done."[49]

H. "The Confrontation": The Conflict Intensifies

From this point, Spence develops the melodramatic conflict and confrontation between Silkwood and the forces of antagonism posed by Kerr-McGee. Spence contrasts the testimony of Kerr-McGee's witnesses against Silkwood's own voice. Spence begins to intimate what *really* happened to Silkwood to counter the defendant's story (pointing the "long, white, bony finger" of blame)[50] that Silkwood intentionally smuggled plutonium out of the plant, poisoning herself to take revenge on the company, effectively committing suicide (although there is scant evidence to back up this theory). Spence's more likely counterstory implicates a dark conspiracy by Kerr-McGee to rid themselves of the union organizer, Silkwood, who has collected evidence of wrongdoing on the part of the corporation (including, perhaps, doctoring images of fuel rods shipped to a breeder reactor in Hanford, Washington).

Spence paints his villainous characters with vivid brushstrokes, usually recalling witnesses with a description of a single detail and then connecting this physicality to the next depiction of villainy. Here, in a sequence, Spence emphasizes how the defendant's evil minions (including Morgan Moore, Silkwood's supervisor at Kerr-McGee and Kerr-McGee's attorney, Mr. Paul) point the "bony finger" of blame at Silkwood: "What did [*Kerr-McGee supervisor*] Morgan Moore do? How does he fit in the picture? He accused her from the beginning—pointed his finger, didn't have any evidence then—and five years later in this courtroom was still willing to point his finger, his long, white, bony finger at her. It is easy to blame."[51] Spence then connects this to how Mr. Paul, defendant's attorney, attempted to put his fingers in the pocket of his coat during his opening statement, intimating to the jury that Silkwood had secreted the plutonium into her pocket, smuggled the plutonium out of the Kerr-McGee plant, and spiked her own urine samples; her apparent motive was to take revenge on the corporation:

> Mr. Paul, you remember him walking up to you in the opening statement and telling you how he blamed Karen Silkwood? He didn't have any more evidence then than he has now. He said first access—first access—you remember he said about her "she had access to it, to her apartment." "Who could get into her apartment?" "Well, she could get into her apartment." The next point is an important one—I'm sure no one of you has wondered about it—"the opportunity to remove small quantities of plutonium from the plant." Then he did this business with his pocket, trying to get your mind ready to blame her and

to join the "company line." ... [A]nd even you remember this business about how he really tried to explain to you that "she did it intentionally to herself."[52]

And then it is back to Morgan Moore, and his "long, white, bony finger" of blame that points to the "only defense they have ... the mud springs."[53]

> Morgan Moore says: "All I have is suspicions. I can't prove a thing." ... Now, I think it is shameful to point the finger in accusation, and know, as Mr. McGee knew clear back in 1975: "It is not likely that the source of her contamination will ever be known." He knew that. The AEC had come in and never came to any such conclusion. They investigated it. Morgan Moore said, "All there are are suspicions."[54]
>
> [I]t is the only defense they have, and they hope to drag you into the mud springs.[55]

While the defendant "make[s] reckless accusations and destroy[s] and desecrate[s] the good name of a decent, honorable, person,"[56] these are not actions that fit the character of a heroic protagonist; her motivations were to protect the workers at the plant, not to poison herself and endanger others by smuggling plutonium out of the plant:

> Her mother said she was crying—she was nervous, something was wrong—she knew something was wrong: "She wouldn't tell me what was wrong. She was afraid of something at the plant. She was contaminated—she said she thought she was going to die. She wanted to come home. She wanted to get away from it, but there was something wrong."[57]

Likewise, Silkwood's sister recalls that not only is Silkwood profoundly upset about her contamination but that she has knowledge about wrongdoings at the plant and must be careful:

> Her sister said: "There is something wrong. Karen wouldn't tell me over the phone. She wanted me to come so I could talk to her. She was afraid to talk to me on the phone. There was something that she knew besides the fact that she was contaminated."[58]
>
> Well, the key question is: "Did she know too much?" "Who contaminated her?" "Did she know too much?" "How much did she

know?" She knew enough to bring this whole mess to an end—the whole Kerr-McGee plant to an end.[59]

The transition to the final section of the argument is again marked by the use of rhetorical questions. The answers are all the same: "she knew enough to bring this whole mess to an end." Spence does not provide the full answer here; he saves this for his rebuttal closing argument. At that time, his "conspiracy" theory is unmistakable, providing the countermotive for the villainous and evil Kerr-McGee, the devouring monster whose lust for profits cannot be sated, to finally rise up from beneath the mud springs, causing Silkwood's death *because* she knew too much. Spence makes this argument by intimation, walking a careful tightrope of evidence, never explicitly accusing Kerr-McGee of authorizing, allowing, or encouraging Silkwood's death; he leaves this for the jury to surmise in deliberations.

Although Spence doesn't pull the pieces together, he leaves the jury to ponder the questions during the defendant's closing argument. Perhaps he chooses this strategy to provide the big ending and dramatic closure to his portion of the tale later. Perhaps his strategy is not to fully play his narrative hand: the defendant will not have an opportunity to respond to Spence's rebuttal argument and cannot then accuse Spence of doing precisely the same thing as Spence now accuses the defendant—that is, of Spence then placing the blame directly on Kerr-McGee with speculation and innuendo.

Nevertheless, Spence systematically identifies the evidence from which the jury might construct this counterstory: Silkwood's reports of doctored defective fuel rods; Kerr-McGee's desperation to obtain the reports that Silkwood planned to turn over to a reporter from The *New York Times*; the search for the never-found documents; forty pounds of plutonium missing from the plant and still unaccounted for; and Kerr-McGee's taking everything in Silkwood's residence "down to the Durkee's dressing"[60] and burying it. Spence does not connect the narrative dots.

Still, Spence can't resist observing, "[t]he cause of [Silkwood's] death isn't an issue, but fifteen minutes after she left" a nighttime union meeting for a meeting with the investigative reporter from The *New York Times*, allegedly carrying evidence of Kerr-McGee's nefarious practices, "she was dead."[61] Although the direct cause of Silkwood's death in the car accident is not an issue in the trial, it *is* potentially important to the narrative logic of Spence's counterstory. The narrative subtext is unmistakable: Kerr-McGee clearly had a motive to do whatever was necessary to stop Silkwood. This certainly provides a stronger and more satisfying story logic than Kerr-McGee's defensive speculations that Silkwood poisoned herself to discredit Kerr-McGee. ("Did she know too much?...She knew enough to bring this whole mess to an end.")[62]

I. Rebuttal Argument: The Final Confrontation

I, during the recess, wondered about whether there is enough in all of us to do what we have to do. I'm afraid—I'm afraid of two things: I'm afraid that you have been worn out, and that there may not be enough left in you to hear, even if you try, and I know you will try, but I know you are exhausted; and I've been afraid there isn't enough left in me, that my mind isn't clear and sharp now, and that I can't say the things that I need to say, and yet it has to be done, and it has to be done well.... And it is the last time that anybody will speak for Karen Silkwood. And when your verdict comes out, it will be the last time that anybody will have the opportunity that you have, and so it is important that we have the strength and power to do what we need to do.[63]

Spence begins his rebuttal with a rhetorical framework identical to the initial argument. First, he reestablishes his dialogic relationship to the jury. Then he reaffirms the historical singularity of the *Silkwood* case: "You know, history has always at crucial times reached down into the masses and picked ordinary people and gave ordinary people extraordinary power."[64] There are retellings of the legal anecdotes ("the lion gets away"—plaintiff's theory of strict liability—and "the mud springs"—defendant's theory of obfuscation and slander). This time, Spence tactically adds an admonition: "I don't want you jumping in mud springs.... [I]t is unnecessary for you to decide how plutonium escaped from the plant, how it entered her apartment, or how it caused her contamination, since it is a stipulated fact that the plutonium in Karen Silkwood's apartment was from the defendant's plant."[65] Although the defendant has the burden of proving how "the lion got away," and it is unnecessary for the jury to decide how the plutonium escaped from the plant, Spence argues that he has a moral responsibility to respond to the attacks and speculations by the defendant's attorney, unsupported by the evidence: "Mr. Paul...stood up here and pointed his finger toward Karen Silkwood.... Mr. Paul doesn't have the right to come into a court and say: 'I think this happened.' And: 'I think *that* happened.'...And to take a whole series of unrelated events and put them together...and to mislead you."[66]

Spence is "angry about *that*," that the corporation "shouldn't hide behind little people."[67] But "[i]f we want to play guess-um—that is, point the finger…I'm willing to play that game. But, when I do it, I want you to know it isn't right, because I can't prove *that* any more than they can prove it."[68] Spence does not explain what "*that*" is; he leaves it to the imagination and speculation of the jury: "What was the motive for them to do *that*? 'She was a troublemaker. She was doing union negotiations. She was on her way— she was gathering documents—every day in that union, everybody in that company, everybody in management knew that.' Nobody would admit it, but they knew it."[69] Spence contrasts the motive for Silkwood contaminating herself suggested by the defendant ("[S]he was furious. We found out that she wasn't furious.")[70] with the motive that Spence suggests for the evil Kerr-McGee: "Compare that motive with the motive of people to stop her. 'She knew too much.'"[71] And then Spence develops his counterstory: who most likely contaminated Silkwood and why.

First, Spence develops Kerr-McGee's motive to stop Silkwood ("What would she [Silkwood] do had she gotten to The *New York Times*?").[72] He then connects this with Silkwood's discovery, and ability to prove, that Kerr-McGee was producing defective and dangerous fuel rods, and her documentation of "leaks," "spills," and "incidents." Silkwood possessed proof that Kerr-McGee was doctoring the x-rays and shipping defective fuel rods. Silkwood was properly fearful for her life because of her knowledge. Spence's intimation is clear: if the jury chooses to enter "the mud springs" of speculation and blame, it is far more plausible that Kerr-McGee caused Silkwood's death to prevent her from revealing what she knew to The *New York Times*' reporter and bringing this whole mess to an end.

Spence intrudes on the narrative, making his point explicit: "You tell me there isn't a hide-up, a cover-up."[73] His comments are overcome by emotion, the force of his own words deeply affecting him emotionally, both as a speaker-narrator of the story and as a virtual member of the jury; he is an observer as well as a participant, and a guide for the jurors on the last leg of their own heroic journey, suggesting his answer to one of the three riddles: "I think she was a heroine. I think her name will be one of the names that go down in history, along with the great names of women heroines. I think she will be the woman who speaks through you, and may save this industry and this progress and may save, out of that industry, hundreds of thousands of lives."[74] Spence redelivers the call to the hero:

Now let me ask you this question: When we walk out of here I ain't going to be able to say another word, and you're going to have to make some decisions, and they are going to be made not just about Karen Silkwood, and not just about those people at the plant, but people involved in this industry and the public that is exposed to this industry. That is a frightening obligation.... Can you do it? Do you have the power? Are you afraid? If you are, I don't blame you, because I'm afraid, too. I'm afraid that I haven't the power for you to hear me. I'm afraid that somehow I can't explain my knowledge and my feelings that are in my guts to you. I wish I had the magic to put what I feel in my gut and stomach into the pit of every one of you.[75]

Initially, it is difficult to contemplate how Spence will move the narrative forward into the final stage of the battle between good and evil; nor is it clear how he will connect the past-tense melodrama about Silkwood with the mythic present-tense story of the trial itself and the heroic quest of the jury to preserve the value of justice itself. Spence solves this creative and aesthetic problem by finally removing the covers from The Beast. Like the shark in the final battle-to-the-death confrontation in *Jaws*, The Beast emerges visible from beneath the mud springs (just as the identity of Karen Silkwood is revealed, and just as Spence has revealed his own vulnerability and fearfulness). In his final revelation appears Kerr-McGee, the antagonistic force, embodied, venal, devouring, and naked at last, dripping radioactive plutonium from the bodies of young and innocent workers, future victims of death by cancer, trapped in its grasp, victims of its insatiable appetite for profits.

In his transition to completing the second act or movement of the narrative—his portion of the telling of the tale and the completion of the past-tense melodrama—Spence identifies Kerr-McGee as the cause of "the immense tragedy in this case that most of us haven't thought about verbally."[76] It is not just Silkwood's tragedy, but a tragedy for the workers still alive. "[T]hese young men may very well die. That is a horrid secret that nobody has told us."[77] The accidents have unleashed plutonium and cancer that will cause even more death if the jury does not listen to Silkwood's prophetic warnings and stop Kerr-McGee.

In this representative excerpt, Spence intersects two discrete parts of the story (the past-tense melodrama about Silkwood and the present-tense story of the trial itself and the jury's heroic quest for justice). The Beast arises from beneath the mud springs, just as Karen Silkwood predicted prophetically:

And I can hear them [agents of Kerr-McGee] saying to you and to those boys and girls that "there has never been a cancer caused by

plutonium, that we know of."...I've prosecuted murderers—eight
years I was a prosecutor—and I prosecuted murderers and thieves, and
drunk and crazy people, and I've sued careless corporations in my life,
and I want to tell you that I have never seen a company who misrepresented to the workers that the workers were cheated out of their lives.
These people that were in charge knew of plutonium. They knew what
alpha particles did. They hid the facts, and they confused the facts, and
they tried to confuse you, and they tried to cover it, and they tried to
get you in the mud springs. You know and I know what it was all about.
It was about a lousy $3.50 an hour job. And if those people knew they
were going to die from cancer twenty or forty years later, would they
have gone to work? The misrepresentations stole their lives. It's sicken-
ing. It's willful, it's callous....

...Karen Silkwood, before she died, before this case was thought of,
said that "these young men don't know." You heard her voice: "These
young men, eighteen, nineteen, twenty, twenty-one years old don't
understand."[78]

J. "The Resolve" by the Jury

Spence leaves it to the jury to do what Karen Silkwood could not do. He
resounds her prophetic warning: what will happen in the future if the jury
does not stop Kerr-McGee. But he is not quite done: Spence returns to his
opening, offering his own dark vision of "the Cimarron Syndrome" before
the arrival of "the prophet." Here, his nightmare foreshadows the future,
flash-forwarding twenty years to what will be if the jury does not stop
Kerr-McGee here and now:

Now I have a vision. It is not a dream—it's a nightmare. It came to
me in the middle of the night, and I got up and wrote it down, and
I want you to hear it....Twenty years from now—the men are not old,
some say they're just in their prime, they're looking forward to some
good things. The men that worked at that plant are good men with
families who love them. They are good men, but they are dying—not
all of them but they are dying like men die in a plague. Cancer they
say, probably from the plutonium plant. He worked there as a young
man. They didn't know much about it in those days....Nobody in top
management seemed to care. Those were the days when nobody in

management in the plutonium plant could be found, even by the AEC, who knew or cared. They worked the men in respirators. The pipes leaked. The paint dropped from the walls. The stuff was everywhere. . . .

. . . Some read about plutonium and cancer in the paper for the first time during a trial—the trial called "The Silkwood Case"—but it was too late for them. Karen Silkwood was dead, the company was trying to convince an Oklahoma jury that she contaminated herself. They took two and a half months for trial. The company had an excuse for everything. Blamed it all on the union. Blamed it all on everybody else—on Karen Silkwood, on the workers, on sabotage, on the AEC. It was a sad time in the history of our country.[79]

Spence then looks into the future and sees the "time of infamy" as "worse than the days of slavery" when "the government held hands with these giants, and played footsie."[80] He describes it as "a sad time, the era between '70 and '79—they called it the Cimarron Syndrome."[81] By projecting forward into time, Spence visualizes the alternative resolution to the story if Kerr-McGee is not stopped, and he now assumes Silkwood's prophetic role himself. Then Spence suggests answers to riddles the jury must solve in its deliberations. The first riddle: who was Karen Silkwood? Answer: she was "a brave, ordinary woman who did care. And she risked her life, and she lost it."[82] Then he suggests an answer to the second part of this riddle, of what she was trying to tell the world: "And she had something to tell the world, and she tried to tell the world. What was it that Karen Silkwood had to tell the world?"[83] Answer:

I think she would say, "Brothers and sisters. . . ." I don't think she would say ladies and gentlemen. I think she would say, "Brothers and sisters, they were just eighteen- and nineteen-year-olds. They didn't understand. There wasn't any training. They kept the danger a secret. They covered it with word games and number games." And she would say: "Friends, it has to stop here today, here in Oklahoma City today."[84]

Spence intuitively understands that there is nothing more to say, no place left to go with his story. His work is complete: "I've still got half an hour, and I'm not going to use it."[85] Spence uses an oral formulary, a stock anecdote that empowers the jury to write the final ending to the story—preferably a big Hollywood "up" ending—and to impose a coda upon the tale; it is "a simple story, about a wise old man—and a smart-aleck young boy who wanted to show up the wise old man for a fool":[86]

> The boy's plan was this: he found a little bird in the forest and captured the little bird. And he had the idea he would go to the wise old man with the bird in his hand and say, "Wise old man, what have I got in my hand?" And the old man would say, "Well you have a bird my son." And he would say, "Wise old man, is the bird alive, or is it dead?" And the old man knew if he said, "It is dead" the little boy would open his hand and the bird would fly away. Or if he said, "It is alive," then the boy would take the bird in his hand and crunch it and crunch it, and crunch the life out of it, and then open his hand and say, "See, it *is* dead." And so the boy went up to the wise old man and he said, "Wise old man, what do I have in my hand?" And the old man said, "Why it is a bird my son." He said, "Wise old man, is it alive, or is it dead?" And the wise old man said, "The bird is in your hands, my son."
>
> Thank you very much. It has been my pleasure, my God-given pleasure, to be a part of your lives. I mean that.
>
> Thank you, Your Honor.[87]

III. *Concluding Observations*
A. "Every Story Is Over Before It Begins"

As observed initially, beginnings and endings are deeply interconnected; beginnings must be carefully selected and developed in anticipation of the ending at the other end of the trajectory of plot.[88] The ending—the point of a story—gives the plot closure and meaning. This is especially so in law stories, like Spence's *Silkwood*, where the plot drives forward toward an implicit and unstated final ending. This ending must be all but inevitable to the jury, ever the more so because the final resolution is left for the jury to impose on the case outside the presence of the storyteller—an ultimate thumbs up or thumbs down, declaring which storyteller will emerge successfully from storytelling combat in the courtroom.

For example, in Spence's heroic melodrama, the true ending that Spence proposes is not the death of the protagonist Silkwood but rather her resurrection and redemption. The heroic jury is compelled to compensate Silkwood's family, punish Kerr-McGee, save the community, and subjugate the evil corporation by declaring that the heroic protagonist did not die in vain. It is here, outside the courtroom, where the jury finally solves Spence's three mythic riddles, slays the evil beast of Kerr-McGee, and provides justice with a satisfying narrative outcome and closure to the tale. Teachers of storytelling like John Gardner advise young writers—and this advice is affirmed by narrative theorists including Peter Brooks—that stories, especially stories with the hard and predictable trajectories such as genre-based melodramas, are best constructed backward, knowing exactly what the desired ending is and then developing the story line by working backward from the ending.[89] Thus, beginnings typically foreshadow all that will occur afterward, often suggesting how the story will end, although the ending is not explicit and may not be apparent in a jury trial until the moment when the jury provides the ending and imposes a final coda of meaning on the tale.

The beginning is crucial for another reason; it typically provides a narrative "hook" that engages and captures the imagination of the listener or reader, and it shapes and defines the world of all that transpires afterward. This "hook" also compels the audience to ask the storytellers the question "what happens next?" in initiating the trajectory of a plot.

Spence's complex argument in *Silkwood* opens slowly. There are many false, yet purposeful, starts before he arrives at the story. But Spence speaks to a captive audience that has already listened to the testimony and the presentation of evidence at trial over many weeks. He has been given four hours for his initial and rebuttal arguments. He can afford to be patient, to take his time before he finally arrives at the beginning. Likewise, he can simply reference evidence and fragments of testimony to evoke the fullness of imagery, characters, and scenes, drawing implicitly on the jury's recollections of the materials presented during the past eleven weeks of the trial. Thus, he can be economical in his re-presentation of the narrative particulars; he does not have to revisit every detail, although it is crucial to sequence the narrative events into a plot that takes into account all the evidence and defendant's counterstories. And Spence must, of course, be meticulous, truthful, and comprehensive. He must be—or appear to be—completely ethical and fair-minded to maintain credibility with the jury, or he risks losing everything.

Initially, he reestablishes his interactive or "dialogic" relationship with the jury, building his own credibility and his caring about and respect for the jurors and, also, reemphasizing the singularity and profound importance of this case: "It's the longest case in Oklahoma history, they tell me. And…this is probably the most important case, as well.…[A]nd it's the most important case of my career.…And, I have a sense that I have spent a lifetime, fifty years, to be exact, preparing somehow for this moment with you."[90] This is Spence's hyperbolic version of the standard lawyer's warm-up, or "proem," that Spence has incorporated into numerous closing arguments. Yet it seems spontaneous and sincere; rhetorically, Spence's credibility is crucial. Likewise, he endeavors to engage the jury "dialogically." Spence then frames his story in terms of his legal theory of the case (the "lion gets away" and strict liability) and characterizes the defendant's theory and evidentiary counterstory (the analogy of "the mud springs"). The law is transformed alchemically into narrative. Finally, Spence delivers an initial narrative "hook" and develops the "setup" for the melodramatic confrontation that follows. He begins a highly stylized and self-consciously literary pronouncement, signaling the start of the story: "It was a time of infamy, and a time of deceit, corporate dishonesty. A time when men used men like disposable commodities—like so much expendable property."⁹¹

Here, in contrast to the idyllic depictions of the anterior steady state in *Jaws* and *High Noon*, the trouble has already arrived onstage; it is already a dark and troubled time. The evil corporation has already taken over Crescent, and the survival of the community is at risk. The story is clearly not just about Silkwood and compensation for her injuries; far larger values are at stake.

Structurally, the beginning defines the outer boundaries of the narrative frame within which the ending must be achieved. The trajectory of the plot later returns specifically to this dark and foreboding place (an anterior steady state) when Spence reveals his nightmare vision for the future if the jury does not intervene on Silkwood's behalf. The initial foreboding simultaneously suggests an alternative, preferable, and irresistible "up" ending for the melodrama—a transformed steady state where the community has been liberated from the forces of antagonism and Silkwood's prophetic warning finally heeded; justice (literally the value of justice) will prevail and "law and order" will be restored in the Wild West.

But where is Silkwood in these initial paragraphs? She is not cast onstage initially. Spence first personifies the villain and the forces of antagonism of the dark, powerful, and sinister corporate giant Kerr-McGee; he brings it alive, giving it powers of thought, intentionality, and language: "well, I guarantee that corporation does not speak 'South,' it doesn't speak 'Okie,' it doesn't speak 'Western,' it doesn't speak 'New York.' ... It speaks one language universally. It speaks the language of money."⁹²

Finally, in the third portion of Spence's initial setup, protagonist Karen Silkwood, the prophet, is cast onstage to finally confront the evil villain, The Beast Kerr-McGee:

Who is Karen Silkwood? Who was she? ... I say she was a prophet, an ordinary woman who cared, and could understand, doesn't have to be anything other than an ordinary woman who cared and understood in order to be a prophet.... [A]nd she prophesied it this way.... She says this to you, ladies and gentlemen: 'Something has to be done.' "[93]

This completes the beginning or setup. Now the action begins.

Let's compare Spence's gradual setup with several more economical and compressed beginnings or openings (two from literature and one from the movies) and observe how these openings all achieve similar objectives in dissimilar ways. In "Beginning," a chapter in a primer for young writers, the novelist, critic, and teacher David Lodge identifies several illustrations of strong literary openings: the first from Jane Austen's *Emma* and the second from Ford Madox Ford's *The Good Soldier*:[94]

[From *Emma*]
Emma Woodhouse, handsome, clever, and rich, with a comfortable home and happy disposition, seemed to unite some of the best blessings of existence; and had lived nearly twenty-one years in the world with very little to distress or vex her.

She was the youngest of the two daughters of a most affectionate, indulgent father, and had, in consequence of her sister's marriage, been mistress of his house from a very early period. Her mother had died too long ago for her to have more than an indistinct remembrance of her caress, and her place had been supplied by an excellent woman as governess, who had fallen... little short of a mother in affection....

... The real evils indeed of Emma's situation were the power of having rather too much her own way, and a disposition to think a little too well of herself; these were the disadvantages which threatened [to] alloy her many enjoyments. The danger, however, was at present so unperceived, that they did not by any means rank as misfortunes with her.[95]

[From *The Good Soldier*]
This is the saddest story I have ever heard. We had known the Ashburnhams for nine seasons of the town of Nauheim with an extreme intimacy—or, rather, with an acquaintanceship as loose and easy and yet as close as a good glove's with your hand. My wife and I knew Captain and Mrs. Ashburnham as well as it was possible to know anybody, and yet, in another sense, we knew nothing at all about them. This is, I believe, a state of things only possible with English people of whom, till today, when I sit down to puzzle out what I know

of this sad affair, I knew nothing whatever. Six months ago I had never been to England, and, certainly, I had never sounded the depths of an English heart. I had known the shallows.[96]

Lodge describes the beginning of *Emma* as "classical: lucid, measured, objective, with ironic implication concealed beneath the elegant velvet glove of the style. How subtly the first sentence sets up the heroine for a fall. This is to be the reverse of the Cinderella story, the triumph of an undervalued heroine.... Emma is a Princess who must be humbled before she finds true happiness."[97] The opening clues the reader in to the steady state of lazy luxury that has existed for two decades (akin to the steady state of decay and corruption that exists in *Silkwood*) and, also, that this steady state is due for a reversal (or why would it be mentioned?). The opening is of a *maturation* or *coming of age* plot.[98] Typically, in Hollywood parlance, this is either an *education plot* (if the story ends well, with Emma's character changing after learning from her experience) or a *disillusionment plot* (if the story ends badly, with Emma's fall from grace).[99] Lodge identifies the meticulous word choice and allusions that, before the end of the first sentence, prefigure all that will take place thereafter:

> "Handsome" (rather than conventionally pretty or beautiful—a hint of masculine will-to-power, perhaps in that androgynous epithet), "clever" (an ambiguous term for intelligence, sometimes applied derogatively, as in "too clever for her own good") and "rich," with all its biblical and proverbial associations of the moral dangers of wealth: these three adjectives, so elegantly combined...encapsulate the deceptiveness of Emma's "seeming" contentment. Having lived "nearly twenty-one years in the world with very little to distress or vex her," she is due for a rude awakening.[100]

In contrast to Austen's cool elegance, Lodge observes, "Ford Madox Ford's famous opening sentence [in *The Good Soldier*] is a blatant ploy to secure the reader's attention, virtually dragging us over the threshold by the collar."[101] Unlike *Emma*, this opening is somewhat mysterious with a "characteristically modern obscurity and indirection" and an "anxiety about the possibility of discovering any truth" that "infect[s] the narrative."[102] There is, as in *Emma*, an emphasis on "the disparity between appearance and reality in English middle-class behaviour; so this beginning strikes a similar thematic note to *Emma*'s"; however, it is "tragic rather than comic in its premonitory undertones. The word 'sad' is repeated towards the end of the paragraph, and another keyword, 'heart' (two of the characters have supposed heart-conditions, all of them have disordered emotional lives), is dropped into the penultimate sentence."[103] Both *Emma* and *The Good Soldier*, as novels, focus more on the internal consciousness of the protagonist than on external actions, as in melodrama, and anticipate changes within the consciousness of various actors.

Citing an example perhaps more closely akin to Spence's genre-based beginning, Anthony Amsterdam identifies the *cinema noir* opening of the masterful film *Double Indemnity*.[104] Walter Neff, insurance salesman (according to the sign on his office door), staggers into the office with a gunshot wound in his upper chest, loads a spool into his dictating machine, and dictates this:

[Walter Neff (dictating into machine)]
Office memorandum. Walter Neff to Barton Keyes, Claims manager.
Los Angeles, July 16, 1938.

Dear Keyes. I suppose you'll call this a confession when you hear it. Well, I don't like the word confession. I just want to set you right about something you couldn't see because it was smack up against your nose.

You think you're such a hot potato as a claims manager, such a wolf on a phony claim. Maybe you are, but let's take a look at the Dietrichson claim. Accident and double indemnity.

You were pretty good in there for a while, Keyes. You said it wasn't an accident. Check.

You said it wasn't suicide. Check.

You said it was murder. Check.

You thought you had it cold, didn't you? All wrapped up in tissue paper with a pink ribbon around it. It was perfect. Except it wasn't, because you made one mistake, just one little mistake. When it came to the killer, you picked the wrong guy.

You want to know who killed Dietrichson? Hold tight to that cheap cigar of yours, Keyes. I killed Dietrichson. Me, Walter Neff, insurance salesman. Thirty-five years old, unmarried, no visible scars—[glancing down at his chest]—until a while ago, that is.

Yes. I killed him. I killed him for money. And for a woman.

And I didn't get the money, and I didn't get the woman.
Pretty, isn't it?[105]

This opening is the most compressed and complete of all the examples. It has none of Austen's sly subtlety or Ford's suggestive ambiguity. Yet it is extremely forceful and straightforward, employing the clipped speech and hard-boiled style characteristic of Raymond Chandler and similar detective fiction. Like *Silkwood*, it immediately and unmistakably clues the viewer in to the genre of the story, providing a strong narrative framing and a clear set of anticipatory expectations in the viewer. But it also resembles *Emma* and *The Good Soldier*, as well as *Silkwood*, in several important and relevant aspects.

First, like the other beginnings, it develops an initial situation of instability; there is the arrival of a "trouble" that cannot be easily resolved by the protagonist who is placed strategically at the center of the situation. In both *Double Indemnity* and *Silkwood*, this trouble is established external to the narrator. In *The Good Soldier* and *Emma*, similar to many classical modern novels, the trouble is more complex and also internal, within the consciousness of the protagonist who is or is not affected and transformed by the gradually unfolding events. That is, the subject of the novel and the movement of the narrative take place within the consciousness of the narrator and the true subject of the novel (unlike *Silkwood* or *Double Indemnity*); they are consciousness itself.

The Russian folklorist and narrative theorist Vladimir Propp famously distinguishes two alternative versions of the trouble by which the movement of a story is launched—"Villainy" and "Lack."[106] The beginnings of the novels *Emma* and *The Good Soldier* signal stories that are about a "lack" within the character of the protagonist, while the beginning of *Silkwood* is clearly a story about villainy.

The point is that all these beginnings now demand narrative propulsion or movement and change to push the plot forward through the progressive complications of the middle toward resolution. In all these beginnings, the audience (whether a reader, a viewer, or a juror) is led to ponder the precise directions that the movement will take. Enough is said about the situation and characters so that certain lines of movement are foreclosed; the audience speculates as to what specific trajectory the plot will take ("what happens next"). After the story is over, it is apparent that the ending is clearly embedded and prefigured in the beginning.

All these storytellers (Austen, Ford, Billy Wilder, Chandler, and, of course, Spence) are adept, within the constraints of their various storytelling forms and the unstated expectations of their diverse audiences, at teasing out and maintaining narrative tension in the pacing and trajectory of the respective plots. They ultimately satisfy the expectations established by the initial setup with aesthetically satisfying endings and compelling narrative payoffs. And the final payoff to Spence's story is literal; it must be translated into and spoken in the only language the villain understands, the language of money.

B. Making the Narrative Move: The "Forces
of Antagonism"

Earlier I presented the concept of narrative movement or *profluence* in plot-ting, characterized by a forward narrative momentum that is more than inertia. The concept of purposeful motion is crucial in all storytelling: the narrative must be directed toward a culmination—some ending or termi-nation (either restorative or transformative) that the sequence of events anticipates. But unlike the moviemaker or novelist, the legal storyteller faces constraints (ethical and strategic) and must fulfill obligations. For example, the story is systematically anchored in the theory of the case in addition to an aesthetically satisfying narrative theme. These two must be fitted and comple-mentary; the narrative must satisfy the legal elements presented in the theory of the case.

Often, the legal storyteller will stop the narrative and step outside the story, purposefully zigzagging from the story to the theory of the case to reveal specifically how a particular sequence of the narrative events satisfies specific elements of legal theory of the case. Spence, for example, is extremely adept at moving from his narrative to his theory of the case, repeating a short-hand phrase or referencing how a piece of the story connects with or fulfills a crucial component of his legal theory, and then returning to the story. He internalizes a psychological awareness of his audience's imaginative attention and artfully maintains his place in the progress of the plot, maintaining his listener's attention and avoiding gaps in the narrative logic of the story. He walks tightropes of language and imagery and emotion; nevertheless, it is the profluence of the plot of a well-shaped and carefully preestablished story structure that ultimately determines the success of his closing argument.

Spence's plot is shaped on a careful yet readily identifiable and prede-termined trajectory. This is especially so because the genre of the story is a familiar melodrama, and the plot of such a story is, by its very nature, highly formulaic and predictable. In this sense, the ending of a successful melodrama is clearly predetermined—the black-caped villain must lose the final and cli-mactic battle to the death, the community must likewise be saved (in a heroic "rescue" narrative), and the voice of the wise prophet finally heeded and her memory redeemed—she must be vindicated and her sacrifice must not be in vain (perhaps Spence's three-word "telegram" about the theme might be "prophets over profits").

How does Spence make the narrative move in a satisfying (yet predictable) way within a complex framework of legal and aesthetic constraints? Let's look briefly at the development of one of the characters, the villain, Kerr-McGee, within the plot and how it shapes the plot and determines the success of the story.

Let's begin with an observation about the nature of character suggested by Michael Roemer, the postmodernist notion that "we no longer believe in character."[107] Our recent neurology and behavioral psychology may suggest that in "real life" actions are often largely determined and shaped by external forces and environments rather than by the internal attributes of the actors, and that the choices are compelled by circumstances and not made exclusively by autonomous actors who must assume complete personal responsibility for their actions. This is a type of narrative framing that some attorneys may occasionally employ to persuade judges and juries. For example, in death penalty mitigation arguments, attorneys often employ stories explaining how a convicted defendant was a victim himself of "environmental" causes or human "ecology" (e.g., a backstory of horrific childhood psychological abuse, a distressing and inescapable personal situation, etc.) that helps explain, but never justifies, the acts committed by the convicted defendant. Consequently, the audience is urged to have some sympathy for the convicted at sentencing; the punishment should be mitigated and the defendant spared the death penalty. This story is connected to specific elements of the applicable legal rules, typically statutorily identified mitigating factors or circumstances.

Melodrama, however, provides a different type of framing story: characters are cast into the roles of autonomous actors and held personally accountable for their actions and choices. The trajectory of the plot then centers on the battle between the monolithic forces of good and evil embodied in clearly presented heroes and villains who are held personally responsible for the consequences of their actions. This is why torts attorneys, like Spence, typically employ the hard trajectory of the plot of a melodrama; in doing so, they attribute actions to the free will of powerful and antagonistic actors. The story eventually turns on the outcome of the battle between the hero and the villain; the conflict is between good and evil, and, in the well-framed torts law story, the value at stake in the battle to the death is typically justice itself.

In effective melodrama, the villain and the villainy are crucial to fashioning the trajectory of an effective plot. Thus, Spence patiently and purposefully transforms the corporation into the unitary and readily recognizable villain long before Silkwood is brought onstage. Systematically, the corporation is personified and given free will. Kerr-McGee is also given the power of language and, implicitly, with it comes the power of thought and intentionality (and with it the jury is charged with speaking the only language Kerr-McGee understands, the language of money). This is all in accordance with the demands of melodrama, and Spence confines his telling to the genre conventions of this highly circumscribed form.

But there is more to it than this. For the story to work fully, there must be narrative movement within the story itself, and this calls for a carefully structured but symbiotic relationship between hero and villain. As Ernest Hemingway observes about characterization in well-constructed plots, "Everything changes as it moves."[108] In courtroom melodrama, this motion requires typically that the villainy becomes ever more sinister as the plot progresses and the sum of the forces opposing the will of the heroic protagonist become more powerful so that it is imperative and urgent that the villainy be ended. Thus Spence implores his jury at the end of his closing argument (as he does in many of his cases): "Friends, it has to stop here today, here in Oklahoma City today."[109] Of course, this villainy must be built exclusively on a true depiction of the evidence and plausible inferences from that evidence.

As the screenwriting guru Robert McKee observes, in melodrama especially, the conflict must "provide progressively building pressures that force characters into more and more difficult risk-taking choices and actions, gradually revealing their true natures."[110] McKee identifies the specific "steps" in the trajectory of the plot of a compelling melodrama. According to McKee, for the story to be compelling, the conflict must be about more than merely a battle between good and evil; there must be the battle over a specific and readily identifiable value that is at stake in the story.[111] The protagonist represents the positive charge of this value, and the "forces of antagonism" (the sum of all the forces opposing the will of the protagonist, including, but not limited to, a specific antagonist or victim) represent the negative charge of this value.[112] In *Silkwood*, Spence specifically identifies the value at stake: it is justice itself. McKee observes accurately that the "stock" narrative progression in the plot of a melodrama about "justice" "moves" from the positive identification of this value (the steady state of justice) through an intermediary depiction of the corruption of this value (unfairness) toward the contrary value—the direct opposite of the positive value (injustice).[113] Finally, the story heads toward "the end of the line" where there is "a force of antagonism that's doubly negative . . . at the limit of the dark powers of human nature."[114] Specifically, the "negation of the negation" for the value of justice, according to both McKee and to Spence, is a vision of "tyranny."[115]

This template provides a suggestive framework that accurately anticipates how Spence propels the story forward by developing Karen Silkwood's progressive conflict against the forces of antagonism aligned against her. Initially, there is Kerr-McGee's "unfairness" (negligence) toward the workers at the plant. This negligent inattention allows dangerous plutonium to escape from the plant, contaminating the workers with carcinogenic plutonium; Kerr-McGee does not take precautions to protect the workers and turns a blind eye to the problems, more concerned about profits than the fate of the workers. This disturbance of the anterior steady state and the depiction of the initial trouble manifest the "contrary" value of unfairness. Then Spence's storytelling moves further down an ordered progression, from unfairness toward a "contradictory" value of illegality and injustice. Here, protagonist Karen Silkwood is cast onstage to fight against the corporation with her efforts at unionization, with her prophetic warnings, and with her revelations about nefarious and intentional misconduct authorized by Kerr-McGee covering up defects in the crystallography of the fuel rods shipped to a breeder reactor in Hanford, Washington, which she plans to turn over to a reporter from The *New York Times* at a final meeting. Kerr-McGee responds to her efforts by attempting to discredit and then silence her. ("What was the motive for them to do that?... [T]he motive of people [was] to stop her. 'She knew too much.'")[116] The illegality and injustice of Kerr-McGee's conduct spills over into the courtroom, where Kerr-McGee's attorneys and witnesses go beyond merely attempting to drag the jury down into the mud springs, when defendant points the "long, white, bony finger at [Silkwood]. It is easy to blame."[117] There is no evidence to support these allegations—"Not one person said she contaminated herself as a motive to get even, or to help the union. Not one from that witness stand...it was only Mr. Paul [defendant's attorney]. They are all his theories.[118]...They accused her then, and they accuse her now, and they continue to accuse her."[119]

Finally, in the last movements of the plot, the full articulation of the value of justice at stake in the story reaches the end of the line—tyranny—as The Beast finally emerges visible from beneath the surface of the mud springs and Spence proposes his vision of the future in the Cimarron Syndrome, where workers are "dying like men in a plague" to satisfy the ravenous appetites of greedy and profiteering Beast Kerr-McGee.[120] It is a time where Silkwood's warnings have gone unheeded, a "time of infamy," "worse than the days of slavery" when "government held hands with these giants, and played footsie."[121] This appears to complete the progression, but it is a false ending, a premature closure; it is a negative ending that, in fact, suggests that it is not too late for the possibility of a big "upbeat" ending that only the jury can provide.

The point here is not that Spence employed McKee's formula intentionally as a structured model or form on which to construct his story structure and create profluence in the narrative. Rather, it is that the conflict develops along a continuum shaped by the genre conventions of melodrama, and this

trajectory is all but inevitable as soon as Spence chooses the genre for his storytelling. That is, narrative conventions shape his storytelling in this closing
"argument" every bit as much as do legal rules and theories, the rules of evidence, or even the evidence itself that was introduced at trial. Consequently,
in retelling his story in his closing argument, Spence cannot begin easily by
initially articulating the most extreme version of the value at stake—tyranny—and then working backward in his story to discuss the lesser values.
As McKee explains, "A story must not retreat to actions of lesser quality or
magnitude, but must move progressively forward to a final action beyond
which the audience cannot imagine another."[122] Spence's story is also shaped,
of course, by the constraints of his legal theory of the case, the judge's instructions, and the requirement that he tell a story that comprehensively and fairly
represents and references the evidence presented at trial. Otherwise, he risks
destroying his credibility and losing his case in the battle of competing storytelling at trial.

As a final note, let me add that the fact that both legal and popular storytelling practices are genre-bound does not diminish the power or gravity of
these forms. Popular melodramas, whether in cinema or the courtroom, are
also attempts to approach an understanding of important cultural values. As
Peter Brooks observes about melodrama (in art and, perhaps, in life as well):

> We do not live in a world completely drained of transcendence and
> significance. Melodrama daily makes the abyss yield some of its con-
> tent, makes us feel we inhabit amid (larger) forces, and they amidst us.
> A form for secularized times, it offers the nearest *approach* to sacred
> and cosmic values in a world where they no longer appear to have any
> certain ontology or epistemology.[123]

Likewise, we employ courtroom storytelling practices, melodramas, and
myths to find the truth, to do justice, and to answer profound questions about
ourselves in the process. The fact that the stories told in the courtroom are
often repeated, often formulaic, and often developed through conventional
forms does not diminish their power or significance. Nevertheless, it is curious that to find the truth, to do justice, and to discover meaning in complex
courtroom cases such as *Silkwood* we rely on myth and melodrama to answer
riddles about a protagonist's identity, to visualize a Beast emerging from
beneath the surface of rural western mud springs, and to track the development of the forces of antagonism through a progression that often seems borrowed from a commercial Hollywood entertainment film.

Character Lessons

CHARACTER, CHARACTER DEVELOPMENT, AND CHARACTERIZATION

> *The Western conception of the person as a bounded, unique, more or less integrated motivational and cognitive universe, a dynamic center of awareness, emotion, judgment, and action organized into a distinctive whole and set contrastively against a social and natural background is, however incorrigible it may seem to us, a rather peculiar idea within the… world's cultures.*
>
> —CLIFFORD GEERTZ, "THE NATURE OF ANTHROPOLOGICAL UNDERSTANDING"

I. Introduction: Why Emphasize Movie Characters in Legal Storytelling?

Character has been called "arguably the most important single decision" made by practitioners of many modern storytelling forms, especially the novel.[1] The novel elevates and dramatizes the art of psychological characterization, of character development, and of motivation; as a form, it squarely places the art of characterization at the forefront of storytelling practice. Indeed, theorists have observed that the primary subject of the modern novel is consciousness and that "[t]he center…of all great literature…is character."[2] In the somewhat reductionist vocabulary of more recent practitioners of visual cinematic storytelling and screenwriting, modern realist novels are typically "character driven." Movies, however, are not; movies are typically "plot based." The focus, especially in commercial entertainment films, is on developing a compelling plot; the characters are shaped and developed in character "arcs" constructed in relationship to, and in service of, the core narrative structure of the plot. Characters are subservient to the demands of plot. Some of the reasons for this are pragmatic: there simply isn't the room or the time available in a commercial two-hour plot to flesh out fully developed characters and characterization. And there isn't the need since the actors are already visible on the screen and can be seen and interpreted by the audience. The audience for a film, absorbing the story in a single viewing, typically does not have the inclination to sift through a gradual novelistic unfolding of character, especially when much of this material may be "irrelevant" or superfluous to the demands of a carefully circumscribed narrative "plot" structure.

Additionally, there are no apparent structural mechanisms or visual techniques typically available in film that allow the story to go within or extensively explore the "consciousness" of the various characters, to radically shift perspectives from character to character, or to provide extended internal or descriptive ruminations on the "character" or internal psychology of the various players in a story; these are the strengths of the novel. In contrast to the novel, there is a certain reductionist and pragmatic approach to character development typical in popular film. It is also why novelists, including those who have also written superb screenplays, often denigrate cinematic storytelling practices. As the novelist E. L. Doctorow puts it:

> Fiction goes everywhere, inside, outside, it stops, it goes, its action can be mental. Nor is it time-driven. Film is time-driven, it never ruminates, it shows the outside of life, it shows behavior. It tends to the simplest moral reasoning. Films out of Hollywood are linear. The narrative simplification of complex morally consequential reality is always the drift of a film inspired by a book. Novels can do anything in the dark horrors of consciousness. Films can do close-ups, car drive-ups, places, chases and explosions.[3]

Now here is the curious rub about legal storytelling practices: storytelling in the law is equally reductionist and plot driven, strongly akin to conventions of commercial entertainment storytelling practices. Indeed, often characters in law stories seem borrowed from a repository of "stock" film characters.

This relationship between character in popular film and legal storytelling practice is not coincidental: as in commercial Hollywood films, characters in legal stories are developed in close relationship to plot. There is simply insufficient room, and typically few literary techniques available, for developing fully formed characters (at least, fully formed within the tradition of the realist novel). Indeed, characters in law stories are subservient in their actions to the demands of the plot. Typically, characters presented in law stories simply lack the psychological complexity and the interior life of characters depicted in the novel. The primary concern in legal storytelling is how the story will end, often embodied in the decision or verdict of a jury at trial, or announced in the words "it is so ordered" in an appellate opinion. Consequently, the focus is not on creating interesting characters who will compel the imaginative attention of the audience; rather the emphasis is on characters and characterization as means to a particular plot outcome. Does this mean that character development in legal storytelling practice does not matter? Of course not. As we explore in this chapter, especially in a close reading of a carefully constructed closing argument in a criminal case, the effective creation, depiction, and casting of characters is profoundly important and often outcome determinative.

II. What Is Character, and Why Is It Important to Legal Storytellers?

In the movie *The Maltese Falcon*, Sydney Greenstreet observes to the detective-protagonist portrayed by Humphrey Bogart, "My word, you certainly are a character, aren't you?"[4] The audience knows intuitively that he is referring to some intrinsic quality within the detective that makes him compelling and provides a core psychological identity to him as a player in the drama. But what exactly is character? Is it a composition or cluster of various "characteristic" psychological traits and attributes? Is it the shell of appearance or physical description? Is it some controlling myth that dominates us, inhabits our soul, and compels us mysteriously in our conduct and our behavior? Or is it somehow the distillation and transposition of "real life" onto the page or screen or into the courtroom? Perhaps character is primarily a function of storytelling practice itself. Let me begin by observing that "character" has multiple, disparate and, often, conflicting meanings. Heraclitus observed that "[c]haracter is fate for a man."[5] At that time, the gods were thought to be in control of the fates and, consequently, of character. Any individuality was stolen at the expense of the gods. Sophisticated and literary notions of complex psychological characterization, motivation, and individuated personality were simply not an order available on the narrative menu of the day.

Character is no longer controlled by the gods. In modern storytelling forms, complex psychological notions of character became most pronounced in the modern novel. As Edith Wharton famously pronounced, character has been the "main concern...of the novel" for the past two centuries; "the test of the novel is that its people should be *alive*," and "[n]o subject in itself, however fruitful, appears to be able to keep a novel alive; only the characters in it can."[6] According to David Lodge (and the illustrations are endless) the high-water mark for "character" was the "European" novel of the seventeenth through nineteenth centuries: "nothing can equal the great tradition of the European novel in richness, variety and psychological depth of its portrayal of human nature."[7] In more recent days, and in more recent storytelling practices, including the literary novel in the twentieth century, character was often streamlined, as if in anticipation of the form of the movie, compelling F. Scott Fitzgerald to observe that "[a]ction is character."[8] Most recently, in many popular storytelling practices, including in literary fiction, the importance and relevance of character and characterization is in decline. Characters are often reduced in complexity or presented in shorthand forms. It may be that there is no longer a shared cultural belief in the power of the individual to shape or control narrative outcomes. As Bob Dylan celebrated ironically in song, "Take what you have gathered from coincidence."[9] That is, implicitly, character and the actions that appear to reflect a person's character are more a function of circumstance and environment. As the filmmaker and postmodern literary theorist Michael Roemer claims, "WE NO LONGER BELIEVE IN CHARACTER."[10] Put another way, our characters no longer control their own fate or destiny. Here is how Jerome Bruner states the proposition in expository form:

> I want to begin by proposing boldly that...there is no such thing as an intuitively obvious and essential self to know, one that just sits there ready to be portrayed in words. Rather, we constantly construct and reconstruct our selves to meet the needs of the situations we encounter, and we do so with the guidance of our memories of the past and our hopes and fears for the future. Telling oneself about oneself is like making up a story about who and what we are, what's happened, and why we're doing what we're doing.[11]

For many recent storytellers, character is constantly in flux and seldom static or fixed. But others have gone even further, in their belief that fate is shaped by forces far beyond our comprehension or control, that our character has little to do in determining the outcome of our stories. As the novelist Irwin Shaw observed:

> It's no accident that Kafka has become so popular. He's enjoying the popularity of a prophet whose prophecies have come true. He prophesied the emergence of the Victim as the archetype of modern man—the Victim who is slowly teased and tortured and destroyed by forces that are implacable and pitiless and that cannot be understood.[12]

However, in our legal storytelling practices, character still matters; it matters profoundly. In legal storytelling WE STILL BELIEVE IN CHARACTER, especially in the economical and persuasive depiction of sympathetic and compelling characters, clearly defined and recognizable, with coherent psychological motivation, fulfilling their purposes within a highly structured and composed plot. In this sense, creation and effective depiction of characters (characterization) is a vital tool of narrative persuasion, especially in legal storytelling. In legal storytelling practice, plots do not open outward on a postmodern confusion, nor do environments outside the intentionality of the various players in the story typically dictate the unfolding of events. We emphasize free will in legal stories; causation results from the deliberate and purposeful choices and actions of the various players in the story. Legal stories are tightly wound, compressed, and plot-based realist narratives; we invite our readers and listeners to judge actions, make inferences about causation, and assign legal responsibility all based on their understandings of a character's "character."

Here is a brief sampling from an inventory of reasons why a character's "character" is especially important in most legal storytelling practice:

1. It is a pervasive habit of thought in society to regard people's behavior as determined by their innate character traits and propensities rather than by their situations or circumstances. When trying to understand "events"—who took what actions and why—we look for explanations in the character of the actor, that is, in the actor's *personal disposition*.[13] Social psychologists call this tendency "fundamental attribution error"[14] or "correspondence bias."[15] A story may depict the character of its central player or players in a subtly nuanced way, as we will see in Jeremiah Donovan's depiction of defendant Louie Failla, or in a gross, stereotypical way. Regardless, what human being X will do is seen as a product of what

human being X is like. Therefore, to make the plot action of stories persuasive, it is crucial to create characters whom the audience will expect to act in particular ways.

2. Judges and juries in criminal cases are particularly given to seeking explanations for behavior in character. For example, judges who impose severe criminal sentences take comfort in the belief that convicted defendants are the type of people who deserve these sentences. Some judges, perhaps, become jaded and lose interest in the many-faceted, complex circumstances of individual cases and find it easier to think about individual defendants as repeat performances of stereotypical perpetrators. Judges are accustomed to administering legal rules that assign great importance to mental states in the grading and punishment of crimes—particularly serious crimes—and it is easy for them to think about particular mental states as attributes of particular types of minds.

3. In criminal trials, just as in popular stories, *motivation* is simultaneously a mainspring of action and a reflection of character. David Lodge puts it this way in discussing motivation and character in the novel:

> Motivation in a [classic realist] novel is a code of *causality*. It aims to convince us that the characters act as they do not simply because it suits the interests of the plot... but because a combination of factors, some internal, some external, plausibly cause them to do so. Motivation in the realist novel tends to be, in Freudian language, "overdetermined," that is to say, any given action is the product of several different drives or conflicts derived from more than one level of the personality.[16]

In this regard, literary and popular storytelling conventions are based on the same premise as legal theory—the model of "the unique, autonomous individual responsible for his or her own acts."[17] According to this model, motivation serves as a two-way bridge between character and action: it enables the reader-viewer-fact finder to infer what a character will do from what kind of person the character is and vice versa. Consequently, it is typically necessary to create coherent, intelligible characters to persuade our judges and juries that our plot makes sense and produces a satisfactory ending to the story of the case.

4. Finally, judges and juries, akin to movie audiences, will root for the characters in a story whom they come to like. Therefore, it often behooves legal storytellers to create sympathetic protagonists with whom the audience can at least identify. On the other hand, the audience will typically long to

witness the downfall of characters whom they come to dislike, whether or not these characters are clearly identified antagonists and often regardless of whether the legal rules governing the legal issues make the personalities or mental states of these characters relevant.

III. Flat and Round Characters and Static and Changing Characters—High Noon *Revisited*

A. Flat and Round Characters, Static and Changing Characters

E. M. Forster famously postulated in his classic dictum in *Aspects of the Novel* that there are both flat and round characters.[18] A dictionary of narratology defines a flat character as "[a] character endowed with one or very few traits and highly predictable in behavior."[19] As Forster puts it, a flat character is "constructed [a]round a single idea or quality."[20] He or she "can be expressed in one sentence" and "has no existence outside it,... none of the private lusts and aches that must complicate [even] the most consistent human lives."[21] Simply put, flat characters are monochromatic or one-dimensional, often cast onstage to express a single idea or to serve a specific plot function—keeping the plot on track or causing an important "twist" or turn in the plot. Alternatively, this character may keep alignment within the story structure, cast onstage to push the narrative inexorably forward.

The townspeople in *High Noon* are all clearly flat characters, each expressing one idea reducible to a single sentence. They push the protagonist Will Kane ever forward in his failed quest for allies so that he must, ultimately, face the villain Frank Miller and the Miller gang alone. Take, for example, the hotel clerk; his single line might be: "The town was better off when Frank Miller was in charge, before Will Kane sent him to prison; I can't wait until he returns and finishes off Kane, and we get back to business once again." Another flat character is Kane's young former deputy sheriff, Harvey. Harvey is cast onstage repeatedly to serve plot functions, reveal crucial backstory, and keep the plot moving forward. His more complex sentence, depicting the source of all his motivations and actions, might read: "I'm as good a man as Kane; either I'm given or I take what was his (and what is now rightfully mine)—both his mistress and his job—or I am out of here."

"Flat" characters may have some aspect or trait that makes (and keeps) them interesting or compelling, but what they lack, typically, is psychological complexity or the ability to change; they are fixed entities and typically do not develop or change in the course of the plot. Flat characters display no distracting internal conflicts; their actions embody and manifest the single-sentence idea that makes them come alive and gives them purpose. Often, the character is brought onstage, especially in film, to advance a crucial sequence of the narrative design. Afterward, this flat character may simply disappear. This does not mean that flat characters are intrinsically uninteresting as characters. Indeed, just the opposite may be the case; there may be some compelling aspect to a flat character that makes him come alive momentarily, or allows the image and identity of the character to linger in the mind of the audience long after the character fulfills her purpose and departs from the story. Further, flat characters often have great utility within the story; the books of some classical novelists (e.g., Charles Dickens) and that of many effective legal storytellers are populated with vivid flat characters cast into crucial secondary roles within the story.

Forster observed subtly about flat characters in the novel:

> One great advantage of flat characters is that they are easily recognized whenever they come in—recognized by the reader's emotional eye, not by the visual eye, which merely notes the recurrence of a proper name.... It is a convenience for an author when he can strike with his full force at once, and flat characters are very useful to him [in doing this], since they never need reintroducing...and provide their own atmosphere....
>
> A second advantage is that they are easily remembered by the reader afterwards. They remain in his mind as unalterable....We all want books to endure, to be refuges, and their inhabitants to be always the same, and flat characters tend to justify themselves on this account.[22]

These observations are, in large measure, also applicable to flat characters in legal storytelling practices, making the use of well-formed flat characters invaluable.

Forster also speaks of "round" characters.[23] Typically, round characters are located at the core of the story; they are more fully developed than flat characters and reveal different aspects or facets as the story develops. The narrative logic and the constellation of secondary flat characters circulate around these core round or complex characters. The story is, in large measure, often—but not necessarily—"their" story. A round character is "[a] complex, multidimensional, unpredictable character."[24] Forster observes that "[t]he test of a round character is whether it is capable of surprising in a convincing way."[25] To create convincing round characters and to make them come alive, it is necessary to provide sufficient information about the character's internal tensions, contradictions, and complications so that the audience will understand the character's actions as "the product of several different drives or conflicts derived from more than one level of the personality."[26]

There is a second important aspect about understanding and depicting round characters. In addition to their psychological complexity, these characters are typically not static within the structure of the plot; they tend to move or evolve or change internally just as the plot develops. As Hemingway observed, when asked about characters and characterization in his novels, "Everything changes as it moves.... Sometimes the movement is so slow it does not seem to be moving. But there is always change and always movement."[27] The change in characters in most legal storytelling, akin to the trajectory of character arcs of many round characters in films, is more scripted and predictable than in the classic novels that are more about character development than plot.

Nevertheless, complex characters may change during the course of a legal story or even the typical commercial popular entertainment film. They mature or degenerate, they have an epiphany or at least an attitudinal shift, or they gain control or lose control of their actions. Regardless, their actions and choices affect their worlds causally and, more important, determine the movement of the plot and the outcome of the story. This is especially so in law stories that, like the popular entertainment film, employ the model of "the unique, autonomous individual responsible for his or her own acts."[28]

The transformation or character shift in law stories typically occurs on a clearly identified and circumscribed trajectory, in Hollywood screenwriting terminology a "character arc."[29] This shift or clear and apparent movement signifies more than the fact that the audience simply knows more about who the character is at the end of the story than at the beginning. Rather, the plot works internally on the character, compelling the character to make crucial choices or take actions that, in turn, shape the plot and the outcome of the story. In doing so, the story compels important internal changes or personal transformation within the character's psychology so that the character is not the same person at the end of the story as at the beginning, as is apparent, for example, in the transformation of the "complex" characters of Helen Ramirez and Amy Kane in *High Noon*. The story inevitably works upon the character's character, and the audience observes and perceives the "reverberations"[30] of the plot within the story.

Other characters are static. They remain frozen in the same mold from start to finish. There is some apparent relationship between the flat-character–round-character taxonomy and the static-character–evolving-character taxonomy. Flat characters *must* also be static. Round characters can be either static or evolving. And especially in legal stories, the character arc of a round character, especially the protagonist, is often left intentionally incomplete.

The next section, as an illustration of this terminology, offers one suggested analysis of how some of the important characters from *High Noon* fit into this typology.

B. The Heroic Protagonist—Will Kane

The protagonist is typically at the center of a Hollywood movie (akin to a law story told about a plaintiff in a tort case or a criminal defendant). The story is typically his or her story; the plot is "protagonist driven," and the movie is primarily about the protagonist. The film is usually "shot" (told) from the "point of view" (perspective) of the protagonist, and, although there may be some scenes or sequences of scenes without the protagonist in them (e.g., the perspective may temporarily shift away from the protagonist), the protagonist's experiences are usually at the center of the film. Even when there are scenes, or sequences of scenes, where the protagonist is not present, these are typically about the protagonist and fill in important pieces of the protagonist's story (or backstory). The protagonist is, invariably, the subject of these scenes. Other characters develop through their relationships with the protagonist; characters diminish in significance in the plot as they orbit farther away from their interactions with the protagonist, who remains at the center of the constellation of characters.

Will Kane is the protagonist in *High Noon*; the story is his story. He is a somewhat complex character. The plot is about his internal development (his character arc) as he moves from honoring his pledge to Amy and leaving town to desperately attempting to enlist the assistance of the townspeople, to finally doing what the hero must do—standing up alone against the evil Frank Miller and the villainous Miller gang. Most of the film is not about the final confrontation and showdown; it is about what happens (or fails to happen) as Kane awaits the arrival of Frank Miller and the Miller gang.

Will Kane, and Gary Cooper's portrayal of Kane, is clearly not a "flat" or "static" character. He has some depth and complexity; it is apparent that he is not a two-dimensional or stereotypical Western melodrama hero. But is he a fully realized, "complex" character—in Forster's literary sense in that his actions in response to the progressive complications of the plot are unpredictable in a way that is both convincing and sometimes surprising? In the end, Kane must respond to his plight and fulfill his heroic narrative destiny; Kane must resolve his internal conflicts and rise to meet the challenges of the melodramatic plot and the expectations of the audience. Kane is an archetypal hero and must do what heroes always do; he is not free to choose to do otherwise. Here, the novelist Edith Wharton's observations about heroes are relevant: the protagonist-hero "tend[s] to be the least real" of characters because the protagonist is a "survivor... of the old 'hero' and 'heroine' whose business it was not to be real but to be sublime" and also because the story being "*about them*,... forces them into the shape which its events impose."[31]

Kane's actions are constrained by his role in the story; Kane must fulfill his narrative destiny and the "logic" of the plot. As a Western melodramatic hero, he must act to save the community, and he must do what a hero must do. Likewise, his internal life and his psychological characteristics—that is, his character arc—are ultimately shaped by his role and by the expectations of the audience. Michael Roemer reflects thoughtfully on how actions inform the character of the Western hero:

> The Western hero often saves an entire community. He guides wagon trains through Indian territory, knows how to ford raging rivers, and protects women, children, and the infirm. But while he is the leader, he remains a "common," democratic man, and his actions, unlike those of King Lear or Julien Sorel, meet with the approval of the audience. If he opposes his fellow townsmen to prevent the lynching of an innocent prisoner, the community will eventually see the light. Conflicts and problems are invariably solved by courage and reason, and there is no need for suffering or self-division.[32]

Superficially, Kane presents the psychological and physical characteristics of the stereotypical Western hero; he is handsome, strong-willed, fair-minded, and willing to sacrifice himself in service of the community. But Will Kane also possesses certain psychological and physical characteristics atypical for the traditional Hollywood Western hero; Gary Cooper plays Kane "against type." Will Kane is a much older man than the audience is used to seeing Cooper portray. He is also a more complex character, capable of betraying the women he loves, Helen and Amy, and capable of contemplating self-betrayal as well. Kane is initially fearful—he races out of town upon hearing of Frank Miller's anticipated arrival—and then must overcome his fear to act heroically at the end of the movie, regardless of the consequences. He is certainly a much less commanding figure, and not a pure heroic archetype, as the more comfortable and predictable heroes Cooper frequently portrayed in earlier films.[33]

C. Amy Kane and Helen Ramirez: Complex "Round" Characters

There are other vivid, fluid, and complex characters in *High Noon*. As Edith Wharton observes, these subordinate characters are often freer than the protagonist to "mov[e] at ease," changing and developing within the "interstices of the tale, and free to go about their business in the illogical human fashion."[34] Amy Kane and Helen Ramirez are such complex characters, although their "movements" are not so "free" and never so "illogical" as in Wharton's estimate of the movements of complex characters in the novels of an earlier time. In popular movies, akin to legal storytelling practices, all characters, including complex characters like Amy and Helen, exist on much tighter narrative tethers, constrained in their movements by character arcs established in service of, and subservient to, the plot. Like Kane, Amy and Helen are both compelling characters. They represent oppositional archetypes: the blonde, patrician, and initially dependent Amy; and the darker, street-smart, mercurial Mexican businesswoman Ramirez. Both women are betrayed by Kane. These betrayals, and the women's responses to them, are at the core of their characters' "character" and the form of their respective developmental arcs.

Both Amy Kane and Helen Ramirez have complex inner psychologies revealed through their dialogue and, more important in film, through their choices in action. Both are "fluid" rather than "static" characters who develop and change through the course of the movie. However, this development is shaped in a clear progression of a purposeful and carefully composed character arc typical of the conventions of cinematic—and of legal—storytelling practices. As Margaret Mehring explains about characterization in the popular movies: "Character traits have to be compressed and condensed. All non-essential character traits must be eliminated and [the essential ones] then compacted—layered—into a denser form."[35] This is also typical of legal storytelling practice: the depiction of character is streamlined; there is simply no narrative "time" allotted for psychological digression. Character arcs are economically developed in law stories; character is visible and apparent.

So, for example, Amy begins the film as a Quaker who does not believe in violence. She has her good reasons for her deeply held pacifist beliefs; her motivations are sketched in through the backstory provided in dialogue in just a few simple lines: both her father and her brother were killed in gunfights. She has married Kane, the marshal, but her marriage vow is conditioned on Kane's promise to hang up his guns after the ceremony, give up violence, and leave Hadleyville to become a shopkeeper in another town. Initially, Will Kane honors his promise, and literally hangs up his guns; the two newlyweds leave town in their buckboard before Frank Miller's arrival. But they don't get far before Kane turns his rig around and heads back to Hadleyville ready to resume his job as marshal. He declares to Amy: "I've got to go back.... They're making me run. I've never run from anything before."[36] Amy is thus betrayed. Amy leaves Kane, and plans to leave Hadleyville. But when she is already on the train and preparing to depart (it is the same train that brings Frank Miller to town), she undergoes an apparent character reversal: at the sound of the gunfire she rushes off the train to assist her man. Although Amy is a pacifist, she picks up a gun and shoots the outlaw Corey in the back to protect Kane. And when Frank Miller takes her hostage, Amy defends herself. She claws at Miller's face—freeing herself physically and perhaps also liberating herself from the constraints of her pacifist beliefs—so that Kane has a clear shot at Miller and can kill him in the final shoot-out. She makes a choice that redefines her character. At the end of the movie, Amy leaves town with Kane, completing her character arc. She has moved from dependency and passivity to strength and action, her internal beliefs and convictions modified and tempered by the knowledge that she has gained from experience. This enables her to overcome her past, change her beliefs, and reconcile with her beloved.

D. Frank Miller (Antagonist/Villain): A "Flat" and "Static" Character

The villain in *High Noon* is Frank Miller, the leader of the Miller gang. He is the primary oppositional force, the force of antagonism, that creates the conflict and compels the other round characters to act and to change. He is the crucial character; the plot of the film could not develop without him. Yet as is typical of villains, Frank Miller is a flat and static character. Miller's obsessive single sentence, his uniform motivational mantra throughout this movie, might be stated: "I'm gonna get Will Kane for sending me to prison and take back the town, my mistress, and all that was once mine." His strength, like the shark's obsession for human flesh in *Jaws*, is in his evil nature and in his ability to impose his will upon the story: his single-mindedness of purpose. Peter Brooks puts it nicely: "Melodramatic good and evil are highly personalized: they are assigned to, they inhabit persons who indeed have no psychological complexity but who are strongly characterized. Most notably, evil is villainy; it is a swarthy, cape-enveloped man with a deep voice."[37] The aesthetic question is how to keep the audience interested in a true villain for the course of the entire plot. In *Jaws* the answer is to have the shark become ever more evil and brazen in its rapacious attacks on vulnerable townspeople, and even to focus meticulously on the details of these attacks, allowing the audience to become voyeuristically engrossed, participating in the attacks often viewed from the underwater perspective of the shark. In the *Silkwood* closing argument the structure builds, shifting the identity of various underlings until the identity of the true culprit is revealed; the devouring corporation rises up from beneath the mud springs.

In *High Noon* the aesthetic solution sustaining the compelling power of the villain is just the opposite: the villain is kept offstage until just before the ending, building the villain's power and strength by employing the reactions of the community to his memory and to the prospect of his return. His identity and character are established consistently by what others say about him, by his reputation, and by the townspeople's (and Kane's) fear of him. Visual imagery (ticking clocks, railroad tracks pointed toward town, black smoke, and meetings of the outlaw gang) foreshadow and set the stage for Miller's arrival, and the ultimate showdown and final confrontation between good and evil that is at the core of melodrama.

The final movement of the plot (the "third act" or the climax and resolution) takes place when Miller steps down from the train and moves out of the shadows and into the sunlight. His power and villainy is anticipated by the audience; we are confident that Miller will prove a worthy adversary for Will Kane. Although Frank Miller is a flat and static character, he maintains a compelling interest for the length of the movie; he serves his purpose in wrapping up the plot of a Hollywood Western melodrama. In legal storytelling the effective use of compelling flat and round characters is equally important to moving the audience forward in resolving the story's plot.

IV. Techniques of Character Development and Characterization: Excerpts from Tobias Wolff's This Boy's Life

Closely related to the subject of types of characters is the subject of how to develop vivid and compelling characters, that is, the use of techniques for effective "characterization." We can identify three primary techniques for character development. These techniques are common to all forms of popular storytelling, regardless of whether the storyteller is writing a brief, short story, or novel, employing an oral storytelling form as in the depiction of character to a judge or jury at trial, engaging in visual storytelling as in a movie, or, ever more often these days, a mixture or blend of various forms. These three basic storytelling techniques for creating and developing effective and compelling characters are: (1) selective use of physical detail and physical description, (2) employing dialogue to reveal character, and, most especially, (3) use of action to reveal character.

1. *Description.* Vivid characters are often initially presented through economical use of selected details. Depiction of character through description need not be comprehensive in design. Indeed, just the opposite—an overload of psychological or physical description, employing the baggage of too many descriptive details, too many adjectives, and too much motivational backstory detracts from effective characterization, especially in plot-driven legal and popular stories. That is, the explanation of a character's character is usually ineffective because this strategy slows the propulsion of the plot; and because it slows the plot, the story is made suspect and distrusted by the audience.

Nevertheless, effective characterization captures appropriate traits, often in arresting imagery or in vivid detail that calls forth character. Carefully selected details can imply, or even reveal, the character whole cloth. Often, the audience assembles for itself the accretion of pieces into the composition of the character's character. What is left out of the composition is often as important as what is included. Characterization flows from the story itself, as if the narrative or argument compels the relevant details. Effective depiction of character through description is a composition of meticulous and intentional choices that compel the attention and interest of the audience and simultaneously, allow the audience to complete the composition.

2. *Dialogue.* The critic and essayist James Wood comments that "[w]e can tell a great deal from a character by how he talks and whom he talks to—how he bumps up against the world."[38] That is, we bump up against the world through our verbal communications and interactions with others, in dialogue. Likewise, we read an individual's character into what that individual says and how he or she says it. As Anthony Amsterdam tells his students, especially when the students are young legal practitioners preparing appellate and postconviction briefs, dialogue is frequently the legal storyteller's single most effective instrument for creating believable characters. Some students, especially in attempting to understand the art of brief writing and creative

advocacy, respond that "you can't submit a brief in written dialogue," to which Amsterdam, in turn, replies, "Sure you can."[39] He follows up: "That is what quotation and paraphrase [which narratologists call 'indirect discourse'[40]] are all about."[41] Further, records and transcripts are always chock full of "quotable testimony, colloquies, motions, and rulings" that, in Amsterdam's words, "can be used to create a rogues' gallery of characters damned near equal to Shakespeare's."[42] I don't know whether I'd go quite this far. Nevertheless, as we will see in Donovan's closing argument on behalf of Louis Failla, dialogue is a powerful tool to convey character economically and compellingly, and there is often plenty of material available in virtually all forms of legal storytelling (from trial arguments to appellate briefs) to employ dialogue creatively and imaginatively in service of character.

3. *Action.* As previously observed, character is not fixed or static; characters change. Complex characters develop as a story progresses, with the characters' motivations and actions driving the plot forward. Thus there is an interplay between character development and plot. The characters and the conflicts between various characters compel events, and the actions in the plot are, in turn, affected by the plot. Likewise, the fuller dimensions of character are revealed in response to, or in the aftermath of, the events of the story; these are what the novelist and short-story writer Katherine Anne Porter called the "reverberations" of the story,[43] on both the audience and the various characters within it.

Character can and does imply conduct, such conduct not only attributing motivation and explanation for what has already happened in the story, but foreshadowing what will happen next. That is, the audience intuitively draws on notions of character and the character's role within the story to look forward in anticipation of what will happen next, in addition to looking back into the past to fully understand what has happened so far. As Porter watches her characters heading toward their fates, she observes:

> Every once in a while when I see a character of mine just going towards perdition, I think, "Stop, stop, you can always stop and choose, you know." But no, being what he was, he already *has* chosen, and he can't go back on it now. I suppose the first idea that man had was the idea of fate, of the servile will, of a deity who destroyed as he would, without regard for the creature. But I think the idea of free will was the second idea.[44]

It is only through the way a character acts that the audience can come to understand the underlying character traits that brought about those particular actions. This greater understanding of his character then informs how the audience expects him to act in the future.

A. Excerpts from *This Boy's Life*

The use of the techniques of description, dialogue, and action to create, sustain, and develop vivid and compelling stories is apparent in literature, popular storytelling, and legal storytelling practice (including briefs, arguments, and, indeed, even judicial opinions). Several excerpts from Tobias Wolff's masterful memoir *This Boy's Life* illustrate this pattern. There are two characters in the following illustrative sequence of scenes. There is the complex protagonist-hero and narrator, Toby. And then there is the character of the vivid antagonist, Toby's soon-to-be stepfather, Dwight. Unlike the villains in *High Noon* and *Jaws*, Dwight is not a flat or static character; he is a more complex "literary" character caught in an ever-deepening tangle of darkening motives, resentment, and rage. Likewise, Toby has an equally complex and changing character.

The sequence of scenes excerpted illustrate the use of: (1) *description*, (2) *dialogue*, and (3) *action* as tools or techniques of characterization, character development, and character change driving this well-paced and highly charged plot forward.

In the first sequence of scenes, the reader is introduced to the character "Dwight" as a minor and flat character. Dwight is vividly *described*; he is one of the many suitors of Toby's beloved and vivacious mother, Marian. In the next sequences Dwight is further developed. Dwight evolves from a flat and minor character into a central figure in the story—Dwight, the distant suitor, will soon become Toby's stepfather. Toby is being driven from his mother's home in Seattle to his new home with Dwight and Marian in rural Washington. On the way, the *dialogue* reveals darker aspects of Dwight's character: the physical details of the humorous, offhanded earlier depiction of Dwight open, like cracks or fissures, upon the darkness of his character. Finally, his antagonism to Toby translates into *action* and the confrontation between Dwight and Toby intensifies. This confrontation escalates through the remainder of the book as Toby attempts to escape the fate that awaits him with Dwight and to rescue Marian from her fate as well.

From an initial depiction (a physical description) of Dwight

Dwight was a short man with curly brown hair and sad, restless brown eyes. He smelled of gasoline. His legs were small for his thick-chested body, but what they lacked in length they made up for in spring; he had an abrupt, surprising way of springing to his feet. He dressed like no one I'd ever met before—two-tone shoes, hand-painted tie, monogrammed blazer with a monogrammed handkerchief in the breast pocket. Dwight kept coming back, which made him chief among the suitors. My mother said he was a good dancer—he could really make those shoes of his get up and go. Also, he was very nice, very considerate.

I didn't worry about him. He was too short. He was a mechanic. His clothes were wrong. I didn't know why they were wrong, but they were. We hadn't come all the way out here to end up with him. He didn't even live in Seattle; he lived in a place called Chinook, a tiny village three hours north of Seattle, up in the Cascade Mountains. Besides, he'd already been married. He had three kids of his own living with him, all teenagers. I knew my mother would never let herself get tangled up in a mess like that.[45]

Dwight drives Toby to his new home (action and some dialogue)

Dwight drove in a sullen reverie. When I spoke he answered curtly or not at all. Now and then his expression changed, and he grunted as if to claim some point of argument. He kept a Camel burning on his lower lip. Just the other side of Concrete he pulled the car hard to the left and hit a beaver that was crossing the road. Dwight said he had swerved to miss the beaver, but that wasn't true. He had gone out of his way to run over it. He stopped the car on the shoulder of the road and backed up to where the beaver lay.

We got out and looked at it. I saw no blood. The beaver was on its back with its eyes open and its curved yellow teeth bared. Dwight prodded it with his foot. "Dead," he said.

It was dead all right.

"Pick it up," Dwight told me. He opened the trunk of the car and said, "Pick it up. We'll skin the sucker out when we get home."

I wanted to do what Dwight expected me to do, but I couldn't. I stood where I was and stared at the beaver.

Dwight came up beside me. "That pelt's worth fifty dollars, bare minimum." He added, "Don't tell me you're afraid of the damned thing."

"No sir."

"Then pick it up." He watched me. "It's dead, for Christ's sake. It's just meat. Are you afraid of hamburger? Look." He bent down and gripped the tail in one hand and lifted the beaver off the ground. He tried to make this appear effortless but I could see he was surprised and strained by the beaver's weight. A stream of blood ran out of its nose, then stopped. A few drops fell on Dwight's shoes before he jerked the body away. Holding the beaver in front of him with both hands, Dwight carried it to the open trunk and let go. It landed hard. "There," he said, and wiped his hands on his pant leg.

We drove farther into the mountains. It was late afternoon. Pale cold light. The river flashed green through the trees beside the road, then turned gray as pewter when the sun dropped. The mountains darkened. Night came on.[46]

Later in the journey (dialogue and some action)

I played the radio softly, thinking I'd use less power that way. Dwight came out of the tavern a long time after he went in, at least as long a time as we'd spent getting there from Seattle, and gunned the car out of the lot. He drove fast, but I didn't worry until we hit a long series of curves and the car began to fishtail. This stretch of the road ran alongside a steep gorge; to our right the slope fell almost sheer to the river. Dwight sawed the wheel back and forth, seeming not to hear the scream of the tires. When I reached out for the dash-board he glanced at me and asked what I was afraid of now.

I said I was a little sick to my stomach.

"Sick to your stomach? A hotshot like you?"

The headlights slid off the road into the darkness, then back again. "I'm not a hotshot," I said.

"That's what I hear. I hear you're a real hotshot. Come and go where you please, when you please. Isn't that right?"

I shook my head.

"That's what I hear," he said, "Regular man about town. Performer, too. That right? You a performer?"

"No sir."

"That's a goddamned lie." Dwight kept looking back and forth between me and the road.

"Dwight, please slow down," I said.

"If there's one thing I can't stomach," Dwight said, "it's a liar."

I pushed myself against the seat. "I'm not a liar."

"Sure you are. You or Marian. Is Marian a liar?"

I didn't answer.

"She says you're quite the little performer. Is that a lie? You tell me that's a lie and we'll drive back to Seattle so you can call her a liar to her face. You want me to do that?"

I said no, I didn't.

"Then you must be the one that's the liar. Right?"

I nodded.

"Marian says you're quite the little performer. Is that true?"

"I guess," I said.

"You guess. You *guess*. Well, let's see your act. Go on. Let's see your act." When I didn't do anything, he said, "I'm waiting."

"I can't."

"Sure you can."

"No sir."

"Sure you can. Do me. I hear you do me."

I shook my head.

"Do me, I hear you're good at doing me. Do me with the lighter. Here. Do me with the lighter." He held out the Zippo in its velvet case. "Go on."

I sat where I was, both hands on the dashboard. We were all over the road.

"Take it!"

I didn't move.

He put the lighter back into his pocket. "Hotshot," he said. "You pull that hotshot stuff around me and I'll snatch you baldheaded, you understand?"

"Yes sir."

"You're in for a change, mister. You got that? You're in for a whole nother ball game."

I braced myself for the next curve.[47]

The three techniques of character construction and development are illustrated nicely in this sequence. Initially, there is a depiction based on the physical description of a flat yet vivid secondary character, Dwight, who is "cast" onto the stage briefly. Wolff observes Dwight's physical traits: "A short man with curly brown hair and sad, restless brown eyes[,]" placed next to the short and seemingly incongruous sentence "He smelled of gasoline." Dwight is a character captured in fragments and disjunctions, and the pieces of him don't fit together: "His legs were small for his thick-chested body[.]" But "what they lacked in length they made up for in spring; he had an abrupt, surprising way of springing to his feet." Toby then describes Dwight's dress: "He dressed like no one I'd ever met before—two-tone shoes, hand-painted tie, monogrammed blazer with a monogrammed handkerchief in the breast pocket."

At the end of this description is the brief intimation of why Toby initially discounts Dwight's importance in the story and explains why he will never be a successful suitor for his mother: "I didn't worry about him. He was too short. He was a mechanic. His clothes were wrong. I didn't know why they were wrong, but they were. We hadn't come all the way out here to end up with him." And then there is the wonderful line, and Toby's misguided observation: "I knew my mother would never let herself get tangled up in a mess like that." The reader is left with a flat but vivid image of Dwight's character based on Toby's description of him.

Subsequently, this secondary and flat character assumes a more important role in the story. Dwight "bumps up against" the protagonist Toby; incident and action explore the increasing conflict that develops between the two competing characters. There are the actions that occur on the trip to Toby's new home; Dwight intentionally runs over the beaver (a vivid secondary "flat" character in its own right), and then Dwight attempts to compel young Toby into helping out with the roadkill. "Pick it up. We'll skin this sucker out when we get home." This incident, and the subsequent events, reveal the cruelty in Dwight's character as the conflict deepens between Toby and Dwight, captured in dialogue: " 'Don't tell me you're afraid of the damned thing.' 'No sir.' 'Then pick it up.' He watched me. 'It's dead, for Christ's sake. It's just meat. Are you afraid of hamburger?' " It doesn't take us long to understand that Toby is, in the terms borrowed from the Amsterdam-Bruner definition of the progressions of a plot, deep in the "trouble."[48] Action and dialogue are used to add depth to Dwight's character and the reader begins to question the assumptions made about Dwight based on Toby's initial description.

In the final excerpt from this sequence of scenes, Dwight makes a pit stop at a tavern at the "last settlement,"[49] and the conflict progresses in the "reverberations" to the action, again captured primarily in dialogue. Dwight, in an action that complements and reemphasizes the dialogue, swerves side to side on a "stretch of the road [that] ran alongside a steep gorge; to our right the slope fell almost sheer to the river." This is a description of physical setting that provides a literal edge to the dialogue. The dialogue here foreshadows Toby's future under Dwight's authority and the conflict unfolding between them. "You're in for a change, mister. You got that? You're in for a whole nother ball game[,]" Dwight says. To which Toby responds presciently (and metaphorically): "I braced myself for the next curve." Dwight's true character is revealed through further action and dialogue, and he has completed the shift from a flat secondary character to the story's main antagonist.

5

Characters, Character Development, and Characterization in a Closing Argument to a Jury in a Complex Criminal Case

I. The "Backstory"

In 1991, Louis "Louie" Failla, a reputed Mafia soldier in the Connecticut faction of a New England crime family, was one of eight defendants charged with racketeering.[1] The thirteen-count indictment included charges that Failla supervised and operated illegal gaming businesses and engaged in wire fraud in connection with schemes to defraud the customers of these gaming operations. The most serious alleged racketeering act, however, was that Failla conspired with two mob informers to murder Tito Morales, his grandson's father. The prosecutor's case was strong; in fact, the evidence seemed insurmountable. The two informants who testified against Failla had been granted immunity and had reasons for lying—to avoid prosecution for other charges and to receive lenient sentences. Failla's words, however, had been captured on tape. Failla's Cadillac had been bugged and his self-incriminating conversations recorded. These tapes and the transcriptions of what one reporter called "Failla's greatest hits"[2] formed the centerpiece of the government's case against Failla and his codefendants. In these tapes, Failla implicated himself in the conspiracy to murder Morales and bragged about his multiple roles in the illegal business enterprises that were at the heart of other charges in the indictment against him.

The evidence was stacked against Failla, and he had not testified. While Jeremiah Donovan, Failla's gifted defense attorney, had successfully impeached the credibility of the two mob informants on cross-examination,

Failla had not produced evidence to rebut the incriminating testimony on the tapes. The prosecutor, in a five-hour closing argument, a serious dead-pan harangue, had meticulously used these tapes to historically reconstruct Failla's criminality and the criminal activities of the seven other codefendants. In contrast, Donovan's closing argument deemphasized the specifics of the historically reconstructed "plot" created by the testimony and tapes that had been central to the government's case and closing argument. Donovan's story attempted to humanize Failla and to depict him as a sympathetic character.

The material for Donovan's closing argument was provided, primarily, by using the same incriminating tapes that had been played at trial and served as the centerpiece of the government's case against Failla and the other codefendants. But Donovan's approach to this material was different. He imaginatively respliced these tapes and retrofitted the pieces into a newly redefined version of the story.

Donovan depicted Failla as a comic character. The concept of Donovan's Failla character could have been pitched in Hollywood. Failla the Fool, the "bumbling mobster wannabe," is a "character who could have stepped from the pages of Damon Runyon."[3] Louie Failla, clown and exaggerator, engaged in minor criminal activity. Although he was a "made" Mafia soldier, he was an outsider, not really a part of the mob, operating beyond the control and authority of the evil capo of the Connecticut branch of the Patriarca crime family, Billy "The Wild Guy" Grasso. Failla was shunned by the Patriarca crime family, and he struggled to make a living. His activities, although illegal under state law, were technically not violations of the federal conspiracy statute, the Racketeer Influenced and Corrupt Organizations Act (RICO), because they were not Patriarca family mob activities.

The most serious charge against Failla alleged that he conspired and plotted the murder of Tito Morales, his daughter's ex-boyfriend and the father of his grandson. The prosecutor meticulously detailed Failla's involvement in this murder conspiracy. Failla was, the prosecutor asserted, exactly what he appeared to be in the tapes. His words unequivocally revealed his intent to murder Morales and manifested his thought processes. The government portrayed Failla as a "flat" character: a sinister, two-dimensional villain who plotted with other members of the Patriarca crime family to execute Morales. The prosecution's bottom line was equally clear: Failla clearly intended and conspired to murder Morales; but for Failla's ineptitude, the murder of the capo Billy Grasso, and the timely intervention of the police arresting Morales, Morales would certainly be dead.

Donovan's version of the story provided a far more nuanced and complex depiction of Failla. Although Donovan could not completely reverse the polarity of the story and transform Failla into a true protagonist-hero, Failla became the protagonist of a different story, a story about a character trapped between two families, his "real" biological family on one side and his adopted mob family on the other. Rather than being merely a member of a gang of bad guys plotting the death of Morales, Donovan's Failla is an outsider, a complex character of shifting emotions and loyalties who develops and changes during the course of the argument. He is seemingly transformed at the end of Donovan's argument, although his character arc, like the story itself, is left incomplete—it remains for the jury (and the judge if Failla is found guilty and sentenced under RICO) to decipher Failla's motivations, discover the identity of Louie Failla, and write the ending to the tale.

The villain of Donovan's version of the tale is clearly not Failla; it is the murdered mob capo Billy "The Wild Guy" Grasso, who orders Failla, the mob underling, to murder his grandson's father. This also serves the purposes of the other mob defendants accused of murdering Grasso by depicting him as the true villain who meets an all-but-inevitable fate in another subplot of the trial.

In Donovan's version of Failla's story, the "engine of action [is] in the characters rather than in the plot."[4] Donovan redefines Failla's character. Character "is not a bundle of autonomous traits but an organized conception" constructed from "scraps and clues."[5] In the prosecution's simple linear version of the story, Louie Failla is a flat character, his intentions clearly captured on the federal surveillance tapes as he plots Morales's murder. But in Donovan's version of the story, there is a deeper subtext beneath the words. It is as if the action takes place in a Hollywood movie where screenwriters are admonished never to write a scene "on the nose." That is, the dialogue of spoken words must typically cover a deeper and transformative story: in Donovan's version, the dialogue in the respliced tapes contains "scraps" and "clues" through which the jury searches for Failla's true identity. In the final act of his closing argument, Donovan presents a sequence of primitive hand-drawn cartoons depicting Failla supplemented with cartoon "bubbles" that reveal his more complex thought processes supplementing the text of spoken words. This enables the jury to visualize and reconceptualize the story,[6] to look within Louie's mind and into his thought processes, and to see him not as a flat character condemned by his own words, but rather as a round character with complex motivations.

In Donovan's closing argument, Failla stalls the mob and prevents Billy "The Wild Guy" Grasso from taking the murder into his own hands by merely pretending to plot Morales's murder. In doing so, he places his own life in jeopardy, buys Morales the time he needs to save himself, and perhaps even makes a crucial choice (takes an action) that implicitly redefines his character in a far more compelling way than the words he speaks on the surveillance tapes. In Donovan's version of the story, Failla is transformed and implicitly redeemed, discovering integrity and saving himself as well as Tito Morales—just as a character in the movies would do.

II. Annotated Excerpts from Jeremiah Donovan's Closing Argument on Behalf of Louis Failla

A. "The Hook": Where the Character Louis "Louie" Failla Is Cast Onstage

Although Failla has never spoken or testified at trial, the jury has watched and studied him throughout the thirteen weeks of the trial, especially as the incriminating surveillance tapes have been played, clearly implicating him in the plot to murder Tito Morales. But now, as if for the first time, the "character" of Failla is brought to life and embodied in the theatrical and dramatic presentation of his seemingly exhausted attorney as he approaches the jury. A reporter describes the scene:

> Louis Failla, a bewildered-looking Mafia soldier from East Hartford, has been at the heart of the federal racketeering trial of eight reputed members and associates of the Patriarca crime family.
>
> Prosecutors hammered him while presenting their case, playing dozens of secretly made tape recordings on which Failla, in a voice evocative of Ed Norton on "The Honeymooners" television series, implicated nearly all his co-defendants in a variety of offenses.
>
> Tuesday, it was the defense's turn in U.S. District Court in Hartford. They took aim at him during closing arguments to the jury.
>
> Failla, they said, rambles, is given to flights of fantasy, is prone to hyperbole and is disconnected from reality. He cannot be believed, they said, particularly...while ferrying...around in his Cadillac....

...Finally, it was time for Jeremiah Donovan, Failla's attorney, to present his summation to the jury. Donovan wore a look of defeat as he approached the jury box, his head bowed, his voice exhausted. He allowed that he is not sure who has beaten his client worse, the government or the defense. Then, he began the most spellbinding harangue delivered since the trial began.[7]

Donovan does not begin his closing argument with the customary proem or introduction characteristic of closing arguments. He simply tells a story, beginning with the identification of his protagonist, the character Louie Failla, the defendant who sits in the courtroom. Donovan speaks to the jurors, setting the stage for the action that will follow:

> I have sat here this morning and listened to Louis Failla accused of being an exaggerator. If you recall, someone who indulges in wild speculation, in fantasy. I haven't said a word yet, but now I want to come forward and plead guilty to those charges. Louis Failla, with all due respect to you, Louis, is an exaggerator. You heard it throughout the trial in tape after tape after tape.[8]

In his opening, Donovan signals to the jury that, although this is a murder trial and Failla is accused of participating in a murder conspiracy, the jury should be aware that this closing argument will be surprisingly lighthearted—indeed the genre for the telling of this story is that of a comedy, albeit a tragicomedy:

> [T]his is a case that lends itself to superlatives.... [T]his is the first case in which an induction ceremony has been played for a jury. This is a case involving the murder of what may be the nastiest man ever to walk the shores of Connecticut, and it is a case in which the charge, in which the legal principals, are probably as complicated as in any case that's ever been brought in America.[9]

Donovan then refers briefly to the judge's charge. Unlike Spence's recurring mantra about strict liability in the *Silkwood* closing argument, Donovan's references to the law are playful and ironic. It is as if Donovan implies that the jury should set aside the legal particulars and the law that may stand in the way of enjoying the compelling story; indeed, this story is the jury's reward for paying close attention to the evidence during the thirteen preceding weeks of trial. Perhaps Donovan intimates that strict application of the law would be misguided since it would ignore the subtleties of the motivations and actions of the various characters within the plot:

> The Judge's charge will probably last for a whole day, and the Judge will be as hoarse by the time he's finished than I was when I finished questioning Jack Johns [the mob informant who testified against Failla], who was happy that my voice had disappeared. But that charge is going to be really crucial, because it's in the charge in the principles of law, it's there that lie [*sic*] Louie Failla's defense.[10]

Donovan acknowledges that "Failla has committed some crimes."[11] For example, "he ran a gambling den in New York in violation of [state] law," but these were not crimes committed in furtherance of a mob conspiracy under RICO.[12] Then he repeats, "So it's in the charge and the elements of the offense that our defense lies. I'll get to that in a little while."[13]

B. Who Is Louis Failla? A Story within a Story Depicting Failla's Character

Then Donovan breaks from his story. It is as if he is tired from the beating he and his client have taken at trial up to now. Like his client, he needs the relief of a joke, for his own sake as well as the jurors'. This storytelling appears spontaneous, as if he is merely stumbling upon this story within a story as he goes along. But he is methodically articulating and crystallizing a theme that serves as the spine of the narrative structure; it is embedded in his presentation of an archetypal comedic character who, the jury will soon see, will be transformed into Donovan's version of the "character" of defendant Louie Failla. Donovan begins with a well-delivered version of a classic Irish barroom story, apparently borrowed from a repertoire of such "stock" stories that can be readily inserted into closing arguments as appropriate: "As I make this defense...I feel a little bit like the legendary O'Toole."[14] Donovan now assumes an Irish brogue and begins as if he is in the pub himself; his voice breaks the tension, and the juror-audience relaxes:

> [Y]ou all know, who—well, in a bar in Dublin in walked a fellow who was about as tall as Ted, the judge's clerk, broad as Jackie Johns [the Mafia informant who testified against Failla]. He had that glimmer in

his eyes of craziness that I think you may have seen in Phil Leonetti. He walked into the bar and said, "Alright, where's O'Toole?"

All the patrons from the bar kind of looked in their drinks. They didn't want to be mistaken as O'Toole, except one little guy, seventy years old, five foot two, in the back, "I'm O'Toole. What is it to you?"

Well, the big guy picked up O'Toole, ran him down the length of the bar knocking off the glasses all the way and threw him through the plate glass window, walked outside, picked him up, threw him through another plate glass window and left him for dead. All the patrons looked at the poor old boy in the bloody mess on the floor. Guy looked up and said, "I sure pulled a fast one on that big fellow. I'm not O'Toole at all."

Now I feel like O'Toole, because in tape after tape after tape Louie Failla says, "I am O'Toole. I'm the guy you're looking for. I'm the new capo for Connecticut."...And I'm getting up and saying he's not O'Toole at all. He's not. He's not guilty of the RICO offenses with which he's charged.[15]

Donovan's opening "hook" takes ten transcript pages (approximately ten minutes or one page per minute). According to a standard Hollywood formula for successful screenwriting: "You've got to hook your reader immediately. You have approximately ten pages to let the reader know WHO your MAIN CHARACTER is, WHAT the premise of your story is, and WHAT the situation is."[16] As the audience determines how it reacts to the story within the first ten pages of a script, a reader likewise knows "whether your story is working or not; whether it's been set up or not."[17] Donovan's opening fulfills the aesthetic commands of the screenwriting manual. He establishes a sympathetic character and creates the point of view from which the story unfolds: Failla's perspective. He also foreshadows the dramatic situation: the bumbling everyman, the low-level Mafioso struggling to make a living, trapped by the orders and commands coming down from the Connecticut capo above him.

C. Excerpts from the "The Setup" and "The Confrontation": Trouble Breaks the Steady State and the Villain Is Cast Onstage

In the next stage after this initial set piece, Donovan creates the dramatic situation and establishes the conflict between Louie Failla (the complex protagonist) and the flat yet compellingly sinister villain, Billy "The Wild Guy" Grasso, and the power of the Patriarca crime family (the forces of antagonism compelling Louie to display his loyalty to the mob by plotting to murder Tito Morales). Initially, Donovan reintroduces Failla through the technique of description. Louie Failla, the Mafia outsider and small-time operator, struggles, often ineptly, to make a living. He is a tenderhearted man, filled with pretense and false bravado, and his actions always fall short of his words. He is deathly afraid of Billy Grasso, his Mafia capo. Nevertheless, he engages in unauthorized minor criminal activity, always fearful that his small scams will be discovered by Grasso and the leadership of the Patriarca crime family (who are not receiving any tribute or profits from these activities).

Through the conflict between Failla and Grasso, Donovan contextualizes the dramatic tension as he, simultaneously, establishes his defenses to the various lesser RICO charges that have been brought against Failla for these activities. Each of these racketeering acts serves as an inciting incident (building the tension between Failla and Grasso as Failla moves ever farther outside the mob to conduct his various nefarious crime-related activities), setting up the ultimate confrontation or showdown between Failla and the mob in the final act. This final act is akin to Kane's showdown with Frank Miller and the Miller gang in *High Noon* or the heroic confrontation with the ravenous man-eating shark in *Jaws*.

For example, one of the charges in the indictment against Failla is that he ran an illegal gaming operation in New York for the Patriarca crime family. Donovan's defense is simple: Failla ran the gambling operation in New York; and there is no denying this, as Failla brags about the scam. Although illegal gambling is a violation of New York State criminal law, Failla is not charged under state law. Further, this game, like Failla's other criminal activities, is not a part of the Patriarca family mob-controlled criminal enterprises as alleged in the indictment. It is unrelated to the crime organization's activities; indeed, Failla would be severely sanctioned and punished if his various scams were discovered by the Patriarca family.

After marking the jury's laughter at his opening hook, Donovan tells the next part of his story, depicting the character of Failla and the villain Billy Grasso through the technique of description, employing vivid and carefully selected details from the tapes presented at trial:

> First of all let's talk about chronology here. With respect to Louie Failla, this case begins in about February of 1989. What do we know about Louis Failla at that point? Well, he's living in ... [a] rented duplex

out in East Hartford. Hasn't been painted for eighteen years.... He is living essentially in poverty....

Why is he living in poverty? A made member of the Patriarca crime family, how could he be living in poverty? Because something has happened, and William Grasso has essentially shunned Louie Failla.... They keep him out of all activities. Grasso has done that.... [He] wouldn't let Louie be involved in anything.[18]

Donovan also speaks anecdotally, describing the antagonist and villain, Billy Grasso, with vivid details taken from evidentiary surveillance tape transcriptions. Grasso, "the nastiest [man]...who's ever walked the shores of Connecticut," tells one of his henchmen that, after he assassinates a person, he will bury him with his hand up out of the ground, "'so I can kick it every day as I walk by.'"[19] Donovan continues, "walking through a McDonald's with one of his men, and enraged, [he] picks up a kid's hat and throws it down."[20]

Louie Failla is petrified by Billy Grasso. To depict Failla's fear, Donovan assumes Failla's voice and borrows edited sequences of Failla's monologue from the dialogue captured on the surveillance tapes. The use of dialogue, of course, is the second technique employed in a planned and carefully constructed sequence of scenes used to establish Louie Failla's character. Failla's words are made more compelling as Donovan assumes the Italian Mafia voice of a movie actor in a typical mob picture, to situate the story comfortably with the audience, just as Gerry Spence employed the deep and resonant voice of a Shakespearean actor in an effort to elevate and defamiliarize the circumstances of his version of Silkwood's character. Donovan's voice is akin to Failla's voice on the surveillance tapes. And, as observed by the press covering the case, it is also strongly "evocative of Ed Norton on 'The Honeymooners' television series":[21]

I didn't have no money. Couldn't do nothing. And I was never called in to defend myself. I used to go home at nights worried that he'd [Grasso] say the next day,... "I got a fucking hole dug for you already. Go get my fucking money." I was living in fucking fear. Nobody to turn to. Not a fucking soul except Louie Failla. If I was going to get banged, I would get banged alone. I was afraid to take my wife in the car, the baby in the car. Couldn't take my grandson anywhere. I looked in his [Grasso's] face and I saw a fucking totally insane man. I saw a totally insane man.[22]

The next scenes are based on the characters' "actions." These are comedic episodes typical of Hollywood "buddy" pictures taken, again, from the transcripts of the surveillance tapes and spliced together into the careful structure of a purposeful plot. Donovan then casts onstage two "flat" yet vivid "secondary" characters, drawn from a vast assortment of potential supporting characters depicted in the repository of FBI surveillance tapes: Jack Farrell and Patty Auletta, who are depicted as if they are all outlaws from an updated suburban mob version of *Butch Cassidy and the Sundance Kid*.[23]

> And he had his friend Jack Farrell. Jack Farrell is a master mechanic... in the sense that this guy had all the natural moves to be a card shark and a dice shark. Jack Farrell and his pretty girlfriend Patty Auletta, defraud you just by being so quiet you would never think that he had a shoe there where she could feel the next card coming up was a high one or a low one.[24]

Jack Farrell is described with just a few well-chosen phrases as "a master mechanic" with "all the natural moves." And, likewise, Donovan depicts his "pretty girlfriend" who could "defraud you just by being so quiet." Neither has testified at trial. Yet it is doubtful a novelist could have reduced their essentials to a description any better or more concise. The initial function of these two characters—the old Irish card shark and his "pretty" girlfriend—spins the plot forward into action. This enables the audience to better visualize Donovan's version of Louis Failla "in action."

Simply put, we derive a deeper understanding of who Louie Failla is from the way he conducts his business. Here, Donovan not only admits Louie's participation in the New York gambling operation but, since these activities are outside of Patriarca family activities and not covered under RICO, he lovingly embraces and revisits the details of the scam. These activities are depicted in a much different way than the prosecution's rendering of criminal activities. In contrast to the flat tonality of the prosecutor's narrative about a monolithic mob, Donovan's description is colloquial and playful, encouraging listeners to establish a sympathetic relationship with these characters: "[I]t was a sting.... [T]hey tried to get these extremely rich, high rolling gamblers,... real high rollers, guys with a lot of money to burn, to come and play blackjack and to play dice, craps, and they would try to play....The problem was that when Louie Failla got involved, it didn't work very well."[25] Only at the end of this sequence, or the other sequences of scenes about Failla's various criminal escapades, does Donovan tie his story back into legal defenses. At the end of the New York gambling caper Donovan depicts "a real cartoon-like picture of the statute" admitting that the game is "in violation of New York laws."[26] It is not, however, in violation of RICO, the Racketeering-Influenced and Corrupt Organization statute:

> Here's what I mean. You not only have to have a participant in a RICO organization commit a crime. It has to be a crime that furthers the enterprise....
> ... The crimes have to be related to the organization. They have to further the policies of the organization. They have to bring money into the organization. They have to be done with respect to the person's role in the organization.[27]

The organization is, like the villain Billy Grasso, antagonistic to Failla's enterprise. Indeed, the serpentine Patriarca crime family and the local capo *are* the forces of antagonism that oppose the will of the protagonist. Donovan argues that the New York gambling game, and Failla's other well-documented criminal activities and schemes that serve as the basis of the multiple counts in the RICO indictment, are outside organization activities: "This New York gambling game put money in Louie Failla's pocket, put money in Jackie Farrell's pocket... money in various people's pockets, but didn't put any money in Billy Grasso's pocket and didn't put any money in the pockets of the alleged Patriarca crime family."[28]

Donovan works back and forth, from description to sequences of scenes and action and then to dialogue and back again, employing excerpts from the tapes to make the story come alive. For example, Donovan moves from incident and action back to dialogue in Failla's taped conversations with Jack Farrell, once again assuming a version of Failla's gravelly mob voice from the surveillance tapes.

Here, for example, Donovan illustrates Failla's fear of the risk of what would happen should Grasso and the Patriarca family ever discover the New York gambling operation: "We're all fucking done as far as I'm concerned."[29] To emphasize and make explicit the meaning of Failla's observation, Donovan adds an ironic and understated editorial aside that, "as far as Louie Failla went, boy, that would be an offense that would be a harsh one, harsh."[30]

D. Excerpts from the Climax and Resolution: Where Failla's Loyalty Is Tested and He Is Compelled to Make a Crucial Decision Redefining His "Character"

Just as in the movies (*High Noon* or *Jaws*) and strongly akin to the illustration provided by *This Boy's Life*, the plot progresses forward based on the unfolding conflict between Louie Failla, the rogue outsider, on one side and Billy "The Wild Guy" Grasso, the villain and capo of the Connecticut faction of the Patriarca crime family, on the other, as the action heads toward the final confrontation. Here, Donovan constructs his defenses to the various lesser RICO conspiracy counts as Failla moves farther outside the sphere and control of the Patriarca crime family in conducting his various criminal enterprises. But there is more complexity to the plot than this: the forces of antagonism are aligned against Failla achieving his goal of becoming a major mobster in Connecticut. There are now the demands of Failla's adopted Patriarca crime family and Billy Grasso calling on Failla to prove his loyalty by executing his grandson's father; there are also the competing demands of his "real" family, his affection for Tito Morales, and his love for his grandson. These countertensions create a compelling dramatic conflict that puts Failla's character under intense pressure, seemingly compelling him to make a definitive choice. Regardless of which choice he makes, it will have devastating consequences.

Thus, this is the final act that leads toward the final crisis, resolution, and climax. But akin to Gerry Spence's legal story in the *Silkwood* closing argument, and unlike the films *High Noon* or *Jaws*, Donovan does not complete his story, and does not provide closure to the tale. It will be up to the jurors in their deliberations and, perhaps, the judge at sentencing (if the defendant is convicted) to finish the story and inscribe a final coda of meaning on the tale. Donovan takes special care not to complete the "arc" of Failla's character.

This final or third act of a movie-like plot structure provides Failla's defense to the murder conspiracy charge, which is the most serious charge against him. Its success turns upon the jury visualizing the scenes (aided by cartoons) and interpreting the subtext of what Failla does not say. It provides a fuller understanding of Failla's complex character, or, at least, Donovan's reinterpretation of who Louie Failla is, and how he responds to the conflicting loyalties and the forces of antagonism aligned against him.

Donovan marks the beginning of the third act—as he has in each of the prior movements of the plot—with another anecdotal story within a story. This is the most complex of his stories within stories (and far more complex than the simple and abbreviated analogies employed powerfully by Gerry

Spence in *Silkwood*). This final story foreshadows strategically the meaning of Failla's words and provides an unstated subtext for understanding Failla's motivations in his willingness to go along with and, indeed, take the lead in plotting Morales's murder (in the various dialogues captured in the surveillance tapes). Donovan maintains the same comedic tonality in his delivery, as if all this material is part of a single overall narrative:

> And this brings us finally to the murder of Tito Morales, and this, ladies and gentlemen, is the most serious crime that faces Mr. Failla. Before I start, I'll get my breath back.
>
> I'll tell a story about Frankie Roosevelt, who was apparently an absolutely brilliant fellow at making different sides believe that he was leaning toward their position. There was a coal strike during the depression in West Virginia, and it had turned violent. The President decided that he would attempt to mediate the dispute in order to end the violence, and he got the workers back into compliance. It was a cause that Mrs. Roosevelt, Eleanor Roosevelt, was very much interested in, so what she decided she would do would be to hide behind a curtain and listen to the meetings that the President had.
>
> So first the owners of the mine come in and they explain that, "Look, it's the depression. We're not getting much money for our coal. We admit the conditions are bad. We're doing the best we can to improve them. The wages are low, but we can't possibly pay more. We'll go out of business. The violence in the strike is over."
>
> President Roosevelt listened and said, "You know, you're absolutely right. You're absolutely right." They left.
>
> John L. Lewis, the head of United Mine Workers, came in, and he said, "These workers are not making a living wage. Children are being used in the mines. The conditions are absolutely horrible. They've brought in strike breakers. The strike breakers are causing the violence."
>
> The President said, "You know, John, you're absolutely right. You're absolutely right." He left.
>
> Eleanor Roosevelt was enraged. She came out from behind the curtain. She said, "Franklin, you told the miners [mine owners] that they were absolutely right, and you told John L. Lewis that he was absolutely right. What are [you] doing?"
>
> Roosevelt looked at her and said, "Eleanor, you're absolutely right. You're absolutely right. You're absolutely right."

Louie Failla does this all the time. He doesn't just exaggerate. He is a verbal chameleon. He adopts the coloration of whoever is with him. We see it all over. . . . When I said that, you [Donovan directly addresses the jury] were supposed to say, "You're absolutely right, Jeremiah. You're absolutely right."[31]

In telling this story, Donovan acts the different characters. Several reporters describe how he interacts physically with the jury. Edmund Mahony observes the theatricality and physicality of the performance: "Donovan sometimes strode and other times tip toed in front of the jurors. He shouted, then whispered and waved wildly with his arms. U.S. District Court Judge Alan H. Nevas hid his face to cover a smile and the audience guffawed out loud."[32] This story embodies Donovan's conceptualization of Louie's character at this point in the story: Louie will use deceits of language to avoid confrontation and violence; he is a people pleaser, determined to give his audience what they want through story. This anecdote also foreshadows Failla's role as mediator between the violent mob impulses.

E. Character in Dialogue and Action

Donovan now transitions back into his story:

The most significant example of Louie's being a verbal [chameleon] has to do with Tito Morales. With respect to Tito Morales I'm going to argue to you that except for Louie Failla, Tito Morales would be dead. I feel really off trying to argue to you that he didn't conspire to murder somebody when, in fact, in our view it's Louie's action, I should say, more precisely, his inaction, that has permitted Tito Morales to be alive and happy in prison, however happy he might be.[33]

In this final act, the conflict peaks. Failla confronts Billy Grasso and the Patriarca mob, specifically, Grasso's two violent henchmen, the father-son mob informants who testified against Failla in exchange for a plea bargain, Sonny Castagna and Jackie Johns. These are also "flat" and monochromatic characters, evil antagonists, akin to the various members of the Miller gang, who are plotting to execute Tito Morales.

After arguing that "except for Louie Failla, Tito Morales would be dead,"[34] Donovan tries briefly to explain the legal basis of his theory that Failla did not participate in the conspiracy to murder Morales. He does not lecture the jury;

he merely invites their participation in understanding the law. To provide a
legal framework for this portion of the story, Donovan briefly recites a legal
theory of conspiracy that anticipates the judge's charge, connecting these to
the motivations of Sonny Castagna and Jackie Johns to execute Morales on
the command of Billy Grasso:

> In order to determine whether Louie is guilty of a conspiracy to
> murder Tito Morales, you're going to have to make a decision about
> whether the conspiracy existed and what Louie's intent was. Now in a
> conspiracy it's seldom true that one act taken by itself can be detected
> as tending to prove the unlawful agreement. What I mean by this,
> I mean there was an agreement. There was an agreement between
> Sonny Castagna and Jackie Johns. Sure, they wanted Tito Morales
> dead, but Louie did not.[35]

Donovan then moves to another action sequence: nine months prior to the
conversations in the car, the two mob enforcers close to Billy Grasso are talking about killing Morales. "Why was it going on?" Donovan asks the jury.[36]
"What was the motive to kill Tito Morales?"[37]

Donovan employs sequences of scenes depicting the characters through
their actions to answer his own rhetorical question. First, a sequence of
scenes displays the bad blood between Morales and the mob henchmen. In
one scene Morales, who had once been a partner with young Jackie Johns
in various Hartford crime activities, was arrested. In another scene, the dialogue between Castagna and Johns reveals their belief that Morales thought
that they had turned him in to the police. In another scene, again reenacting
transcripts from recorded surveillance tapes, Johns and Castagna tell Failla
that Morales can implicate them both in the murder of a young boxer named
Eric Miller (who was assassinated by Johns and Castagna under Billy Grasso's
order, because Miller had foolishly gotten into a fight with Billy Grasso in
the parking lot of a Hartford restaurant). Donovan details Castagna's and
Johns's motivations to get rid of Morales through edited dialogue. Donovan
concludes with characteristic understatement and irony: "Tito Morales, who
knows about what happened with the other kid [Eric Miller], can get Sonny
and Jackie into some pretty serious trouble."[38]

Finally, Donovan caps off this sequence of scenes by describing, from
Castagna's and Johns's point of view, the visual shot of Morales "seen going
into the federal building."[39] Donovan underscores the meaning of the scene
described: "Tito [Morales] was seen going into the federal building, and

very shortly thereafter... there's a real rough call to Jackie Johns [from Sonny Castagna]... to get over here fast."[40] Donovan shifts tonality from the comedy of Louie Failla's scenes; there is a serpentine quality to the depiction of the actions now defining the characters of Johns, Castagna, and especially Billy Grasso:

> What are [these guys] worried about? They're worried Tito Morales is going to go in and spill the beans that these were the guys who murdered Eric Miller [on the order of Billy Grasso]. They're scared that he's going to go in and tell them all about... Jackie Johns's counterfeiting and drug activity.... And besides, Jackie Johns doesn't like [Tito] too much, anyway, because [Tito] put the moves on his girlfriend.[41]

Donovan cuts to the next sequence of scenes. Initially, there is more dialogue between Failla and his friend Jack Farrell while riding in Failla's Cadillac: "[t]hey're reminiscing back to the days when Billy Grasso controlled everything."[42] Donovan reenacts the scene captured on the tape of when Failla tells Farrell about how he once made an excuse to Grasso, presumably about temporarily refusing to carry out the order to execute Morales:

> Failla says, "I didn't do what he said. That's why I walked away from the table once... [h]e came flying right back, 'You motherfucker.'"
> "I said, 'Look, you don't see the eyes around. I've got people watching me. I know when to fucking move and [when] not to. You're not supposed to tell me when to move.'"
> "'You do what I tell you, you yellow motherfucker.'"...
> ...Grasso's furious at him that he's a yellow motherfucker. What he's doing is he's saying, "Eyes all around me. I can't do it." He is making an excuse.[43]

"But why did Louie Failla not carry out this order of Grasso?" Donovan asks the jury.[44] "Because he and Morales were close."[45] Donovan's answer to his own rhetorical question provides the transition into another scene and more dialogue in the car between Failla and Morales, dialogue in a scene that starkly contrasts the characters of Failla and Morales with the characters of the father and son mobster henchmen, the murderous team of federal informants, Johns and Castagna. This is evidence that Donovan painstakingly introduced during the defendant's case at trial. In these surveillance tapes, Failla and Morales reveal aspects of a far more complex relationship in their dialogue. For example, while driving in Failla's Cadillac, soon after he has been ordered to murder Morales, Failla tells Morales, "All right, you take care of yourself, kiddo. I love you. You know that, don't you?"[46] Donovan then steps outside of the scene and observes, "I don't know. It's not often, I think, that grown men tell each other they love each other."[47] Donovan cuts to the next scene in the sequence:

> The great one is, I think, on August 28th, and they're talking about Jason [Morales's son, Louie's grandson]. [Donovan assumes Failla's gravelly mobster voice.] "You should see their fucking tape. They took him to Lake Compounce yesterday, and they made a videotape of him, and he gets up and he starts playing fucking good times, singing and dancing. That was, [the] whole fucking thing. You should see this fucking tape. He should send it to Hollywood. That was, this kid did everything. He looked at the audience and people and give him a fucking scowl like this [Donovan imitates Failla imitating his grandson's scowl] with his face." Morales laughed. "I got to show you."[48]

Donovan briefly frames the scenes and marks the end of the sequence describing the relationship between Failla and Morales: "There's a tenderness between them. I said tenderness is too strong. There's a mutual respect and affection between them. Louie has been placed in a terribly, terribly difficult position. His life is in danger if he does not carry out the order, and he's the father of his grandchild."[49] This sequence leads to a turning point and the climax of the "third act" of Donovan's three-part narrative structure. First, Donovan observes Louie's paralysis and inaction:

> So what does Louie do? Louie does nothing. Nothing happens....[N]othing happened in April, nothing happened in May, nothing happened in June, July, August, or September. Nothing at all happened...[b]ecause Louie Failla didn't do what Billy Grasso said....
> ...Tito Morales is alive and happy in prison because of Louis Failla...[who] disobeyed an order from Grasso at peril to his own life. "You yellow motherfucker." Because of the affection that he had for Tito Morales.[50]

Finally, Donovan ties the story into the legal issue of intent—what did Louie Failla intend to do; what did he mean to do? Donovan instructs the jury that "to figure out his [Failla's] intent, you got to think what he was thinking...you got to see this."[51]

Donovan playfully uncovers a larger-than-life cartoon depicting an image of Louie Failla, one of many sequential cartoons in a thick pad of exhibits. "There's Louie," Donovan speaks to the picture and then confides intimately to the jury, "I tell you, you got to convict a guy on a look, Louie would spend the rest of his life in jail."[52] Donovan looks at the exhibit, with the "real" Louie Failla carefully positioned behind the pad in the unobstructed sight line of the jury. The jury and spectators chortle. Donovan continues, "Two things you got to do. What did Louie say, or what was Louie thinking when he said it."[53]

Donovan sets up the tension, filling in the spaces between what Louie says and what Louie intends—the distance between the explicit text of his spoken words and the unspoken and interpretive "subtext" of the scene, that is, "what happens below the surface of a scene; thoughts, feelings, judgments—what is *unsaid* rather than *said*."[54] Donovan's technique enables him to go within the mind and thoughts of the "complex" character of Louie Failla. Although Failla has never taken the stand to testify at trial, Donovan effectively testifies on Louie's behalf and articulates his thought processes and motives in an easy-to-visualize linear text encapsulated into cartoon "thought bubbles." Donovan's storytelling strategy is so engaging and seamless that it is not broken by the prosecution's objection that there is no evidence to substantiate Donovan's assertions about Failla's thought processes.

Donovan proceeds through the many seemingly incriminating conversations recorded on the FBI surveillance tapes. Employing his theatrical version of Louie Failla's mob voice, Donovan speaks Failla's words and then articulates and clarifies Failla's purported thought processes. As he speaks the words he provides the larger-than-life illustration of Louie Failla facing right in profile with a "hard" solid-line cartoon bubble of Failla's recorded words emerging from Failla's mouth. Then Donovan provides the subtext of Failla's purported thoughts, a counterstory, atop a chain of smaller "thought bubbles" emerging as if from inside Failla's head from a parallel left-facing side profile. The bubbles of testimony capturing Louie's thoughts establish the subtext underlying the meaning of his spoken words and reveal Failla's true motivations—to stall the mobsters and save Tito Morales's life. This newly redefined version of the story eclipses the prosecution's literal interpretation of Failla's words, which implicate him in the murder conspiracy.[55] These same words now suggest that Failla's own complicity in the murder conspiracy were efforts to stall the mobsters by inaction and vindicate him of the most serious charge against him.

After Mafia soldier Louis Failla ran afoul of an FBI bug planted in his car, Donovan took on his defense. Part of Donovan's courtroom performance involved telling jurors what Failla really meant by his recorded statements — that Failla didn't have homicidal intent. Donovan drew poster-sized cartoons to make his argument.

FIGURE 5.1 "What did Louie Say? What Did Louie Think?" Illustration a courtroom exhibit. N.p. in transcript.

F. Failla's Character Arc Is Not Completed

The cartoon bubbles, together with Donovan's reenactments of Failla responding to the murderous mobsters time and again, provide the denouement to the carefully scripted two-hour performance. Donovan has redefined crucial elements of the plot of evil mobsters (flat monochromatic characters) whose words mean precisely what they say, conspiring to execute Morales in a plot that fortuitously never reaches resolution. While in the prosecution's version of the story the characters of the various mobsters are psychologically undifferentiated in their dark motivations, Donovan's story provides an alternative rendering of these characters, especially Louie Failla.

At the end, Donovan does *not* take the final step and resolve the drama by providing closure to the "character arc" of Louie Failla, completing the plot and inscribing a meaningful coda on the tale. Instead, Donovan leaves it for the jury and judge to resolve the issue of Failla's identity: in a final visual cartoon the two divided halves of Louie Failla's profile are posed in opposition while, just behind the exhibit stand, the "real" Louie Failla sits at the defense

WHAT DID LOUIE DO?

NOTHING.

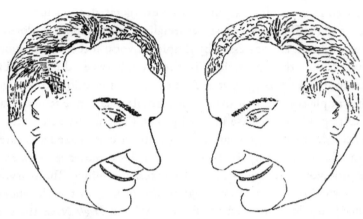

FIGURE 5.2 "What Did Louie Do?" Illustration a courtroom exhibit. Quotation, transcript, 75–76.

table studied by the judge and jury in a carefully crafted visual montage of the simulation set atop courtroom "reality."

In a voice-over, Donovan concludes his portion of the storytelling dramatically:

> What did Louie do? Nothing. No evidence of going out and buying a gun. No evidence of a real plan that would bring Tito out at this time to this place.... No evidence of any of the kind of actions that one would expect that Louie should have been engaging in if he had really conspired to kill Tito Morales. He talked, and by talking he saved Tito Morales's life. By making Johns and Castagna think that he was going along with the plan, he got Tito Morales that one more month he needed....[56]

Donovan refers only briefly to the legal implications of his story, leaving it largely to the jury's charge.[57] Likewise, Donovan only briefly emphasizes the standard of reasonable doubt.[58] It is up to the jury first to determine who Louie Failla is at the end of the story and then to provide narrative closure by formulating their own ending to the Louie Failla story.

III. Concluding Observations
A. Louie Failla's Character and the Movies

Cinematic characters seldom display the depth of literary characters. They are reduced in psychological complexity, exaggerated, and shot out across hard plot lines. The protagonists, especially in contemporary plot-driven Hollywood films, are possessed by simple univocal forces that respond to external pressure through action. This tension, between the internal force that motivates the protagonist and an external oppositional force, generates the simple conflict that shapes the formulaic narrative structure at the heart of popular film. These internal forces, like the characters, are readily identified. The resulting narrative exploits are compressed and carefully configured to fit and surprise (yet never defy) the audience's expectations as the protagonist struggles to resolve external conflict. The storyteller's point of view is almost always that of the protagonist with whom the audience is implored to identify. For example, in *High Noon* the story is told primarily from the perspective of Will Kane, although there are some shifts to scenes between Amy and Helen where Kane is not present on the screen. Likewise, in *Jaws* the perspective of the film is that of the heroic human protagonists attempting to stop the shark, although the film shifts to the underwater perspective of the shark where the audience vicariously and guiltlessly enjoys the shark's attacks on the naïve and innocent bathers in the world above.

The dominant and almost exclusive perspective in Donovan's closing argument (in contrast to the prosecution's story) is that of Louie Failla. The jurors observe and then inhabit Failla's thoughts and character, although Donovan effortlessly slides out into several important sequences of scenes "shot" from the perspective of mob henchmen Jackie Johns and Sonny Castagna. (For example, the two mobsters consult with Billy Grasso and then watch Tito Morales going into the federal building fearing that he is about to "roll over" on them, establishing their "motivation" to execute Morales.)

The formulaic conventions for defining character and establishing motivation in popular films provide a template for better understanding the dynamics of Donovan's Louie Failla and, more generally, the dynamics of character construction in legal storytelling. Donovan employs a familiar and viewer-friendly compositional structure in his depiction and representation of Louie's character. Although Louie Failla is a simple man, he is a "complex" character. Nevertheless, he is a readily recognizable archetype already familiar to this audience from the movies.

His character is initially presented and then refined in the progressive stories within stories that serve as place markers for each of the three discrete and purposeful acts of Donovan's story. Failla's motivations are, likewise, carefully scripted, and internally consistent: he is a comic protagonist, an exaggerator, a fabulist. His stories are big Mafia dreams, filled with chronic self-distortion and self-deception. When Louie attempts to execute a scheme, however, his actions seldom achieve the consequences that he anticipates. He is not a brutal man or an effective Mafia tough guy. He is an inept and comic character, easily differentiated from the villainous "flat" characters, the henchmen Jackie Johns and Sonny Castagna and, especially, the evil and powerful Patriarca mob capo, Billy "The Wild Guy" Grasso. Unlike Grasso, Failla is a conflicted character; he is ineffective *because* he is neither venal nor cruel. Louie drives around in his big Cadillac, telling big stories, while engaging in small scams to survive, keeping out of the way of Billy Grasso and operating outside of, and ostracized from, the power of the Patriarca crime family.

During the "third act"—the climax and resolution—of Donovan's clearly marked three-part narrative structure, Louie Failla appears initially as a two-dimensional visual cartoon, supplemented by Donovan theatrically delivering his lines edited from the FBI surveillance tape transcripts in a gravelly and stereotypical mob voice. Here, another strand of Failla's character emerges in the subtext from beneath Failla's words; Donovan makes Failla's thoughts explicit in the cartoon bubbles that emerge from Louie's mind in contrast to the words that come from his mouth. Akin to Will Kane in *High Noon*, Failla's character undergoes a subtle reversal at the moment of crisis; he must make a choice that redefines his character.

The multiple and discrete audiences (e.g., the jury, the judge, Failla's "real" family and his "adopted" mob family, and the other codefendants at the trial who are accused of murdering Billy Grasso) are left to interpret and fully understand his motivations and actions as a component of a carefully constructed and dramatic story. At the moment of deepest crisis and climax, it is apparent that Donovan's Failla makes the crucial choice to save Morales's life. He engages in doing so by not doing anything beyond pretending to go along with the order. As Donovan proceeds through the extensive surveillance tapes, he contrasts Louie's thoughts with his words; he emphasizes Louie's strategic failure to follow through with the plan to execute Morales, despite the pressure from the mob. In doing so, Failla saves Morales's life just as he intends to do. In the end, Donovan's version of Failla transcends the cartoon and becomes almost heroic, choosing to protect the life of his grandson's father by stalling the mobsters (Johns, Castagna, and Grasso) by using his storytelling skills and abilities. Just as in the movies, Donovan's Failla chooses his real family over the orders of the villainous faction of his mob family led by Billy Grasso. It is at this moment that the audience sees who the "real" Louie Failla is.

Of course, Donovan's version of Failla is not a "real" person. He is an artistic creation existing in a narrated dream state framed by popular cinematic representations of Mafia archetypes and the codefendants in the trial. Screenwriting texts and Hollywood practices provide a theoretical framework for better understanding Donovan's work. In popular films that adhere to the Hollywood formula, characters, including complex protagonists like Louie, must be centered, and their motivations must be apparent and consistent. The plot must be kept on track by the protagonist's pursuit of the object of his univocal narrative desire. Screenwriting manuals suggest that this outer goal—the plot goal—must be clarified by an internal goal—the personal goal.[59] That is, "[a] good [effective] character has compelling personal goals. These personal goals spring from very deep emotional needs, deprivations, and scars. The need for self-respect; for self-actualization. The need to be loved; to be respected."[60]

In *The Screenplay*, Margaret Mehring analyzes the Hollywood formula for constructing character and effective characterization, describing the "personal goals" that "drive the characters to reach their plot goals."[61] These goals are "the voices within the character that yearn for fulfillment, that must be satisfied. They're the needs that create the energy to overcome obstacles."[62] These forces, like the characters themselves, are exaggerated and distilled, and they provide apparent motivation for the protagonist.

Hollywood screenwriters also speak of the protagonist's "inner contradiction" that accompanies the internal personal goal.[63] This is the conflict within the protagonist that, according to Hollywood folk wisdom, makes the protagonist's character compelling. Usually, like the personal goal, there is one primary and identifiable inner contradiction that determines the protagonist's identity and shapes the character's cinematic destiny or fate.

Failla's personal goal is partly material and partly psychological: Failla struggles for those Hollywood staples of "fortune and fame" as well as for professional recognition, respect, and self-esteem. The inner contradiction in Failla's character, however, is more subtle. Donovan's not-so-tough guy Louie Failla tells big stories to capture and please his audience. He does so because he lacks something within himself and needs something that he is missing desperately. This psychological need interferes time and again with the achievement of his personal goal and, perhaps, contributes to his

self-destructive confessions in a car that he could have and should have anticipated was "bugged." This missing element cannot be fully deciphered, however, until Donovan intimates it at the end of his closing argument by reading
the complex progressions of cartoons and suggesting the true nature of Failla's
character.

The inner contradiction within Failla's character is between Louie Failla,
the purported Patriarca mafioso, with his tough guy exterior, his Runyonesque
bravado, and the softer, compassionate, empathetic, and even loving aspects
of his personality. This tension is revealed in Failla's confessional dialogue
with Jack Farrell, and especially, in his conversations with Tito Morales about
his grandson. This contradiction is most apparent in the final act or movement of the story when the audience sees Failla's character depicted as the two
contradictory and conflicting halves of a personality.

When the screenwriter is constructing the dynamics of a protagonist's
character, according to the Hollywood template, the audience sees the character "in action" in the struggle toward a clearly defined outer plot goal. Plot
goals, like personal goals, are specific and apparent. They include "[t]hings
like becoming a famous pilot, being married to a wealthy woman, capturing a
notorious criminal, or earning a higher education degree."[64] Initially, the plot
goal may appear simply as an external and visible representation of the personal goal. Tension between the protagonist's personal goal and the plot goal
results in the "darkest moment" or the "final crisis" and ultimately moves the
protagonist to the climax "when the protagonist *must* make a decision that
will reflect a substantial change within him or her and will create a substantial change in the situation.... The moment the change manifests itself...the
moment when the theme of the story becomes clear."[65]

Failla seeks a specific external plot goal. Failla wants to become a capo of
Connecticut organized crime activities. Failla, like the legendary O'Toole in
Donovan's story, pretends to be who and what he is not. In the final act, he has
the opportunity to achieve this external plot goal; he can ingratiate himself
with and prove his loyalty to the leadership of the Patriarca crime family by
completing the conspiracy to murder Tito Morales. In Donovan's version of
the story, however, he does not do so, and it is at this moment that the narrative theme becomes clear.

B. Character and Theme

The theme of a popular movie or an effective law story is often deeply connected to the development of the central character, typically cast as the

protagonist of the story (especially in a criminal law or torts story). This is especially so in a sophisticated law story akin to Donovan's narrative on behalf of Failla. This is a story that ultimately turns on the audience's perception and understanding of Louie Failla's character: at the start of the story, Louie is a narrative trickster, who tells his stories for effect (akin to "O'Toole" in the barroom anecdote), as compared to who he becomes at the end of the story, a character (akin to "Roosevelt") who uses storytelling skills to save Morales's life and maintain his own integrity. That is, the theme of Failla's story concerns Failla's motives and contradictory impulses and how this internal psychological conflict is translated into action (more specifically, in Failla's case, into inaction).

It is Failla's self-defining "choice," at the moment of crisis and climax, not to murder Morales that reveals his true identity. The jury will complete the story with a verdict; the judge with a sentence, if Failla is convicted. Failla's real family will complete the story by determining whether they believe Failla had their best interests at heart and in how they will respond to him after the argument. Likewise, Failla's adopted mob family, especially the codefendants on trial with Louie who are now charged with the murder of Billy Grasso, will complete their version of the Failla story by assessing whether they believe Donovan's story assists them in their defense to murder charges by implicating that, simply put, Grasso is truly a villain who deserved to die.

6

Style Matters

HOW TO USE VOICE, POINT OF VIEW, DETAILS AND
IMAGES, RHYTHMS OF LANGUAGE, SCENE AND
SUMMARY, AND QUOTATIONS AND TRANSCRIPTS IN
EFFECTIVE LEGAL STORYTELLING

*Every sentence has a truth waiting at the end of it and the
writer learns how to know it when he finally gets there.*
—DON DELILLO, MAO II

I. Backstory: Grading Law School Examinations

As I revise this manuscript, I am simultaneously grading blue-book examinations and ExamSoft examinations in a large doctrinal criminal law class. The process is labor intensive and often painful. One reason why grading examinations is so difficult is the importance of grades to the students. Law school examinations and law school grades provide the psychic undercurrent of law school. First-year law school grades, typically based on one end-of-semester examination, often shape law school identities and self-perceptions by determining law school honors, including law review membership. This can have long-term effects on a student's confidence, ability to create a professional persona, and perception of self-worth. Increasingly, first-year law school grades have profound practical significance as well: first-year grades affect directly how students will fare in an increasingly competitive employment market. First-year students have a great deal riding on their examination performance, and they know it, and their professors do, too.

Simply put, my job is to determine who will be the law school winners and losers. Typically, I give four-hour in-class essay examinations. Often (in criminal law and torts courses), I give two long "issue-spotting" questions employing complex fact-based problems, sometimes derived from "real" cases, and other times fabricated based on doctrinal coverage. In my criminal law class, for example, I tell stories about murders, rapes, robberies, thefts, conspiracies, and so on. As is traditional, students must translate these narratives into doctrinal frameworks, "spotting" or identifying the relevant issues— picking them up like Easter eggs on an elaborate Easter egg hunt—articulating accurately the relevant legal rules necessary to solve these legal problems, then systematically applying these rules to resolve the issues correctly.

Generally, there are two pedagogical approaches to grading students' examinations: (1) employing an objective checklist and grading criteria *or* (2) employing a more "holistic" approach that emphasizes an individualized assessment of the quality of students' writing and analytical abilities. Like most law professors, I opt for the latter approach; it simply provides more room for my own subjective judgment and flexibility. Of course, I tell my students the rules of the game before the exam and in the written instructions to the examination.

As I grade these examinations, as best I can articulate it, the singular difference between the mediocre examination answers (C and below) and the middling to good examination answers (B-range grade) is primarily in the "substance"—whether the students can identify the relevant issues and accurately articulate the relevant legal rules necessary to analyze the problem. The distinction between the B exams and the A exams is, however, primarily in the "voice" and "style" of presentation. Voice and style, however, mean something much different in the context of law school examination taking than in the artful trial and appellate narratives that litigation attorneys construct in a factually far more complex and indeterminate world. (This, I think, speaks to why excellent litigation attorneys were often poor law school test takers.) For law school examinations, stylistic concerns are based on the limitations and constraints on possibilities, about clamping down intellectually and authoritatively on the facts. Students are evaluated on the cleanness and effectiveness of the organizational structures they select and employ, on analytical precision and accurate presentation of complex legal doctrine, and on adherence to grammatical rules and the King's English. Excellent students avoid colloquialism and humor, and avoid reading too deeply between the lines of the story, getting lost in the story. Students must present normative analysis cleanly, developing a legal voice that appears neutral and does not call attention to itself but conveys simultaneously an underlying authority and confidence, transforming the narrative into legal analysis. The story is made subservient to the rules, and the events depicted in a law school examination hypothetical case are, as one of my students observed, merely the "floating factoids" that drift atop the law. The shrewd and adept student employs the facts to reveal the law, speaking with a lawyer-like authority and precision, manifesting knowledge of doctrinal law and a newfound forensic confidence and authority that borders on arrogance.

But what has all this to do with the subject matter of this chapter? Simply put, voice and style are profoundly important in oral and written legal storytelling practice. But style and voice in storytelling practice are not the same as the stylistic concerns and disciplines developed in law school. Indeed, style in legal storytelling is liberating; the facts at trial are typically indeterminate, and the choices and possibilities available to legal storytellers are different and far more complex than those exposed or developed in the normative analytical practice successful students employ in law school. This chapter focuses on some of the stylistic concepts and techniques that are often crucial to effective legal storytelling, in both written and oral argumentation at trial and on appeal. This chapter presents a compressed and representative selection of topics from a far more extensive narrative menu. It merely provides a starting point, an introduction, rather than a comprehensive exploration of this complex subject. Unfortunately, these topics are seldom, if ever, foregrounded systematically in law school, even in legal writing or clinical and advocacy courses. Nevertheless, effective law students intuitively understand the importance of style and voice in determining examination grades. More importantly, techniques of style and the power of voice are often at the core of narrative persuasion and legal storytelling practice, and employing technique effectively is often crucial to determining the outcome of many cases.

II. Preliminary Note: "Voice" and "Style"

As Henry Miller observed, what one has to tell may not ultimately be as important as the telling itself. The two are clearly intertwined in all types of storytelling practice, including legal storytelling. The telling itself is embodied in the "style" or "voice" of the storyteller.

To illustrate, in an oral trial or appellate argument, the audience typically listens closely to, and is persuaded by, the literal voice or persona of the attorney-storyteller; it is profoundly important, yet seldom discussed or analyzed as a persuasive tool. Here, however, when analyzing voice I refer to something more than just the "sound" of the voice; legal storytelling voice is composed of instrumental stylistic choices, carefully selected in relation to the material of the story, fitted to the narrative's plot and characters. In many ways it is akin to the voice of a popular singer interpreting a song, the lyrics and melody shaping inflection, modulation, and phrasing. Likewise, the legal story affects voice, influencing choices made from a repertoire of alternative stylistic possibilities. This is true in both oral and written storytelling practices; the qualities of voice are deeply related to other aspects of the narrative.

For example, the audience for Spence's closing argument in *Silkwood* is captured by the power and confidence of Spence's literal voice; there is deliberateness, pacing, and confidence in his rhythmic yet theatrical delivery. It is through Spence's voice and presentational style that Spence elevates a simple and not atypical torts melodrama (the story of the heroic "prophet" sacrificed to the greedy corporate Beast's hunger for profits). Spence employs his voice and presentation, reshaping the material into a story with almost biblical dimensions. Spence's closing argument in *Silkwood* presents a homiletic or teaching story with a moral message about what happens when corporate greed and hunger (The Beast in the free market) goes unchecked and unregulated and devours and destroys a rural community as well as the young workers and innocents within it. Spence's voice and his presentational style are intentionally magisterial, signaling carefully that this is an important story capturing a crucial historical moment.

Spence's story, like most torts stories, is fundamentally a simple melodrama. And Spence's Silkwood character is a simple hero without the depth of character of, for example, a complex tragic hero. Indeed, attempting to transform Silkwood's story into the genre of tragedy by adding another dimension to Karen Silkwood as protagonist would diminish the story's persuasive power. There are, nevertheless, clearly tragic victims in Spence's story: the young workers who, Spence argues, will suffer horrible struggles with cancer if the jury does not intervene heroically to give Silkwood's life meaning by speaking the only language the Beast corporation understands, the language of money.

It is a presentational style and voice that Spence marries intentionally to his theme and story. Spence's voice is appropriately respectful, reverential, and lawyer-like. Spence chooses a third-person omniscient *perspective* for telling most of his story. Spence strategically employs edited audiotapes, however, to shift purposefully from the third-person omniscient voice into Silkwood's own first-person voice and perspective, and, likewise, incorporates vignettes or stories within stories to strategically readjust his narrative frame. Spence purposefully and effectively varies the rhythm and cadence of his speech on various levels, from the rhythms and word choice within sentences to the modulated, shifting use of *scene* and *summary* throughout the story.

The selection of details and images for story elaboration is an equally strategic part of a presentational style. Thus, for example, Spence contrasts rural and bucolic details that characterize the innocent townspeople with the details that mark and signify the big city corporation and its evil minions. These are all shrewd stylistic choices.

This chapter attempts to provide an understanding of these alternative stylistic possibilities through analysis of short literary illustrations and also excerpts from selected legal stories. I choose as narrative illustrations examples primarily taken from creative nonfiction and from criminal appellate and postconviction briefs. Although a primary focus here is on writing, these examples could have been drawn equally from oral stories and oral arguments and from other areas of practice. The nonlaw examples include analysis of excerpts from James Ellroy's autobiography *My Dark Places*,[1] Norman Mailer's *Executioner's Song*,[2] Truman Capote's *In Cold Blood*,[3] and Frank McCourt's *Angela's Ashes*.[4] The choice of examples from creative nonfiction is purposeful: legal storytelling often seems stylistically akin to the practices of creative nonfiction storytellers. The journalism of Mailer and Capote and Ellroy's and McCourt's memoirs are all presumably bound by the constraints of evidence and memory. Although all are truthful and factual storytellers, akin to legal advocates, all are also situated storytellers, purposely telling their stories to persuade and move their readers emotionally; none purport to be telling purely "objective" stories.

III. Voice and Rhythm: "Staying on the Surface"

There are many different styles and voices manifest in effective legal storytelling, although we do not typically label or deconstruct these styles as such. The legal stories told in criminal cases are often presented as detective mysteries. One of the characteristic voices is that of the hard-boiled detective. This is a voice that creates a distinctive rhythm and, as David Lodge puts it, typically "stays on the surface" of events.[5] It is a style that "focuses obsessively on the surface of things.... The dialogue is presented flatly, objectively, without introspective interpretation by the characters, without authorial commentary, without any variation on the simple, adverb-less speech tags *he/she asks/ says*."[6] The effect, as Lodge observes, is often "at once comic and chilling."[7] It is a style that, as Anthony Amsterdam observes, "hustles the reader rapidly across a catwalk above a pit, giving him or her no pause to look down."[8] The style conveys a sense of a dangerous world out of balance; it is simultaneously riveting and disturbing.

It is not coincidental that lawyers purposefully embody the voice, rhythms, and stylistic conventions of the "hard-boiled" detective mystery story in many criminal appellate briefs. Indeed, the very purpose of these stories is to draw the reader into a mystery that activates the imagination; they are successful when they compel the reader to, as Jerome Bruner puts it, go "beyond the information given."[9] This style invites readers to dig beneath the surface of the language and solve the unsolved or wrongfully solved puzzles of meaning.

What does this style look like? I take, as an initial example, a brief excerpt from James Ellroy's autobiographical memoir *My Dark Places*. Like many criminal defense attorneys, Ellroy uses a style or voice akin to that employed in detective fiction, albeit for a different purpose: Ellroy uses this voice to tell his deeply personal story, a memoir. Initially, the plot of the story appears to match that of a typical genre "whodunnit": James Ellroy's mother was murdered, and the murderer was never apprehended. Many years later, Ellroy, the narrator-detective, must return to the past and attempt to retrace the steps of the criminal to rediscover the story of what happened to her. In retelling the story, Ellroy hopes to reassemble the clues and evidence in a way that points to the murderer. Ellroy's story operates on a second level crucial to the memoir (akin to Tobias Wolff's story in chapter 4): the purpose of Ellroy's narrative quest is to understand who his mother was and, in doing so, to navigate his own artistic identity, and understand how his own voice and vision were shaped by these long-ago events.

Stylistically, Ellroy's autobiography initially assumes its power through the authority of the voice. *My Dark Places* begins with the subtitle "The Redhead" and the disturbing and graphic crime photo of Ellroy's murdered mother, lying facedown in the brush, her dress partially undone, the ligature marks from the strangulation around her neck.[10] The use of the subtitle from detective fiction supplemented by an actual image of Ellroy's deceased mother is a striking choice for framing the story.

Ellroy begins by speaking directly to his mother, seemingly bypassing the reader, employing a second-person voice. It is a voice that delivers a cry of anguish that also frames the story that he will tell. He puts these paragraphs into italics to differentiate this voice from that of the third-person detective story that follows:

A cheap Saturday night took you down. You died stupidly and harshly and without the means to hold your own life dear.

FIGURE 6.1 Credit: James Ellroy, *My Dark Places* (New York: Vintage Books, 1997).

Your run to safety was a brief reprieve. You brought me into hiding as your good-luck charm. I failed you as a talisman—so I stand now as your witness.

Your death defines my life. I want to find the love we never had and explicate it in your name.

I want to take your secrets public. I want to burn down the distance between us.

I want to give you breath.[11]

Although it is only the second page, Ellroy has made several bold stylistic moves: First, Ellroy has used significant "white space" on the page to focus on the horrific visual image of his mother. He has framed the image with an attention-gathering, tabloid-like header. He then employs short sentences and short paragraphs containing one, two, or no more than three sentences. He arrests the reader's attention with the plea of the son for the mother whose "death defines my life" who "want[s] to find the love we never had and explicate it in your name." Yet even here, the hard-boiled style "stays on the surface" of the images, with the beat of short rhythmic sentences pushing the reader compulsively forward over the chasm below: "A cheap Saturday night took you down. You died stupidly and harshly and without the means to hold your...life dear."[12]

Next, the narrative voice shifts abruptly from the first to the third person. Hard-edged visual details pile one atop another as if in a montage of photographs or a sequence of cinematic images:

Some kids found her.

They were Babe Ruth League players, out to hit a few shag balls. Three adult coaches were walking behind them.

The boys saw a shape in the ivy strip just off the curb. The men saw loose pearls on the pavement. A little telepathic jolt went around.

Clyde Warner and Dick Ginnold shooed the kids back a ways—to keep them from looking too close. Kendall Nungesser ran across Tyler and spotted a pay phone by the dairy stand.

He called the Temple City Sheriff's Office and told the desk sergeant he'd discovered a body. It was right there on that road beside the playing field at Arroyo High School. The sergeant said stay there and don't touch anything.

The radio call went out: 10:10 a.m., Sunday 6/22/58. Dead body at King's Row and Tyler Avenue, El Monte.

A Sheriff's prowl car made it in under five minutes. An El Monte PD unit arrived a few seconds later.

Deputy Vic Cavallero huddled up the coaches and the kids. Officer Dave Wire checked out the body.

It was a female Caucasian. She was fair-skinned and red-headed. She was approximately 40 years of age. She was lying flat on her back— in an ivy patch a few inches from the King's Row curb line.

Her right arm was bent upward. Her right hand was resting a few inches above her head. Her left arm was bent at the elbow and draped across her midriff. Her left hand was clenched. Her legs were outstretched.

She was wearing a scoop-front, sleeveless, light and dark blue dress. A dark blue overcoat with a matching lining was spread over her lower body.

Her feet and ankles were visible. Her right foot was bare. A nylon stocking was bunched up around her left ankle.

Her dress was disheveled. Insect bites covered her arms. Her face was bruised and her tongue was protruding. Her brassiere was unfastened and hiked above her breasts. A nylon stocking and a cotton cord were lashed around her neck. Both ligatures were tightly knotted.

David Ware radioed the El Monte PD dispatcher. Vic Cavallero called the Temple office. The body-dump alert went out:

Get the L.A. County Coroner. Get the Sherriff's Crime Lab and the photo car. Call the Sherriff's Homicide Bureau and tell them to send a team out.…

…Her face had gone slightly purple. She looked like a classic late-night body dump.[13]

Ellroy's opening stays compulsively on the surface of the details. Although his voice is now cast in the third person and an omniscient perspective, Ellroy avoids descending into the consciousness of his characters and providing their thoughts other than his brief observation that a "little telepathic jolt went around" when the boys discovered the body. The freestanding details have sufficient power to hold the reader; any emotion of Ellroy for his mother is compressed into "hard" visible objects and a matching hard-edged voice. Ellroy employs short concussive sentences, equally short and arresting paragraphs, and the rhythms of the prose are derived from the colloquial street language characteristic of a contemporary detective mystery. The surface of language is foregrounded by the absence of any commentary by Ellroy on the images he depicts and splices together almost cinematically. This stylistic form of presentation encourages the reader to function as a detective-investigator. Images are clues to be sifted through by the reader and not ascribed specific meanings by their author. These images are tethered back to the initial image of Ellroy's dead mother, who serves as the focal point and emotional pivot of the story. Ellroy looks down from outside the experiences and images with a detached and hardened clarity, whether he is engaged in revisiting and investigating the circumstances of his mother's death or in investigating the equally harrowing circumstances of his own life as it takes shape—in an almost predetermined manner—after her murder.

In his chapter "Staying on the Surface" in *The Art of Fiction*[14] David Lodge observes that this is a form of story elaboration where "the narrative discourse impassively tracks the characters as they move from moment to moment towards an unknown future."[15] The "text's refusal to comment, to give unambiguous guidance as to how the characters should be evaluated," may be "disturbing" but "may also be a source of power and fascination."[16] The qualities and techniques that are compelling in Ellroy's prose, drawing the reader into the story and activating the imagination of the reader to resolve a complex puzzle of meaning, often serve the legal practitioner as well, especially in effective appellate and postconviction relief briefs.

For example, here is how some of these same techniques are employed in a postconviction defense brief in *Riggins v. Nevada*.[17] The story in the "Statement of the Case" begins with the visual depiction of the defendant, heavily drugged and unable to participate effectively in his own defense at trial. The legal issue turns on whether the defendant was denied due process when he was placed on trial only after being "forced to ingest high dosages of the antipsychotic drug Mellaril"[18] over the objections of his attorney. The images and concrete details are embodied in a strong and hard-boiled detective voice, akin to Ellroy's, that stays primarily on the surface of events. Although it is hard-edged and coldly objective, the voice conveys a strong sense of emotional involvement with the material, so that the reader perceives and responds with a shared yet unstated moral outrage about the injustice of the defendant's legal predicament. How does the defendant's brief accomplish its purpose? The stylistic voice matches the narrative and circles repetitively back to a crucial core image ("The Zombie" in the petitioner's brief is akin to "The Redhead") that is the emotional pivot of the story.

The evocative "Statement of the Case" begins:

> Petitioner David E. Riggins is presently under sentence of death after he was so heavily drugged by the State of Nevada that he appeared like a zombie throughout his trial. Despite Riggins' objection while competent to receiving medication during his trial, and despite substantial evidence that Riggins would have been competent to stand trial without medication, the State of Nevada forced Riggins to ingest extremely high dosages of the antipsychotic drug Mellaril each day of his trial. The medication sedated Riggins; it made him appear apathetic, uncaring, and without remorse. Riggins was therefore prevented from presenting the best evidence he had—his unmedicated demeanor—to support his only defense—that he was legally insane at the time of his crime.[19]

After compressing the legal particulars of the case, and providing the backstory of Riggins's illness with a vivid and straightforward explanation of the psychiatric diagnosis, the writer presents an equally brief and clear description of the effects of the antipsychotic drug Mellaril. The writer then returns to the image of "The Zombie"; the repetition of the image does not appear calculated and the voice does not call attention to itself, or explicitly reveal the writer's beliefs. Instead the voice stays on the surface of events, emphasizing repetitively the images of Riggins after he had been force-fed Mellaril, and the voice presents the responses of various actors in a style similar to the hard-boiled voice of a Raymond Chandler novel:

> Accordingly, Riggins was forced to ingest 800 milligrams of Mellaril each day of his trial, a dosage every psychiatrist considered excessive. Dr. Jurasky...described this dosage as enough to "tranquilize an elephant."...It was no surprise, therefore, that Riggins was seen closing his eyes during his hearing on a motion to terminate the medication and had a zombie-like appearance throughout his trial.
>
> Riggins' sole defense was insanity, and he took the stand to prove this. [The writer then presents a vivid selection of Riggins's delusions from his testimony that allegedly provided the reasons why he was compelled to kill the victim.] The state exploited Riggins' drug-induced demeanor during his trial, and in doing so directly contradicted its pre-trial representations to the court.[20]

The writer explains how the state's expert witnesses and closing argument focused on Riggins's demeanor at trial, a condition the state had authorized, although it had promised not to do so, by quoting from the prosecutor's closing argument: "Does Riggins express sorrow, no. Does he express remorse, 'no.'"[21] And then the brief returns to the image of the zombie, observing how Riggins's Mellaril-induced demeanor undermined mitigation arguments based on "extreme emotional disturbance" and "remorse" at sentencing. Although the voice stays on the surface of images, it dips momentarily, effectively, and almost unnoticeably into the consciousness of Riggins to observe that he wanted to express grief and sorrow, but was prevented by the drug from doing so:

> Rather than looking like the emotionally disturbed individual that he is, the heavily sedated Riggins sat calmly and impassively through the sentencing hearing. Although he wanted to express the grief and sorrow he felt for killing Wade [the victim], the medication prevented him from doing so, and, in fact, prevented him from reading a statement he had prepared expressing these sentiments.[22]

The brief initially describes the various ways the state may permissibly "advance a compelling interest to restrict a defendant's fundamental right to testify" by the "least restrictive [alternative] available," including the least acceptable alternative, "binding and gagging the witness."[23] And then, in the body of the argument, the brief compares the zombie-like Riggins to the witness "bound and shackled" by the forced ingestion of Mellaril and made to "effectively present evidence against himself by compelling him to appear unremorseful, apathetic and sane."[24] Stylistically, this story is translated into a legal argument that is equally hard-boiled, flat, and coldly objective.

Is this the only voice available or employed in criminal defense brief writing? Of course not. It is but one of a wide range of possible styles available to legal storytellers; but it is certainly one that fits well with the subject matter and with the legal argument.

IV. The Use of Scene and Summary: "Showing and Telling"

Stories, whether in law or creative nonfiction, are constructed through a rhythmic alternation and carefully structured interplay between "scenes" and "summaries." Just as in commercial films, scenes are constructed by employing visual details (images), dialogue (quotations), and depiction of events (action).[25] Indeed, the fundamental building block in film is the scene; scenes are constructed from shots that then, in turn, are built into compositions or sequences of scenes and then into acts. There is, obviously, little if any authorial summary in a movie. In this way, film is a pure form of "showing."

Summary, however, is different; language summarizes and encapsulates events, compressing images. Consequently, events are typically compressed as well, and specific scenes are not called forth readily in the mind of the listener or reader.

Another way of distinguishing between scenes and summaries is in terms of narrative time (a separate chapter in this book). In a scene the discourse time is roughly equivalent to story time—whether the scene is presented in dialogue or as a straightforward account of moment-to-moment visual action. In contrast, in a summary, the story time significantly exceeds the discourse time; that is, the pacing of events is compressed, and images and individual events are seldom evoked with particularity.[26] In a scene, events are typically clearly displayed, formed into visual images. In summary, however, particularity is lost or blurred as the events are sped up over time.

Thus, for example, in his closing argument on behalf of Louis Failla, Jeremiah Donovan often speeds up narrative time in summaries that gloss over many months of time, while at other points he meticulously reconstructs specific conversations between Failla and various mobsters while plotting the murder of Tito Morales. These conversations between Failla and Morales fit into carefully constructed sequences of scenes that focus the listener's attention on crucial evidence presented in the trial, providing an alternative interpretation of the meaning of Louie's spoken words in the context of a cinematic and visual narrative landscape.

There is also a third type of movement in written and oral storytelling that narrative theorists call *stretch*. Here, the storytelling is typically slowed down so that the discourse time significantly exceeds story time. The meticulous *showing* or the extended *telling* accompanying this movement exaggerates the importance of this piece of the story; the pace of the telling clues the reader into the relative importance of specific sections of the story. The slow motion of a stretch is not frequently employed in legal storytelling, except on occasion to revisit a crucial event and dissect and elaborate on the moments within it. One famous and illustrative use of stretch within a legal story was the slow-motion replay of the videotape in the Rodney King trial,[27] supported with explanation and commentary on the individual frames of the sequence. Another illustration of the use of stretch is, of course, Jeremiah Donovan's extended revisitation of portions from the transcripts of Louie Failla's audiotaped conversations plotting the murder of Tito Morales; Donovan carefully supplements the dialogue with strategic first-person commentary, revealing Louie's internal thought processes.

All stories, including legal stories, establish rhythmic interplay or pacing by alternating scene and summary. Legal briefs and written legal stories typically emphasize summaries over scenes. This is because there is often a great deal of information to convey to the reader and, although much of this information is important, it is not sufficiently important to warrant an entire scene. Also, of course, there are limitations on space, time, and the willingness of the audience to engage with the story. Nevertheless, scenes are extremely significant in all legal storytelling practices, just as they are crucial in fiction and creative nonfiction: we are drawn into the story not through flat, abstract summaries but rather through the detailed depiction of events. Thus, David Lodge admonishes young writers that overuse of authorial summary is not only deadening, it may also be "unreadable."[28] Nevertheless, summary is important structurally because "it can, for instance, accelerate the tempo of a narrative, hurrying us through events which would be uninteresting, or *too* interesting—therefore distracting, if lingered over."[29]

As a teacher of legal writing and a clinical supervisor, I have observed that many legal briefs (written both by students and experienced practitioners) are often unreadable because the writer simply does not know how to construct or employ appropriate and strategic *scenes* to supplement *summaries*; that is, the legal writer does not know when it is appropriate to use "showing" instead of "telling." It is as if the legal storyteller is often afraid of constructing scenes or of crossing over intentionally into purely narrative territory. Of course, summary has its uses, and it is important structurally; no brief or even a statement of a case is ever exclusively a composition of scenes, akin to a movie. Typically, because of page constraints and the average attention span of a judicial reader, the balance in written legal storytelling tips toward using more summary and less construction of scenes.

Norman Mailer is masterful in striking a balance between *showing* and *telling*; he knows how to develop a scene, where to begin it and how to end it while working within a carefully structured narrative framework. In Mailer's *Executioner's Song* we find a brief, understated, and self-contained scene describing the murder of Max Jensen by Gary Gilmore.[30]

> Gary walked around the corner from where the truck was parked and went into a Sinclair service station. It was now deserted. There was only one man present, the attendant. He was a pleasant-looking serious young man with broad jaws and broad shoulders. He had a clean straight part in his hair. His jawbones were slightly farther apart than his ears. On the chest of his overalls was pinned a name-plate, MAX JENSEN. He asked, "Can I help you?"
>
> Gilmore brought out the .22 Browning Automatic and told Jensen to empty his pockets. So soon as Gilmore had pocketed the cash, he picked up the coin changer in his free hand and said, "Go to the bathroom." Right after they passed through the bathroom door, Gilmore said, "Get down." The floor was clean. Jensen must have cleaned it in the last fifteen minutes. He was trying to smile as he lay down on the floor. Gilmore said, "Put your arms under your body." Jensen got into position with his hands under his stomach. He was still trying to smile.
>
> It was a bathroom with green tiles that came to the height of your chest, and tan-painted walls. The floor, six feet by eight feet, was laid in dull gray tiles. A rack for paper towels on the wall had Towl Saver printed on it. The toilet had a split seat. An overhead light was in the wall.

Gilmore brought the automatic to Jensen's head. "This one is for me," he said, and fired.

"This one is for Nicole," he said, and fired again. The body reacted each time.

He stood up. There was a lot of blood. It spread across the floor at a surprising rate. Some of it got onto the bottom of his pants.

He walked out of the rest room with the bills in his pocket, and the coin changer in his hand, walked by the big Coke machine and the phone on the wall, walked out of this real clean gas station.[31]

Mailer takes great pains to show the murder rather than tell about it; likewise, he avoids "fancy" language that would diminish the impact of the images and the understated scene on the reader. He allows his readers to form their own judgments. But there are apparent narrative strategies in Mailer's use of a minimalist description that captures the action as if through the coldly objective eye of a camera.

In the first paragraph Mailer sets the stage for his movie-like scene: Gary Gilmore comes on stage and meets "the attendant" who is described initially with neutral adjectives as an everyman (as a "pleasant-looking serious young man"). Then the somewhat blurry description emphasizes selected particularized physical details of the attendant's appearance (e.g., the "clean straight part in his hair," the "jawbones…slightly farther apart than his ears," even his nameplate—"MAX JENSEN"). Max Jensen innocently offers to assist Gilmore. Abruptly, the robbery begins; Gilmore orders Jensen into the bathroom. Mailer emphasizes the cleanliness and order of the bathroom. This description, in turn, provides the setup for the ending of the scene, and Jensen is ordered to "get down" on the floor; all the while Jensen is "trying to smile."

Then Mailer takes a paragraph to provide a detailed description of the bathroom, slowing the pace of the telling momentarily. Immediately thereafter, without pause, Mailer details Jensen's violent execution, supplemented with Gilmore's remorseless non sequiturs, naming each bullet fired into Jensen's head with particularity: "this one is for me" and "this one is for Nicole" (Gilmore's girlfriend). And then he adds the disconcerting final detail of Gilmore noticing that some of Jensen's blood has apparently stained the bottom of Gilmore's pants. The scene concludes with Gilmore "walk[ing] out of this real clean gas station," reemphasizing ironically the image presented several paragraphs earlier in a careful sequence.

This structure is shaped to provide a seemingly objective but, nevertheless, prosecutorial condemnation of Gilmore, without ever becoming overtly judgmental. Mailer's sympathy, in this scene, is clearly with the innocent victim Max Jensen; he is akin to an innocent member of the community attacked by the shark in *Jaws* or a worker afflicted with cancer by the Beast's (Kerr-McGee's) plutonium in *Silkwood*. After this scene, however, Mailer has many pages to allow the remarkably self-reflective Gilmore to reach toward the possibility of understanding his own actions and toward a desire to atone for his sins through his own execution, as a partial payment back to society for actions that are inexcusable.

The imagery appears taken from a documentary film shot from the objective perspective of an unseen narrator who, only in the most delicate way, dips into the mind of Jensen, the victim, to observe that just before Jensen was shot "[h]e was still trying to smile." This arrangement of description, action, and character is a carefully structured composition, however, designed to achieve a precise effect on the reader: it is similar to the effect that a skillful prosecutor would desire to achieve detailing the circumstances of a crime.

V. Telling in Different Voices

Often, the strongest and most persuasive legal narratives—especially compelling scenes incorporated into and alongside authorial summaries—are not the product of the voice of the legal storyteller. The advocate assembles and transforms collages of quotations into closely edited structural compositions. For example, Jeremiah Donovan develops scenes from reedited versions of the federal surveillance tapes. Likewise, Gerry Spence in his closing argument in *Silkwood* makes the prophet Silkwood come alive by replaying crucial and carefully edited segments from tapes introduced into evidence. In brief writing, the pieces of the brief are often reconfigured from transcripts and records and—in appellate and postconviction practice—from previous tellings and retellings in judicial opinions. The voices that speak in legal briefs are typically taken directly from other sources. The work of the legal storyteller is thus a practice of bricolage or assembly, as the author arranges which voices come to the forefront of the argument to do their work on the reader or listener. This artistry creates a sense of complete transparency and candor rather than intentional narrative strategy. But this is seldom, if ever, actually so in legal storytelling or in any creative storytelling practice. The art in narrative practice and persuasion is to affirm the appearance of artlessness and of objective transparency in the telling of the tale.

In Cold Blood provides an illustration of meticulous investigation and purposeful assembly of voices in a classic work of creative nonfiction. Capote's voice is that of an objective investigative journalist who relies primarily on direct quotations, transcripts of conversations, and excerpts from journals. In one sequence of scenes, for example, Capote reveals the discovery of a murder scene by employing a purportedly unedited verbatim transcript of an eyewitness who accompanies the sheriff to investigate the possibility of a crime at the Clutter family farm.[32] The witness, Larry Hendricks, is a schoolteacher who had taught one of the murdered Clutter children.[33] Before beginning his dark journey, Hendricks "decided I'd better keep my eyes open. Make note of every detail. In case I was ever called on to testify in court."[34] Hendricks's story within a story begins at his own house, with a scene depicting a steady state of domestic tranquility:

> Well, the TV was on and the kids were kind of lively, but even so I could hear *voices*. From downstairs. Down at Mrs. Kidwell's. But I didn't figure it was my concern, since I was new here—only came to Holcomb when school began. But then Shirley—she'd been out hanging up some clothes—my wife, Shirley, rushed in and said, "Honey, you better go downstairs. They're all hysterical." The two girls [Hendricks's children]—now they really were hysterical. Susan never has got over it. Never will, ask me.... Even Mr. Ewalt [a middle-aged farmer], he was about as worked up as a man like that ever gets. He had the sheriff's office on the phone—the Garden City sheriff—and he was telling him that there was "something *radically* wrong over at the Clutter place." The sheriff promised to come straight out, and Mr. Ewalt said fine, he'd meet him on the highway......
>
> [Hendricks accompanies Ewalt to meet the sheriff on the highway.]
>
> The sheriff arrived; it was nine thirty-five—I looked down at my watch. Mr. Ewalt waved at him to follow our car, and we drove out to the Clutters'. I'd never been there before, only seen it from a distance. Of course, I knew the family. Kenyon [the Clutters' son] was in my sophomore English class, and I'd directed Nancy [the Clutters's daughter] in the "Tom Sawyer" play. But they were such exceptional, unassuming kids you wouldn't have known they were rich or lived in such a big house—and the trees, the lawn, everything so tended and cared for. After we got there...[the sheriff] radioed his office and told them to send reinforcements, and an ambulance. Said, "There's been some kind of accident." Then we went in the house, the three of us. Went through the kitchen and saw a lady's purse lying on the floor, and the phone where the wires had been cut. The sheriff was wearing a hip pistol and

when we started up the stairs, going to Nancy's room, I noticed he kept his hand on it, ready to draw.

Well, it was pretty bad. That wonderful girl—but you would never have known her. She'd been shot in the back of the head with a shotgun held maybe two inches away. She was lying on her side, facing the wall, and the wall was covered with blood. The bedcovers were drawn up to her shoulders. Sheriff Robinson, he pulled them back, and we saw that she was wearing a bathrobe, pajamas, socks, and slippers—like, whenever it happened, she hadn't gone to bed yet. Her hands were tied behind her, and her ankles were roped together with the kind of cord you see on Venetian blinds. Sheriff said, "Is this Nancy Clutter?"—he'd never seen the child before. And I said, "Yes. Yes, that's Nancy."[35]

Notice how Hendricks's composition (and, perhaps, how Capote shapes this testimonial evidence) is intuitively artful, with respect to each of the stylistic topics presented in this chapter. First, there are the concussive rhythms of the short sentences that convey emotion by slowing the reader down so he is encouraged to feel the emotions experienced by Hendricks. It is as if the reader is accompanying Hendricks and is simultaneously discovering the crime scene shortly after the murder. Second, these rhythms are complemented and matched by meticulous selection of descriptive details. Outside, "the trees, the lawn, everything so...cared for." Inside the house, however, there is "a lady's purse lying on the floor, and the phone where the wires have been cut." It is a detail that foreshadows what Hendricks and the sheriff will discover in the next scene in the sequence. As the sheriff goes up the stairs he "kept his hand on it [a hip pistol], ready to draw" as if in anticipation of what he (and the reader) will discover next. And then the description and the scene slow down into a "stretch," with murdered Nancy Clutter first described, the bedcovers "drawn up to her shoulders." Then, as if in slow motion, the sheriff pulls the bedcovers back, and "we saw [what] she was wearing," including the telling details (e.g., "her ankles were roped together with the kind of cord you see on Venetian blinds"). The brutality of the scene is tempered by a pitch-perfect and understated compassion (e.g., the sheriff says he's never seen "the child" before).

Hendricks then describes the discoveries of the victims in the next rooms, Mrs. Clutter, Hendricks's former student Kenyon, and then Mr. Clutter. The same stylistic techniques are employed intuitively (the rhythms, the details, the use of scene and stretch). Hendricks seems to relive the discoveries, as he describes each room filled with a horror more vivid and more frightening than the one before it. The reader experiences the horror with him; it is akin to a narrative told by a victim of posttraumatic stress who rediscovers an immutable past that he cannot let go of. And the reader is taken along with him both visually and psychologically.

The sequence of images and scenes concludes with the arrival of other witnesses. Hendricks completes the story within a story by leaving the house and the images behind him, walking home and along the way seeing Kenyon Clutter's collie "with its tail between its legs, didn't bark or move." This image jolts him out of the dazed shock that has prevented him—up until that moment—from comprehending the full horror of the situation on an emotional level, but being "too dazed, too numb, to feel the full viciousness of it."[36] This paragraph provides closure to Hendricks's testimony and this piece of the story:

> After a bit, the house began to fill up. Ambulances arrived, and the coroner, and the Methodist minister, a police photographer, state troopers, fellows from the radio and the newspaper. Oh, a bunch. Most of them had been called out of church, and acted as though they were still there. Very quiet. Whispery. It was like nobody could believe it. A state trooper asked me did I have any official business there, and said if not, then I'd better leave.... I started walking home, and on the way, about half way down the lane, I saw Kenyon's old collie and that dog was scared. Stood there with its tail between its legs, didn't bark or move. And seeing the dog—somehow that made me *feel* again. I'd been too dazed, too numb, to feel the viciousness of it. The suffering. The horror. They were dead. A whole family. Gentle, kindly people, people *I* knew—murdered. You had to believe it, because it was really true.[37]

Capote steps out of the way and allows other voices to speak; he frames this testimony, assembling the pieces. This composition is a meticulous assembly of edited scenes and images connected with understated authorial summary, and presented in a rhythm that captures and holds the attention of the reader. Capote is masterful as interviewer and investigator, extracting the material and unearthing images and scenes and emotion from his subjects; his is a telling presented in large measure through unmediated voices edited into story.

Proper use of these skills can be very powerful in legal storytelling. Effective advocates, in building their arguments, use different voices to tell strategic narratives, and they do so at all stages from trial to appeal to postconviction relief. Here, for example, is a *scene* created by composition of transcripts and testimony from a well-crafted, effective, and successful death penalty brief.

The legal issue presented in *Atkins v. Virginia*[38] is whether executing a mentally retarded adult violates the Eight Amendment's prohibition of cruel and unusual punishment. The core of the theoretical argument is simple: a mentally retarded defendant is inherently disadvantaged in litigation, and his condition makes it inherently difficult to participate effectively in his own defense. Especially when there are multiple codefendants, it is more likely that the mentally retarded defendant will be convicted of a capital offense and sentenced to death, because he is the least able to protect his own interests and will likely become the fall guy in the litigation, regardless of his actual role in the killing. The defendant's condition makes it difficult for him to effectively tell his story. This allows another version of events to be privileged over his less-coherent story. Moreover, his mental retardation prevents him from possessing the requisite culpability to be sentenced to death and it is therefore cruel and unusual punishment to sentence him to die.

This legal argument is built on an effective story: Daryl Atkins clearly participated in the crime that resulted in the killing of an innocent victim. The question is about Atkins's role in the killing. A second codefendant, the clever and more capable twenty-six-year-old William Jones, escaped the death penalty by testifying against the eighteen-year-old and mentally retarded Atkins, who was convicted of capital murder and sentenced to death.

The brief presents testimonial excerpts as dialogue to illustrate how the mentally retarded defendant is disadvantaged in litigation. The defense attorney presents the story like a radio play, carefully editing testimonial excerpts and arranging them "dialogically"[39] to reenact selected portions of the trial proceedings.

The first section of the "Statement of the Case," subtitled "The Evidence Concerning the Crime," locates the crime itself in the backstory—the narrative time before the presentation of evidence. The first paragraph only briefly references the robbery and murder of the victim, Eric Nesbitt, in a *summary*: "He was robbed of the money in his wallet, driven in his own truck to an ATM and required to withdraw more money, then driven eighteen miles to York County, where he was shot eight times and killed with a semi-automatic handgun."[40] Although the brief does not minimize the horrific circumstances of the crime, it does not indicate who does the shooting or depict the precise circumstances of the killing. After the body is discovered, a videotape from the ATM transactions reveals Nesbitt sitting between two African American men, later identified as William Jones and Daryl Atkins.

The scene then shifts to the investigation and trial, and it is here that the story begins. It is told primarily through the competing first-person voices of Atkins and Jones. The reader is presented with selected excerpts from their testimony, and is invited to weigh the testimony and assess Atkins's ability to assist in his capital defense, despite his apparent mental retardation. The shrewder Jones seems far more capable of directing the outcome of the proceedings by casting blame and responsibility on codefendant Atkins.

The initial paragraphs provide more summary of the investigation and proceedings prior to Atkins's trial: Atkins gives a statement the day of his arrest identifying Jones as the triggerman.[41] Jones, however, does not give a statement, playing his legal cards more carefully.[42] Both are indicted for capital murder, but in Virginia, "only the triggerman could be convicted."[43] A year later Jones tells the authorities that he took part in the robbery and abduction but "blame(s) Atkins for the shooting."[44] Jones pleads guilty to first degree murder, "a plea that made him ineligible for the death penalty—with a requirement that he testify against Atkins."[45] The scene then shifts to the guilt phase of Atkins's trial. The scene is initially presented from Jones's point of view: Jones and Atkins spend the day drinking, smoking marijuana, and watching television.[46] They go to a convenience store for beer and then to a liquor store; running low on money, Atkins panhandles.

Here, the two stories of Jones and Atkins diverge. Their voices are transposed into a purposeful sequence, which enables the reader to assess these two characters in relationship to one another. For example, first Jones asserts that Atkins had a gun in his belt.[47] Then Atkins speaks and the reader is immediately struck by Atkins's voice; he sounds like Lenny in John Steinbeck's *Of Mice and Men*: "Me and William Jones was on the side of the 7-Eleven and we planning to rob somebody. And William Jones had the gun."[48]

On the other hand, Jones's sentences are clear, his grammar is correct, but there seems to be a self-serving calculation and rehearsed manipulation to his responses. In Jones's version of the story, Atkins is the dominant actor and initiator, while Jones is subservient and submissive. For example, when Jones is close enough to hear what is occurring, the robbery is already well under way; and as Jones gets into the car, he realizes "at that point" that he is involved in a robbery.[49]

In contrast to Jones, Atkins's syntax is convoluted and ungrammatical. His speech draws attention to itself and he confuses the events of the story. It seems apparent that he is unable to present the events in a straight, linear, and self-serving way. Nevertheless, Atkins's version is filled with vivid details, sharp imagistic fragments that seem authentic and arrest the reader's attention. Atkins's "voice" foregrounds the mental retardation that limits his abilities and, implicitly, proscribes his culpability.

The "Statement of the Case" walks a careful tightrope of language. The writer is careful not to appear; there is minimal authorial intrusion on the dialogue, and no judgments are made about what is being said. Strategically, the brief cannot present the competing stories in such a way that the reader speculates about why Atkins's version wasn't believed at trial. The reader should not feel manipulated or made suspicious or critical by the form of the presentation. Nor should the reader be invited to challenge implicit assertions about Atkins's character and abilities (e.g., whether Atkins is, indeed, so mentally retarded that his condition prevents him from forming the mental state required for the conviction of capital murder).

Like Capote in *In Cold Blood*, the author gets out of the way and lets the characters speak in their own words. The author carefully selects and places the quotes, building scenes into purposeful sequences. There is no commentary on these testimonial excerpts, no shifts of perspective or movements inside the consciousness or thoughts of the speaker (as there were, for example, in both Donovan's and Spence's closing arguments).

The "Statement of the Case" presents two competing versions of the initial armed robbery and the drive to the bank where the murder victim Eric Nesbitt is forced to withdraw another $200 from an ATM. The roles of Jones and Atkins are reversed in the two tellings, as to who is the dominant initiator and who is the passive accomplice.[50] The two versions of the murder itself are presented dialogically, alternating the perspectives of Jones and Atkins.

The author presents Jones's version of the killing in an active voice with short, grammatically correct sentences that are readily understood by the reader: " 'Mr. Atkins got out. He directed Mr. Nesbitt out'. Atkins still had the gun. 'As soon as Mr. Nesbitt stepped out of the vehicle and probably took two steps, the shooting started'."[51] In Jones's version, Jones even visualizes himself as Nesbitt's protector: Jones goes "around the back of the truck, aiming 'to get the gun away from Mr. Atkins', 'to stop him from killing Mr. Nesbitt.' "[52] Jones's telling seems rehearsed, pat. Jones avoids assuming any major role in the killing, depicting himself as an unwitting accomplice.

Atkins's ungrammatical and less coherent version seems more authentic and persuasive. Here, for example, is an illustrative paragraph from the petitioner's brief, presenting Atkins's version of the same events:

> Atkins' version was that Jones stopped the truck and "told me to get out, me and Eric Nesbitt to switch places. He never said why.

So I hand—he told me to hand him the gun. I hand him the gun. I got out first. Eric Nesbitt got out behind me. I got back in. Eric Nesbitt got back in. William Jones still had the gun. He put it in a holster that he had on his belt, a black nylon holster. Then he drove up the street a little more. And then I noticed it was like a fork in the road. So then he stopped and backed up, and then he backed up, parked the car, and he opened up the door.... He told Eric Nesbitt to get out.... Eric Nesbitt got out." Atkins was in the truck, "in the middle." "As Eric Nesbitt was getting out William Jones got out, too. So by the time Eric Nesbitt got out the vehicle, William Jones was there. He had come around the back of the truck.... He—Eric Nesbitt bend [*sic*] over and William Jones told him to get up. And he didn't get up. And then the shooting started." Jones did the shooting. Atkins was still in the truck. There were a lot of shots. After they started, Atkins' "leg was hurting, so I reached down to look at my leg.... Then I didn't hear no more shots. And then William Jones got inside the driver's—he came back around, got inside the driver's and took off." Atkins asked Jones why Jones had shot him, and Jones tried to figure out how he shot Atkins. Atkins asked Jones to take him to the hospital "[b]ecause my leg was hurting." Atkins also "asked...[Jones] where did he shoot him [Nesbitt] at. He said he shot him in the body."[53]

From this excerpt of the brief, it appears that Atkins is speaking for himself exclusively, with unmediated language and quotations from the transcripts. But this presentation is a composite of edited testimony, of paraphrase, and of alteration between scene and summary: it shifts perspectives, creates a rhythm, and builds scenes into a purposeful sequence. When depicting the murder itself, the writer slows the pace of the telling into a stretch, reconstructing the murder by splicing together and editing transcript into montage. Although the jury apparently disbelieved the veracity of Atkins's testimony, and convicted him of capital murder, the reader is invited to revisit the story, assessing Atkins's abilities to participate effectively in his own defense. The telling is a composition designed to make Atkins appear confused but truthful; it is perhaps as artful, although less dramatic and more understated, than the excerpts from Capote's *In Cold Blood*. This is a clear example of how skillful use of scenes, rhythm, stretches, and detail can subtly lead the reader to view the events and characters in a way that supports the writer's intended result.

VI. Perspective or Point of View

A final important topic closely related to understanding voice and the specific qualities of various voices is *perspective* or *point of view*. The novelist and writing teacher John Gardner observes that, "in contemporary writing one may do anything one pleases with point of view, as long as it works."[54] But what, exactly, is perspective or point of view? And how does it work? How do perspectives affect legal storytelling and argumentation?

Perhaps the simplest and clearest understanding of perspective or point of view may be derived from watching movies. Perspective may be conceptualized and understood simply as: (1) where the cameras and microphones are placed to record the action, (2) who the story centers on (typically, most films track the movements of the protagonist), and (3) the stance of the moviemaker in relationship to the subject matter and theme of the story and the characters within it.

These concerns are equally important to legal storytellers. For example, in the closing arguments of Spence and Donovan, it is the perspective or point of view that determines the appropriate voice for the speaker. Gerry Spence assumes an omniscient third-person perspective sympathetic to the protagonist Karen Silkwood; he stands outside the events and follows her actions, commenting in a godlike and often judgmental way on her activities. He observes from a distance Silkwood's heroic and melodramatic battle against the trouble—the assembled forces of antagonism aligned in opposition to her, as she attempts to protect the innocents in the community. Silkwood is in an epic battle against The Beast, Kerr-McGee, and its many evil minions.

In Donovan's tragicomic Failla storytelling, Donovan assumes a different and more intimate voice embodied within a closer and more limited perspective. Donovan's voice and perspective is cast in a limited third person, more tightly and subjectively aligned with the movements and thoughts of his defendant-protagonist, Louis Failla. From this perspective, Donovan repeatedly slips directly into the mind of Louie Failla, revealing Failla's thought processes, assuming a first-person perspective.

It is helpful to identify alternative perspectives or points of view that are typically employed by both legal and nonlegal storytellers, including: (1) the first-person, (2) the third-person subjective, (3) the third-person objective, (4) the authorial omniscient, and (5) the essayist omniscient.[55]

The first-person perspective provides, perhaps, the most natural voice, in that it enables the writer to write as she actually thinks or talks, and to write simply and directly about how she perceives the world. It provides the most direct form of connection between speaker and reader; it allows for direct expression of the speaker's thoughts. Examples of first-person narrators in the modern novel include, of course, the strong voices and unique interior perspectives of Huckleberry Finn or Holden Caulfield. The perspective of the narrative is fixed within the speaker; the reader perceives what the narrator perceives, and the story moves with the narrator's movements; the camera's lens and the recording microphones are located within the narrator. As we have already observed in the storytelling of Jeremiah Donovan in the Failla closing argument (employing edited transcripts) and in the excerpts from the audiotapes employing the recorded voice of Karen Silkwood (returned from the dead) in Spence's closing argument, the careful use of the first-person voice is an especially powerful tool in legal argumentation. In many effective briefs, including in the "Statement of the Case" of *Atkins*, selective use and incorporation of first-person voices and first-person stories within stories is a powerful tool of narrative persuasion.

The second often-adopted narrative perspective is the third-person subjective, a point of view in which "all the 'I's are changed to 'he's or 'she's and emphasis is placed on the character's thoughts."[56] The objective here is to indirectly embody or convey the consciousness of a clearly identified actor, often the protagonist in the story: "this point of view (style in a sense) goes for deep consciousness, in the hope that the thoughts and feelings of the character will become the immediate (unmediated) thoughts and feelings of the reader."[57] Gardner notes, however, that this perspective also has severe limitations. For example, it "locks the reader inside the character's mind, however limited that mind might be, so that when the character's judgments are mistaken or inadequate, the reader's more correct judgments must come from a cool withdrawal."[58]

This perspective clearly has utility in different types of legal arguments, and lawyers selectively employ it to explain and capture the consciousness of a central character. For example, Spence shifts strategically from an omniscient third-person narration into a more limited and subjective third-person voice to convey Silkwood's motivations and show how she overcame her own fears and self-interest through courageous action on behalf of the innocent workers at the plant. Likewise, Donovan's narrative shift into a sly, darkly comical, and ironic third-person perspective reveals intimately the complex psychological intentionality that undergirds Louie Failla's inaction, and his seeming complicity in the plot to murder Tito Morales. Louie attempts to preserve the appearance of his loyalty to the Patriarca family and, simultaneously, his loyalty to his real family as well;

he cleverly deceives the Patriarca family, deceives his real family, and, perhaps, deceives himself too. Only at the end of his two-hour performance does Donovan shift from a limited third-person into a first-person narration, directly voicing Failla's unexpressed thoughts by translating them into a clearheaded, internal, first-person monologue.

The third perspective that Gardner identifies is the third-person *objective*, which is "identical to the third-person subjective except that the narrator not only never comments himself but also refrains from entering any character's mind. The result is an ice-cold camera's eye recording. We see events, hear dialogue, observe the setting, and make guesses about what the characters are thinking."[59] An example of this limited third-person perspective is in the portions of the *Riggins* brief cited previously in this chapter, where the reader sits as if a spectator in the jury box observing the image of the zombie-like defendant Riggins. The reader never enters the mind and thoughts of the defendant, who has been incapacitated by the forced ingestion of the drug Mellaril. Likewise, in the initial excerpt from Ellroy's *My Dark Places*, the voice shifts from a first-person perspective (and a rarely employed and compellingly intimate second-person voice that speaks directly to his dead mother) to a cold camera's eye third-person "objective" recording of the events, including the discovery of the corpse of his mother. This shift of perspective from the intimacy of the first-person voice to a cold and limited third-person objective detective's voice is striking and initially disconcerting. It is a dramatic movement emphasized with the framing devices of headings and subheadings structurally akin to a technique that skilled writers of legal briefs also employ. In all of these illustrations, the aesthetic relationship between voice and perspective is apparent and functionally correct for effective storytelling. The choice of perspective implicates the voice and, in turn, the voice controls and suggests the appropriate perspective. Although perspective and voice are fused into one, these are two discrete and complementary stylistic components of the story.

VII. Several Functions of Perspective: How Does Perspective (Point of View) Work, and What Work Does It Do?

David Lodge observes that "the choice of the point(s) of view from which the story is told is arguably the most important single decision that the [storyteller] has to make, for it fundamentally affects the way readers will respond, emotionally and morally" to the story.[60] Is this so? How does perspective shape or control the narrative? What are the functions and limitations of various perspectives or points of view?

A. Perspective Controls the Flow of Information

The choice of perspective shapes and predetermines the narrative logic of the story. It is akin to the way the rules of evidence in a courtroom regulate storytelling practice, by predetermining what information comes in and how it may be presented in relationship to and connected with other evidence presented at trial. That is, perspective affects the narrative logic of the story.

For example, an omniscient third-person narrator can reveal information that no person in the story possibly knows—events that occur outside the presence of any individual who might serve as a first-person narrator or beyond the scope of the third-person limited observer. Thus, an omniscient narrator in the excerpt from Norman Mailer's *Executioner's Song* dips into Max Jensen's consciousness and delicately reveals the meaning of the gas station attendant's smile. This is so because an omniscient narrator can describe the thoughts and feelings of everyone in the tale, and can provide insights about an individual's character that the individual may lack the capacity to express. An omniscient narrator can also generalize about the meaning and implications of various events and connect these events to other events or to theory. For example, in the legal argument section of the petitioner's brief in *Atkins,* the voice shifts from a limited to an omniscient third-person perspective, revisiting the story told initially in the "Statement of the Case"; this enables the narrator to generalize about the abilities of mentally retarded individuals to participate effectively in their own defense. The argument describes several cases where an innocent defendant's mental retardation resulted in his wrongful conviction.[61] Likewise, an omniscient Gerry Spence looks into the future and previsions the cancer that will befall the young workingmen continuing at Kerr-McGee, fulfilling the dark prophecy of Karen Silkwood. His omniscient perspective enables him to articulate the historical significance of this trial and to call on the jury's heroism to prevent the Cimarron Syndrome, stopping the Beast Kerr-McGee and its voracious appetite for profits and prophets. Spence even previsions that the jurists can change the course of history through their heroic intervention.

The strength of the omniscient perspective is not only to expand upon and explain; it can equally summarize, compact, edit, reconfigure, and reorganize information in a purposeful way that a first-person or third-person limited narrator can seldom do. For example, it can convey the most content in the fewest words. An omniscient narrator can move in a godlike way that ranges freely across time. For example, Spence moves over time and across space, from the origins of the law of strict liability in England to the popular culture events of the present day in a greedy and corrupt post-Watergate America, and on into a cinematic dream-like vision prefiguring a dark future that will emerge unless the jury can heroically intervene. Neither a first-person nor a limited third-person narrator could make these leaps in time, for the rules of perspective wed these types of narrators to events in a way that compels a different type of systematic unfolding.

On the other hand, the use of a first-person narrator or a third-person limited narrator allows the writer to withhold information or delay its disclosure strategically. This allows for creating the suspense or tension crucial to the construction and propulsion of detective mysteries (which are typically told from first-person or third-person limited perspectives).

B. Perspectives Can Suggest Outcome and Endow the Reader with Responsibility for Determining Meanings

Different perspectives endow the reader with different levels of responsibility for making sense of the events of the story and—perhaps of more importance in legal storytelling—for deriving the point of the story; the audience becomes responsible for determining what the outcome of the story should and will be. Especially since law stories are unfinished stories, with an active decision maker charged with writing the ending of the tale, the choice of perspective implicitly entails different roles or responsibilities for the listener or reader in determining the ending of the story and for imposing meaning upon it.

Specifically, an omniscient narrator who speaks with the authority of God can be quite explicit in telling the reader or listener what happened and what to make of the events that occurred and in specifying the desired outcome or judgment. At other times, an omniscient narrator can strongly direct the reader's moral response to a scene and the characters within it by selecting and depicting details and ordering the presentation of information. For example, Mailer observes Gilmore's angry asides as he pulls the trigger of the automatic leveled against Jensen's head. "This one's for me," Gilmore says, and then again, "this one's for Nicole." Likewise, instead of generalizing about the helpless and vulnerable attendant, Mailer observes that the attendant is "still trying to smile" as Gilmore orders him to the floor. That is, Mailer carefully selects and tightly arranges details from an omniscient perspective in such a way as to evoke a specific emotional response in the reader, one that creates no sympathy for Gilmore. Mailer's depiction of the crime is similar to the narrative strategy of many prosecutors; it is designed to viscerally and powerfully reenact the horror of the crime and to point the reader toward a particular ending: one in which Gilmore deservingly faces conviction and the death penalty.

A possible disadvantage of employing an omniscient voice is that it is often too strongly directive. It may disempower listeners-readers and deprive the audience of the excitement and stimulus necessary to figure out what is going on, determine how to interpret events, and, in legal stories, decide how to write the ending that provides closure to the tale. Employing an omniscient perspective may also unintentionally evoke reader or listener skepticism or create unintended effects. Consequently, for example, in his closing argument on behalf of Karen Silkwood, Gerry Spence seems intuitively conscious of the potential for being perceived as overly directive and manipulative. Thus, he shifts from his omniscient perspective, emphasizing that his vision of the future is his own personal dream of what the future will look like if the heroic jury fails to intervene on behalf of Silkwood.

In contrast, first-person and third-person limited narrators typically appear to provide the empirical data from which readers or listeners can determine for themselves the meaning of events and conclude whether X is true or Y is the point. For example, in a story told by a third-person limited narrator (e.g., in portions of Ellroy's *My Dark Places* or in defendant Riggins's brief) the reader is compelled to make sense of and construct the story from the limited and restricted viewpoint (perspective) of the narrator.

The first-person perspective also typically allows the teller to introduce additional evidence and personal information that might otherwise appear extraneous. The reader or listener is thus encouraged to develop a closer personal relationship with the storyteller and is empowered to sort through this information as a collaborator with the narrator. This allows the reader to better understand why the information is included in the story.

Here, for example, is the opening narrative hook from Frank McCourt's memoir, *Angela's Ashes*.[62] An intimate voice speaks from the narrator's point of view directly to the reader. The prose has an immediacy; the richness of evocative details fits the style and resonates with readers; there is a deep emotional attachment between the writer and his material, as pervasive in the prose as the "Irish" sadness that soaks the images like seawater. McCourt begins:

> My father and mother should have stayed in New York where they met and married and where I was born. Instead, they returned to Ireland when I was four, my brother, Malachy, three, the twins, Oliver and Eugene, barely one, and my sister, Margaret, dead and gone.
>
> When I look back on my childhood I wonder how I survived at all. It was, of course, a miserable childhood: the happy childhood is hardly worth your while. Worse than the ordinary miserable childhood is the miserable Irish childhood, and worse yet is the miserable Irish Catholic childhood.
>
> People everywhere brag and whimper about the woes of their early years, but nothing can compare with the Irish version: the poverty; the shiftless loquacious alcoholic father; the pious defeated mother moaning by the fire; pompous priests; bullying schoolmasters; the English and the terrible things they did to us for eight hundred long years.
>
> Above all—we were wet.[63]

McCourt's voice is cast in a first-person perspective that invites the reader to sort through the past with the narrator as a collaborator to determine the meanings of the images and to travel with him on an evocative journey. This is akin to the strategy Jeremiah Donovan employs when he shifts from a third-person limited perspective directly into the first-person consciousness of Louie Failla, where we are invited to share emotionally in Louie's dilemma. Also similar is Truman Capote's shift to a first-person perspective by employing the recollections of the schoolteacher who travels with the sheriff to discover the bodies of the Clutter family. Through these recollections the schoolteacher returns via the narrative as if attempting to retrieve the emotional meaning of the ministory, telling the story for himself as well as for the reader.

But aren't first-person voices and the first-person perspective disfavored in formal legal storytelling? When a first-year law student prefaces an answer to a question with "I think" or "I believe," isn't the characteristic response of law professors, "Who cares what you believe Mr./Ms.——?" Isn't it part of the imperative of becoming a lawyer to eliminate reliance on the first-person voice? Yes and no. Legal storytellers often purport or appear to assume a neutral third-person voice, an objective, dispassionate, and emotionless stance.

As I have analyzed in the trial arguments of Spence and Donovan and in the dialogue in the petitioner's "Statement of the Case" in the successful *Atkins* brief, however, attorneys often incorporate intentionally strong first-person voices into their arguments.

For a final legal example, the petitioner's brief in [Terry] *Williams v. Taylor*[64] argues that defendant's trial counsel provided ineffective assistance in failing to investigate and present evidence of defendant's childhood environment. As a result of the failure to introduce relevant mitigation evidence at sentencing, defendant Terry Williams was sentenced to death. Initially, the petitioner's brief speaks of this omitted evidence abstractly, of Williams's "traumatic childhood," and a mother who "drank herself into a stupor almost daily while pregnant with him."[65] By themselves, these abstractions have little impact on the reader. However, there is additional evidence included in Terry Williams's "uncontroverted juvenile records."[66] Rather than merely providing a summary or paraphrase of these records, the author excerpts evidence in the form of first-person notes and the firsthand observations of a social worker who had visited the defendant's family home many years earlier, and who was charged with protecting the children on behalf of the state. The social worker's report of the conditions of Williams's family home is framed in a double-indented block quotation. The social worker's testimonial account vividly captures the quality of Terry Williams's childhood, bringing to life "the sordid conditions of Williams' home" for the reader.[67]

> At the hearing, records and testimony were introduced showing that Williams had a traumatic childhood but was able to function well in structured settings and establish positive relationships. He was the sixth of eleven children, and Williams' mother testified that she drank herself into a stupor almost daily while pregnant with him. Uncontroverted juvenile records showed that his parents were alcoholics who supplemented their meager income by selling bootleg whiskey. The records described [from the perspective of the social worker] the sordid conditions of Williams' home:
>> [Here, the brief shifts to the voice of the social worker.]
>> Lula and Noah [the parents] were sitting on the front porch and were in such a drunken state, it was almost impossible for them to get up. They staggered into the house to where the children were asleep. Terry, age 1, and Noah Jr., age 3, were asleep on the sofa. There was an odor of alcohol on the breath of Noah Jr.... Oliver [Olivia] had just awakened and was very sick. She said she was hungry and had been drinking

whiskey. Ohair was completely passed out and never could be awakened. He did not have on any clothes....

The home was a complete wreck.... There were several places on the floor where some one had had a bowel movement. Urine was standing in several places in the bedrooms. There were dirty dishes scattered over the kitchen, and it was impossible to step any place on the kitchen floor where there was no trash.... The children were all dirty and none of them had on any under-pants. Noah and Lula were so intoxicated, they could not find any clothes for the children, nor were they able to put the clothes on them. There was stuffed pickle scattered on the floor in the front bedroom.

Noah and Lulu were put in jail, each having five charges of neglect placed against them. The children had to be put in Winslow Hospital, as four of them, by that time, were definitely under the influence of whiskey. When Dr. Harvey examined them, he found that they had all been drinking bootleg whiskey. They were all hungry and very happy to be given milk, even the baby [Terry] drank a pint of milk before stopping. Oliver [Olivia] said that they had not had any food all day. Ohair was still so drunk he could not talk.[68]

Williams' parents were jailed for criminal neglect, and the children were placed in a foster home where they were badly treated before being returned to their parents three years later.

Even then, the "parents show[ed] no interest in...the children"; "the children are without food or proper clothes often," and "[t]here are many home problems." The family was so poor that Williams' mother could not afford surgery to remove a tumor.[69]

The social worker's narration introduces mitigation evidence omitted at trial more effectively than a summary, a paraphrase, or an omniscient third-person narrator interpreting the images and making explicit the effects of the petitioner's chaotic childhood home life. Instead, the brief simply provides a frame for this mitigation evidence, and presents it in a straightforward way. Nor does the writer comment on the meaning of the ministory in the context of the legal story (e.g., that defendant's counsel was ineffective because he failed to introduce mitigation evidence based on defendant's past). The understated mode of presentation without editorial comment or narrative intervention serves the vivid imagery well; the reader readily comprehends that the fate of the defendant is at least a partial product of his bleak and dysfunctional social history. The imagery conveyed through the observations of the social worker invites, but does not force or compel, the reader to reenter the horrific home life of the defendant as a small boy, alongside the social worker.

C. Perspective Affects the Degree of the Reader's or Listener's Engagement in the Story and Suggests the Degree of Empathy the Reader or Listener Should Hold for Various Characters within a Story

Omniscient narrators can be coolly dispassionate and encourage listeners and readers to exercise a logical judgment; an omniscient perspective often avoids intimacy and emotional involvement in the story. Because there is an emotional remove, an omniscient perspective can encourage the listener or reader to make judgments about the conduct of the various actors in the story. For example, in Mailer's depiction of the murder of Max Jensen, there is no sympathy created for the character of Gary Gilmore. The reader is clearly invited to judge Gilmore's actions harshly, and reach the determination that Gilmore has acted brutally and coldheartedly.

Gary Gilmore in *Executioner's Song* appears gradually as a more deeply layered and nuanced character as Mailer incorporates directly Gilmore's first-person letters and observations, and shifts perspectives. For example, Gilmore introspectively seeks to understand the horror of his actions, acknowledging both society's need for retribution as well as his moral responsibility to pay society for the crimes that he has committed. Thus he writes eloquently in a letter to his girlfriend, Nicole, as he awaits execution on Utah's death row:

> Recently, it has begun to make a little sense. I owe a debt, from a long time ago.... I'm on the verge of knowing something very personal, something about myself. Something that somehow wasn't completed and made me different. Something I owe. I guess. Wish I knew.
>
> Once you asked me if I was the devil, remember? I'm not. The devil would be far more clever than I, would operate on a much larger scale and of course would feel no remorse.... And I know the devil can't feel love. But I might be further from God than I am from the devil. Which is not a good thing. It seems that I know evil more intimately than I know goodness and that's not a good thing either. I want to get even, to be made even, whole, my debts paid (whatever it may take!) to have no blemish, no reason to feel guilt or fears. I hope this ain't

corny, but I'd like to stand in the sight of God. To know that I'm just and right and clean.[70]

Likewise, Donovan brings jurors directly inside Failla's thoughts through a first-person perspective supplemented with an extended commentary on Failla's words. In this stretch, Donovan employs Louie's first-person voice and slows down the action to incorporate additional narration from a limited third-person perspective. Donovan makes jurors feel Louie's predicament, as if they exist inside Louie's skin. Similarly, the use of a close third-person narrator who follows the central character can also make us care about the fate of the character as we witness the unfolding events that affect his life, even if the voice seems objective. For example, in *Riggins* we watch the plight of the defendant Riggins from the limited third-person perspective of a person sitting in the jury, realizing that his zombie-like appearance does not reflect his competence to stand trial, but is rather an effect of the forced ingestion of the drug Mellaril. We also have knowledge of what will happen to him: he will be condemned to death because of this zombie-like appearance. This use of a limited third-person perspective enables the reader to grasp Riggins's plight, and intuitively understand that his trial violates due process and his conviction and sentencing are unfairly predestined.

Closely related to this point, the use of perspective enables the storyteller to purposefully regulate the degree of empathy for various characters. For example, a first-person narrator can explain and express the narrator's experience of the world in the narrator's own terms, giving readers a sense that they understand the narrator's character and plight intimately.[71] This can create feelings for, and empathy with, a character who may initially appear otherwise unsympathetic when her actions are viewed from another perspective.

On the other hand, an omniscient narrator, who readily slips in and out of the minds of various characters, typically limits the ability of the reader or listener to identify with individual characters (and may intentionally keep the reader-listener from knowing where to fully place her loyalties). Thus, a voice cast in an omniscient perspective can be employed to create emotional distance or detachment from the events of the story and the characters within it. In many cases prosecutors intuitively tell their stories through a voice speaking from an objective and omniscient perspective, as the jury watches the events from this distance. The omniscient prosecutorial narrator may slip into and out of the minds of various characters, or, conversely, refuse to slip into any one character's mind, seeming to apply the same narrative rules fairly to the depiction of all events and all characters. The result is, typically, that the audience does not place loyalty with or identify strongly with any one character.

Here, for example, is the opening of the prosecutor's closing argument against Louie Failla (and seven other reputed Patriarca crime family members) as he frames his complex five-hour story summarizing the evidence. Before beginning, the prosecutor thanks the jurors for their attention to the evidence, admonishes the jury not to be deceived by the stories presented by the attorneys in the closing arguments, and emphasizes that the job of the jurors is simply to determine what happened, what *really* happened: "If what the lawyers say... differs from your recollection of the evidence, it's your recollection that controls. The most important job that you have in this case is to find the facts, to decide what really happened."[72]

After referring to the judge's charge, the prosecutor describes the dramatic and dark initiation rituals of the Patriarca crime family (captured on surveillance tapes) as a compelling opening hook. The prosecutor establishes a third-person omniscient perspective for the entire closing argument that looks down at the past events placed into evidence through testimony and in the crucial FBI surveillance tapes. Before examining the specific activities of each of the defendants, the prosecutor addresses the cruelty of the criminal activities of all eight codefendants as members of a shared criminal enterprise:

And all of these activities, all of them, are laced one way or another with their undercurrent of violence that affects everything these guys do, and it spills out from time to time, and we saw it here, too. It spills out when they're burying bodies in a garage. It spills out when people put guns to the back of people's heads and shoot them like they did with William Grasso. It spills out when people plot in cars to kill human beings like they did with respect to Tito Morales.[73]

Subsequently, after Donovan's compelling narrative closing argument employing first-person and limited third-person voices and perspective, a different prosecutor in the rebuttal closing argument attempts to reestablish the jurors' perspective as objective fact finders, their role limited to reviewing the evidence regarding the charge that Failla conspired to murder Tito Morales. He directly refers to the narrative deceits implicit in Donovan's storytelling and, specifically, Donovan's use of the first-person perspective to step inside

Failla's mind and articulate his thoughts. He admonishes the jurors not to be deceived by this trickery, but to limit their deliberations to the evidence:

> With respect to Failla, and I will turn to the murder now, with respect to Mr. Failla and Tito Morales, Mr. Donovan is an excellent lawyer. And Mr. Donovan's final argument in my view was outstanding. But when Mr. Donovan stands here in front of you with cartoons and suggests to you what Louie Failla was thinking I suggest to you that that's [going] too far. Because there is no evidence in this case about what Louie Failla was thinking or saying other than the tape recordings which were admitted into evidence in this case.
>
> That's the evidence in the case.... [A]nd when you listen to those tapes, listen to those tapes and what was said. Is there any doubt in your mind that these people were serious? Mr. Donovan wants to suggest to you that well, what Louie Failla was doing was he was just putting off Castagna and Johns because they were killers.
>
> In another breath he says they can go do whatever they wanted, but that's not the evidence, and you know that's not the evidence. *That's lawyers' games. Lawyers' games.*[74]

Similarly, in a recent New York murder case, analyzed by Janet Malcolm in a magazine article,[75] an omniscient prosecutor-narrator presents a story in a voice filled with the judgmental and moral outrage of a retributive and vengeful Old Testament God. There is none of the subtlety, understatement, or irony in Mailer's artistic depiction of the murder of Max Jensen by Gary Gilmore. Likewise, there is none of the prosecutor's calm or dispassion, the purported objectivity, and his measured words, as presented in the closing argument and rebuttal closing arguments in *Failla*. Instead, the prosecutor is consumed by moral outrage and makes the judgments of his omniscient narrator explicit. There is no doubt about where the jurists are commanded to place their sympathies; the jury is admonished that there is no choice but to share the prosecutor's narrative perspective and to entrust itself to his narrative vision.

Thus, the prosecutor Brad Leventhal begins his opening statement and sets the stage for his depiction of the murder with the initial appearance of the victim:

> It was a bright, sunny, clear, brisk fall morning, and on that brisk fall morning a young man, a young orthodontist by the name of Daniel

Malakov, was walking down 64th Road in the Forest Hills section of Queens county just a few miles from where we are right now. With him was his little girl, his four-year-old daughter, Michelle.[76]

Just as in *Failla*, there is more to the theatricality of the prosecutor's voice and style than merely the recitation of the words. Janet Malcolm, the reporter, describes the composition of words, gestures, and sounds. Leventhal continues: "[A]s Daniel stood outside the entrance to Annandale Playground, just feet from the entrance to that park, just feet from where his little girl stood, this defendant Mikhail Mallayev stepped out as if from nowhere. In his hand he had a loaded and operable pistol."[77]

Janet Malcolm describes Leventhal's gestures and physicality:

When Leventhal uttered the words "this defendant," he theatrically extended his arm and pointed across the room to a thickset man in his fifties with a gray beard and heavy dark eyebrows, wearing wire-rimmed eyeglasses and a yarmulke, who sat impassively at the defense table. Leventhal went on to describe how Mallayev shot Malakov in the chest and in the back, and, as the orthodontist lay on the ground dying, his blood pouring from his wounds, saturating his clothing and seeping into the cement, this man, the defendant, who ended his life, calmly and coolly took his gun, put it into his jacket, turned away and headed up 64th Road towards 102nd Street and fled the scene.

With agitated, outstretched hands, Leventhal asked the jury: "Why? Why should this defendant lie in wait for an unsuspecting and innocent victim? A man, I will prove to you, he didn't even personally know. Why would he lie in wait with evil in his heart?"

Leventhal answered the question:

Because he was hired to do it. He was paid to do it. He's an assassin. A paid assassin. An executioner. A hit man. For who? Who would hire this man, this defendant to murder in cold blood an innocent victim in the presence of his own daughter? Who could have such strong feelings towards Daniel Malakov that they would hire an assassin to end his life? Who?

Leventhal walked toward the defense table and again lifted his arm and pointed—this time at Borokhova [the codefendant]. "Her," Leventhal said, his voice rising to its highest pitch. "The defendant Mazoltuv Borokhova, Daniel Malakov's estranged wife. The woman

with whom he had been engaged in an ongoing and heated, conten-
tious, acrimonious divorce for years."[78]

It is the prosecutor's use of an omniscient perspective that dictates the way in
which the jury will respond emotionally and morally to the characters. The
listeners' moral outrage at the actions of the defendant is a result of the prosecutor's use of perspective.

D. Perspective Directly Affects the Reader's or Listener's Perception of Events, Determining Whether the Reader or Listener Believes the Storyteller's Depiction of What Truly Happened

The prosecutor in a contest of competing stories (in trial, on appeal, or in a
postconviction brief) strategically employs an omniscient perspective affirming an apparent and undisputable "objective" truth. Often the story is told in
an unembellished "just the facts, ma'am," no nonsense rhythm and style: the
narrator employs short and straightforward declarative sentences. This clarity is to be equated with candor and absence of narrative manipulation.
Prosecutors typically tell their stories in straightforward and linear past-tense
constructions. Often the details and specifics are muted, as if the voice does
not need to prove itself to the reader or call attention to itself, and the details
are distractions that might be misread.

This strategy often works best in legal storytelling—just as it does in
nonlegal storytelling—when the omniscient narrator comes across as well
informed, unbiased, and trustworthy; this alone will tend to make his version
of the story believable. A measured tone, together with the absence of any
discrepancy between the narrator's version of events and whatever information is available from independent sources about those events, will invest the
story with believability. Conversely, if an omniscient narrator comes across as
unreliable at all, it completely destabilizes the entire reality of the telling. The
reader or listener is left not knowing what to believe. Especially in the context
of litigation, if the omniscient narrator is unreliable the reader or listener will
usually believe the converse of what the narrator says. In legal storytelling,
the use of an omniscient narrator implies the storyteller can always be trusted
to tell an absolute truth. Furthermore, the use of an omniscient narrator in
legal storytelling also implies that there is a single and absolute "objective"
truth that can be readily captured and depicted in the narrative; it need not
be unpacked and discovered by the listener or reader.

If a first-person or a third-person limited narrator comes across as reliable, however, the story gains the type of truth that comes from an eyewitness account. The world is perceived in subjective pieces and then assembled from these pieces. If, on the other hand, a first-person narrator or a third-person limited narrator appears unreliable, there are two possible effects. First, the reader or listener may believe that all the events are misrepresented and the truth is best ascertained by detecting the distortions that result from the narrator's deceitful motivations or judgmental impairments. Thus, for example, in the *Atkins* brief, once the reader determines that the prosecution's witness Jones is an unreliable narrator who has cast the blame on Atkins to avoid the possibility of a death penalty, the reader reinterprets the seeming coherence of Jones's version of the story and Atkins's role within it.

Second, the reader or listener may believe that the same motivations or judgmental impairments affect the behavior of the first-person narrator (or third-person limited narrator) as an actor within the story. Thus, for example, the unreliability of Jones as narrator not only affects his credibility but also transforms him into a villain within the story and causes the reader to reinterpret the events of the story with Atkins recast as the victim of Jones's villainy.

VIII. Concluding Observations

I began this chapter with an anecdote about grading law school examinations, explaining how style and voice are profoundly important in determining outcomes on these examinations. Specifically, like most law professors, I look for writing that is clearheaded, grammatically precise, and aggressively purposeful. The A student's "voice" is careful, meticulous, and constrained. Beneath it there is an understated confidence and authority, indeed, often a borderline arrogance and analytical certainty, mimetic of the judicial voices excerpted in the law school casebooks. The successful law student internalizes certain repetitive and preconfigured analytical forms to display doctrinal knowledge. The student learns how to analyze, synthesize, and analogize cases, and is able to apply doctrinal analysis to "the facts" within these tightly prescribed and highly organized analytical structures. The successful law student does not immerse herself in the facts to tell a persuasive story; instead, she employs facts as "floating factoids" to display doctrinal knowledge. Stories are subservient to legal analysis, colonized by analytical structure. This mode of presentation, important to law school success, rightfully becomes part of the successful practitioner's tool kit.

Unfortunately, to create problems that permit law students to develop this structured analytical precision and lawyer's voice, something important is typically sacrificed: "the facts"—the multidimensional, complex, ambiguous, and particularistic stories at the heart of legal problems. The practitioner's factually indeterminate world is tipped upside down in law school, so that the facts do not subsume doctrinal and legal analysis. Similarly, in heavily edited law school casebooks, complex and ambiguous stories are reduced and transformed into narratologies that seldom breathe, often have little inner life to them, and are typically merely excuses for exploring fine gradations and distinctions in doctrinal law.

In law practice, however, outcomes turn on storytelling skills and qualities of different storytelling voices. Lawyers intuitively develop new stylistic techniques crucial to their roles as legal storytellers. In this chapter I presented a limited selection from a large menu of relevant stylistic concerns and techniques that suggest a more expansive tool kit relevant to legal storytelling practice. I have used examples to illustrate how these techniques are applied and are relevant in effective legal and literary storytelling. The particular form of legal storytelling, whether a closing argument at trial or an appellate or postconviction brief, will present the storyteller with a large number of stylistic choices. These choices are nearly always determinative of the success of the legal argument and are an important tool of legal persuasion. In short, it is clear from a look at any effective storytelling that *style matters*.

A Sense of Place

SETTINGS, DESCRIPTIONS, AND ENVIRONMENTS

Beyond the lines of printed words in my books are the settings in which the books were imagined and without which the books could not exist.... I am a writer absolutely mesmerized by places;... and the settings my characters inhabit are as crucial... as the characters themselves.
—JOYCE CAROL OATES, "TO INVIGORATE LITERARY MIND, START MOVING LITERARY FEET"

Setting is... a powerful vehicle of thematic concerns; in fact, it's one of the most powerful.
—JOHN GARDNER, INTERVIEW IN PARIS REVIEW

Description... is never just description.
—DAVID LODGE, THE ART OF FICTION

I. Introduction

This chapter explores the significance of settings, descriptions, and the creation of complete environments in storytelling practice. These are closely related aspects of all stories, instigating the events of the story, compelling the shape of the world in which the events can happen, and in some circumstances even determining the outcome of the narrative itself.

The events of stories must fit in the worlds (the settings, the descriptions, and the complete narrative environments) shaped around them and, in turn, these environments are developed only in tandem with the telling of the tale itself. As we will explore, the settings, descriptions, and environments that work well in one story (whether legal or nonlegal) will clearly not fit in another. Indeed, the failure to develop an effective setting and environment can diminish or destroy the persuasive power of the story.

In many stories the settings, descriptions, and environments are crucial to the theme and the plot; the setting allows the events of the story to happen. For example, Spielberg's *Jaws* could obviously only take place in a summer beachfront community on the ocean where innocent summer bathers are naively enjoying the water unaware of the shark lurking beneath. Likewise, Foreman's allegorical *High Noon* fits the Western frontier town where order has yet to be imposed upon anarchy and justice is still meted out in a violent story-ending gun battle between the clearly marked forces of good and evil. The story fits the place or setting and the settings, in turn, suggest or create a complete narrative environment where the story can unfold.

But it is more complex than this: the settings, descriptions, or narrative environments are not merely containers shaped to fit the plots of the stories told within them. Settings and environments are developed and are often strategically affirmed or shaped throughout the story in tandem with the development of the narrative. Think, for example, of the images of the train tracks coming out of the distance that signal the arrival of Frank Miller in *High Noon*, or of the ticking of the clocks as Miller's arrival looms more immediate, or of the desperate marshal pacing relentlessly from place to place in his chaotic search for assistance from the townspeople who refuse to aid him in the battle to preserve their community. This imagery, these places and settings, embody the themes of the story and alert the viewer subtly to the complex and allegorical nature of the plot. In contrast, think of *Jaws*. The settings and shots are technically more elaborate and meticulously constructed, providing complex scenery for the shark attacks on the swimmers and the ultimate and prolonged final battle sequence between the three nautical heroes and the shark. The settings in *Jaws* are stages on which the action takes place, conveying to the viewer that all that matters is what is depicted on the screen; the viewer does not have to go any deeper to comprehend the meaning of this story. The viewer is thus encouraged to enjoy the movie. The settings and environment in *Jaws* provide a simple cartoon realism that integrates with and affirms the theme of this movie. The ending in *Jaws* is an appropriately shallow restorative ending; the town returns to exactly what it once was: a place where innocent swimmers guiltlessly enjoy the pleasures of a summer day in the waters off the Amity Island beach.

Thus setting or environment is developed and operates in tandem with the other narrative components of the story; the setting is aligned with the way in which this particular world works. The same is true in legal storytelling practices; the settings, descriptions, and environments are constructed to fit the story and, simultaneously, to suggest or create the type of world in which the events of this particular story can take place. Further, the type of world that fits one type of story will not typically fit another type of story.

This chapter analyzes discrete settings and environments depicted in creative nonfiction and fiction. The literary examples are provided by: (1) one paragraph from a Joan Didion essay about the Manson murders and Los Angeles in the summer of 1969; (2) a section from a travel story by the writer W. G. Sebald in which the narrator travels from Europe to America retracing the path of the journey taken by members of his family; and (3) an excerpt from a real-life crime story told by Kathryn Harrison about a boy who murders his mother, father, and younger sister. The legal examples include the depiction of settings and environments in a judicial opinion, two briefs from coerced confession cases, and the brief from a death penalty case. The chapter illustrates how some of the same techniques and concepts relevant to the development of settings in literature are applicable to effective brief writing and legal storytelling practice.

The various techniques employed in these illustrations and in practice are so numerous and diverse and so susceptible to invention that I will not attempt to describe or catalog them all. Briefly, they include strategic choices of: (1) whether to include or omit particular categories and groupings of things (physical objects, states of mind) and specific items in each category; (2) the level of detail and the kind of detailing selected; (3) the description of settings and what perspective to use in descriptions; (4) vocabulary, sentence structure, and paragraph structure; and (5) what information will be conveyed in direct statements versus through implication or presupposition. This is merely a general inventory of techniques that are best presented and understood in context of specific illustrations from nonlegal and legal storytelling practice.

II. Dangerous Territory: Contrasting Settings Evoking Danger and Instability in Joan Didion's "The White Album" and the Judicial Opinion in a Rape Case

We put "Lay Lady Lay" on the record player, and "Suzanne." We went down to Melrose Avenue to see the Flying Burritos. There was a jasmine vine grown over the verandah of the big house on Franklin Avenue, and in the evenings the smell of jasmine came in through all the open doors and windows. I made bouillabaisse for people who did not eat meat. I imagined that my own life was simple and sweet, and sometimes it was, but there were odd things going on around town. There were rumors. There were stories. Everything was unmentionable but nothing was unimaginable. This mystical flirtation with the idea of "sin"—this sense that it was possible to go "too far," and that many people were doing it—was very much with us in Los Angeles in 1968 and 1969. A demented and seductive vortical tension was building in the community. The jitters were setting in. I recall a time when the dogs barked every night and the moon was always full. On August 9, 1969, I was sitting in the shallow end of my sister-in-law's swimming pool in Beverly Hills when she received a phone call from a friend who had just heard about the murders at Sharon Tate Polanski's house on Cielo Drive. The phone rang many times during the next hour. These early reports were garbled and contradictory. One caller would say hoods, the next would say chains. There were twenty dead, no, twelve, ten, eighteen. Black masses were imagined, and bad trips blamed. I remember all of the day's misinformation very clearly, and I also remember this, and wish I did not. I remember that no one was surprised.[1]

Joan Didion's essay "The White Album," in her collection of essays with the same title, is partially a retelling of the story of the aftermath of the Manson cult murders in Los Angeles in the summer of 1969. It is also a story about the times in which these killings occurred, depicting a strange and unfamiliar environment, a setting in which these horrific and random acts were somehow predictable even if not logically understandable. To make her story work and to enable the reader to better understand the tabloid-like and horrific murders committed by the Manson cult gang, Didion must evoke, if not re-create, this unstable and dangerous world and draw the reader into it. Didion must make the familiar strange, bringing the physical environment or setting to life to embody qualities that somehow almost invite the characters' horrific actions. That is, the setting calls forth the plot.

The paragraph excerpted above is written in a highly subjective first-person voice that may, initially, seem far removed from the style of the legal story-tellers, but there are many lessons that legal storytellers might learn from it. In the paragraph, Didion begins to construct the cultural environment in which the Manson murders take place. The initial sentences select details to convey the crucial sense of time and place. These are not visual details or a composition built on a meticulous and complete description; rather they are a quick composition of sensate fragments lyrically or poetically presented: sounds, tastes, and smells. In contrast to the eye (a more critical and judgmental faculty), hearing and smell are less critical and more associative functions.

The specific references are to popular music of the day; this music is crucial to the theme of the story. The Manson story is about a multiple murder based upon Manson's delusional misinterpretation of prophecy contained in the lyrics of the Beatles' song "Helter Skelter" on *The White Album*.[2] Didion selects her representative musical selections carefully; Bob Dylan's "Lay Lady Lay"[3] and Leonard Cohen's "Suzanne"[4] are disconcerting because they are romantic and intimate songs, distinct from the horrific nature of the multiple cold-blooded murders at the heart of the story. Likewise, Didion identifies the "smell of jasmine" that enters through "all the open doors and windows," conveying a mixture of sensuality and openness.

Didion locates herself as a character who imagines that her own life is both "simple and sweet." The counterpoint to this simplicity is an interior setting of psychic dislocation and disjunctions. There are "rumors" and "stories." And there is a "mystical flirtation with the idea of 'sin'—this sense that it was possible to go 'too far,' and that many people were doing it." The personal tone manifests aspects of a darker collective psyche: "A demented and seductive vortical dimension was building in the community. The jitters were setting in." The interior observations color the exterior landscape as if in anticipation of what is coming: "The dogs barked every night and the moon was always full."

Here, midparagraph, Didion shifts from describing the surfaces to intimations of dark future events that will occur; these are echoes or reverberations from events that have already taken place elsewhere in the city. These events bounce off of, or resonate from, the settings depicted earlier in the paragraph, setting up the story that will follow. First, Didion watches herself sitting passively, vulnerable, "in the shallow end of my sister-in-law's swimming pool in Beverly Hills" when the phone call comes in "about the murders at Sharon Tate Polanski's house on Cielo Drive." More dark fragments surface in the descriptions and leak out into the world. One caller says, "hoods," the next "chains." One says, "twenty dead, no, twelve, ten, eighteen." There are speculations on motives: "[b]lack masses were imagined, and bad trips blamed." There is, however, one psychological constant about the violent events that have taken place on this strangely configured and unfamiliar landscape—"that no one was surprised."

What is it that lawyers may learn from reading a description or depiction of setting so personal and idiosyncratic as Didion's? Didion's poetic techniques seem far removed from the functional descriptions of settings that lawyers tend to employ. That is, rather than building up the world "slowly and completely," Didion "lights up" the scene "by lightning flashes."[5] Didion depicts her narrative landscape or environment through a composite of sometimes abrupt and unexpected sensate fragments from her personal recollections. This technique draws her reader onto a shared stage, an internal landscape or setting where the reader can more fully experience, rather than comprehend intellectually, the events taking place. This isn't a strategy that is typically attempted by lawyers in legal storytelling. Or is it?

Let's contrast Didion's first-person composite of sensate fragments evoking a dangerous landscape with the depiction of dangerous settings in legal storytelling practice. The judicial opinions excerpted in the casebook in my criminal law course provide a laboratory filled with these places, though these settings and environments are seldom intentionally foregrounded or depicted with Didion's artistic flare.

In *Rusk v. State*,[6] defendant Edward Salvatore Rusk successfully appealed from his trial court conviction for rape to the Maryland Court of Special Appeals. The court determined that there was insufficient evidence in the trial record to uphold Rusk's conviction for rape. The majority opinion turns on the legal issue of whether Rusk's "words or actions created in the mind of the victim a reasonable fear that if she resisted, he would have harmed her, or that faced with such resistance, he would have used force to overcome it."[7] The majority's version of the story emphasizes ambiguous evidence about whether Rusk used force or threat of force sufficient to compel the victim to have sex with him. [8]

The dissenting opinion critiques the majority's story and presents a retelling of its own, reframing events against a different background. In this second telling, a sequence of dangerous places directly influences the plot's unfolding. Here is an excerpt from the dissenting opinion:

Upon this basis, the evidence against appellant must be considered. Judge Thompson recounts most, but not quite all, of the victim's story. The victim I'll call her Pat attended a high school reunion. She had arranged to meet her girlfriend Terry there. The reunion was over at 9:00, and Terry asked Pat to accompany her to Fell's Point. Pat had gone to Fell's Point with Terry on a few prior occasions, explaining in court: "I've never met anybody (there) I've gone out with. I met people in general, talking in conversation, most of the time people that Terry knew, not that I have gone down there, and met people as dates." She agreed to go, but first called her mother, who was babysitting with Pat's two-year old son, to tell her that she was going with Terry to Fell's Point, and that she would not be home late. It was just after 9:00 when Pat and Terry, in their separate cars, left for Fell's Point, alone.

They went to a place called Helen's and had one drink. They stayed an hour or so and then walked down to another place (where they had another drink), stayed about a half hour there, and went to a third place. Up to this point, Pat conversed only with Terry, and did not strike up any other acquaintanceships. Pat and Terry were standing against a wall when appellant came over and said hello to Terry, who was conversing with someone else at the time. Appellant then began to talk with Pat. They were both separated, they both had young children; and they spoke about those things. Pat said that she had been ready to leave when appellant came on the scene, and that she only talked with him for five or ten minutes. It was then about midnight. Pat had to get up with her baby in the morning and did not want to stay out late.

Terry wasn't ready to leave. As Pat was preparing to go, appellant asked if she would drop him off on her way home. She agreed because she thought he was a friend of Terry's. She told him, however, as they walked to her car, "I'm just giving a ride home, you know, as a friend, not anything to be, you know, thought of other than a ride." He agreed to that condition.

Pat was completely unfamiliar with appellant's neighborhood. She had no idea where she was. When she pulled up to where appellant said he lived, she put the car in park, but left the engine running. She said to appellant, "Well, here, you know, you are home." Appellant then asked Pat to come up with him and she refused. He persisted in his request, as did she in her refusal. She told him that even if she wanted to come up, she dared not do so. She was separated and it might cause marital problems for her. Finally, he reached over, turned off the ignition, took her keys, got out of the car, came around to her side, opened the door, and said to her, "Now, will you come up?"

It was at this point that Pat followed appellant to his apartment, and it is at this point that the majority of this Court begins to substitute its judgment for that of the trial court and jury. We know nothing about Pat and appellant. We don't know how big they are, what they look like, what their life experiences have been. We don't know if appellant is larger or smaller than she, stronger or weaker. We don't know what the inflection was in his voice as he dangled her car keys in front of her. We can't tell whether this was in a jocular vein or a truly threatening one. We have no idea what his mannerisms were. The trial judge and the jury could discern some of these things, of course, because they could observe the two people in court and could listen to what they said and how they said it. But all we know is that, between midnight and 1:00 a. m., in a neighborhood that was strange to Pat, appellant took her car keys, demanded that she accompany him, and most assuredly implied that unless she did so, at the very least, she might be stranded.

Now, let us interrupt the tale for a minute and consider the situation. Pat did not honk the horn; she did not scream; she did not try to run away. Why, she was asked. "I was scared. I didn't think at the time what to do." Later, on cross-examination:

At that point, because I was scared, because he had my car keys. I didn't know what to do. I was someplace I didn't even know where I was. It was in the city. I didn't know whether to run. I really didn't think, at that point, what to do. Now, I know that I should have blown the horn. I should have run. There were a million things I could have done. I was scared, at that point, and I didn't do any of them.

What, counsel asked, was she afraid of? "Him," she replied. What was she scared that he was going to do? "Rape me, but I didn't say that. It was the way he looked at me, and said, 'Come on up, come on up;'

and when he took the keys, I knew that was wrong. I just didn't say, are you going to rape me."

So Pat accompanied appellant to his apartment. As Judge Thompson points out, appellant left her in his apartment for a few minutes. Although there was evidence of a telephone in the room, Pat said that, at the time, she didn't notice one. When appellant returned, he turned off the light and sat on the bed. Pat was in a chair. She testified: "I asked him if I could leave, that I wanted to go home, and I didn't want to come up. I said, 'Now, I came up. Can I go?'" Appellant, who, of course, still had her keys, said that he wanted her to stay. He told her to get on the bed with him, and, in fact, took her arms and pulled her on to the bed. He then started to undress her; he removed her blouse and bra and unzipped her pants. At his direction, she removed his clothes. She then said:

> I was still begging him to please let, you know, let me leave. I said, "you can get a lot of other girls down there, for what you want," and he just kept saying, "no;" and then I was really scared, because I can't describe, you know, what was said. It was more the look in his eyes; and I said, at that point I didn't know what to say; and I said, "If I do what you want, will you let me go without killing me?" Because I didn't know, at that point, what he was going to do; and I started to cry; and when I did, he put his hands on my throat, and started lightly to choke me; and I said, "If I do what you want, will you let me go?" And he said, yes, and at that time, I proceeded to do what he wanted me to.

He "made me perform oral sex, and then sexual intercourse." Following that:

> I asked him if I could leave now, and he said, "Yes;" and I got up and got dressed; and he got up and got dressed; and he walked me to my car, and asked if he could see me again; and I said, "Yes;" and he asked me for my telephone number; and I said, "No, I'll see you down Fell's Point sometime," just so I could leave.[9]

If the settings and the environment are so important in this sequence of scenes (first, at the bar; second, in the parked car outside Rusk's apartment; third, inside the apartment), why doesn't the dissent further emphasize the victim's vulnerability and fear by foregrounding the scene with vivid, descriptive details, akin to Didion's narrative strategy? These details are available in the trial record of the victim's testimony and, indeed, this testimony is cited in footnotes annotating the story. There are reasons for the selective use and frequent underinclusion of descriptive detail in depicting settings and environments in many legal stories, especially the stories told by appellate judges.

First, the conventions of judicial storytelling practice impose constraints on how appellate judges tell stories: judges seldom employ language (akin to Didion's) that intentionally directs the reader's attention to the artistic and narrative dimensions of their craft. Appellate judges typically profess that their decisions are limited to review of the legal—not factual—claims.

Second, legal decision making assigns causal significance and responsibility to the free will of individual actors; characters shape events into plots. Many law stories discount the significance of settings and environments external to the various actors, especially judicial stories about the guilt or innocence of actors and the punishments visited upon them.

Nevertheless, in a nicely understated way, the dissent's critique of the majority's story suggests how the victim, "Pat," was affected by her surroundings (the setting or environment) and how defendant Rusk took advantage of these circumstances to compel Pat's submission. In the selection and ordering of scenes, the dissent conveys a shadowy environment. It begins in the appropriately named Fell's Point, a falling-off point where Pat meets Rusk in the bar. The dissent's narrative then cuts to the dark and unfamiliar neighborhood where Rusk pulls the keys from the ignition of Pat's car. Finally, the narrative turns to the bedroom of Rusk's apartment. The bare-bones setting matches the intentional gaps in the physical and psychological depictions of Rusk and Pat. The powerful rhetorical message of the dissent's narrative is centered not on what the majority opinion said but rather what it *omitted* from its retelling of events; these gaps in the narrative cannot be filled in accurately from the cold record of the trial—only the jury, who evaluated the credibility of the witnesses, weighed the evidence, and pieced together the fragments of the narrative, could begin to find and put into place the missing elements of the story.

III. More Dangerous Places Where Bad Things Happen: Use of Physical Descriptions and Factual Details to Create Complex Environments in W. G. Sebald's The Emigrants and the Petitioners' Briefs in Two Coerced Confession Cases

W. G. Sebald writes stories grounded in places and settings; his environments predominate and shape events, narrative outcomes, and the fates of characters within. Sebald travels in his books, vividly evoking places and settings. He supplements his descriptions with visual evidence, including photographs and sketches, pictures of family and relevant historical figures, and depictions of artifacts that document the authenticity and legitimacy of his observations and of his stories. He makes the images, settings, and the characters who inhabit these places come vividly alive in the mind of the reader. The foregrounding of setting and place invites digressions into personal memory and collective history. Setting is always the starting point and ending place for the story; Sebald's art is a meditation on place.

In *The Emigrants*, for example, Sebald retraces the paths of four emigrants, whose stories are embedded in the landscapes or settings mapped by their journeys. Sebald reconstructs these characters' stories through presentation of place; these environments are as alive as the characters who inhabit them.

For example, in one of the four narratives, Sebald retraces the picaresque journey of Sebald's great-uncle Ambrose, a manservant, whose emigrant journey terminates in a sanatorium in upstate New York where Ambrose is treated for depression with a regimen of electroshock therapy.

Initially, this setting is depicted through the perceptions of a character named Dr. Abramsky, now retired. Many years earlier, Abramsky treated Uncle Ambrose as an assistant to a "Dr. Fahnstock," who was the previous director of the sanatorium. Fahnstock, like Uncle Ambrose, is now long dead and the sanatorium is no longer operating. Ambrose had entered the sanatorium voluntarily and submitted to electroshock therapy to treat his depression. There are two interlocking descriptions of this setting and the practices of electroshock therapy within this institution. In the first, the practices at the sanatorium are described somewhat abstractly by the old doctor, Abramsky.

> It was also remarkable how readily Ambrose submitted to shock treatment which, in the early Fifties, as I understood only later, really came close to torture and martyrdom. Other patients often had to be frogmarched to the treatment room, said Dr. Abramsky, but Ambrose would always be sitting on the stool outside the door at the appointed hour, leaning his head against the wall, eyes closed, waiting for what was in store for him.
>
> In response to my request, Dr. Abramsky described shock treatment in greater detail. At the start of my career in psychiatry, he said, I was of the opinion that electrotherapy was a humane and effective form of treatment. As students we had been taught—and Fahnstock, in his stories about clinical practice, had repeatedly described in graphic terms—how in the old days, when pseudo-epileptic fits were induced

by insulin, patients would be convulsed for minutes, seemingly on the point of death, their faces contorted and blue. Compared with this approach, the introduction of electro-shock treatment, which could be dispensed with greater precision and stopped immediately if the patient's reaction was extreme, constituted a considerable step forward. In our view it seemed completely legitimate once sedatives and muscle relaxants began to be used in the early Fifties, to avoid the worst of the incidental injuries, such as dislocated shoulders or jaws, broken teeth, or other fractures. Given these broad improvements in shock therapy, Fahnstock, dismissing my (alas) none too forceful objections with his characteristic lordliness, adopted what was known as the block method, a course of treatment advocated by the German psychiatrist Braunmühl, which not infrequently involved more than a hundred electric shocks at intervals of only a very few days. This would have been about six months before Ambrose joined us. Needless to say, when treatment was so frequent, there could be no question of proper documentation or assessment of the therapy; and that was what happened with your great-uncle too. Besides, said Dr. Abramsky, all of the material on file—the case histories and the medical records Dr. Fahnstock kept on a regular basis, albeit in a distinctly cursory fashion—have probably long since been eaten by the mice. They took over the madhouse when it was closed and have been multiplying without cease ever since; at all events, on nights when there is no wind blowing I can hear a constant scurrying and rustling in the dried-out shell of the building, and at times, when a full moon rises beyond the trees, I imagine I can hear the pathetic song of a thousand tiny upraised throats. Nowadays I place all my hope in the mice, and in the woodworm and deathwatch beetles. The sanatorium is creaking, and in places already caving in, and sooner or later they will bring about its collapse.[10]

What is there for the legal storyteller to see in Sebald's initial description of shock treatments and depiction of the setting of the sanatorium in upstate New York? These two paragraphs introduce the reader to the use of electroshock at the sanatorium. Abramsky's description is presented as a clinical abstraction. There is little physical detail in the initial description of the room, the practice itself, or the machinery employed in electroshock therapy.

Sebald uses the description as a set piece; it is not a complete scene or sequence of scenes in which the characters are actors in control of the actions on a stage. For example, there is only a single sentence about an individual character or identified actor: Abramsky recalls Uncle Ambrose as distinct from the other patients who had to be frogmarched into the room. Unlike other patients, Uncle Ambrose "would always be sitting on the stool outside the door at the appointed hour, leaning his head against the wall, eyes closed, waiting for what was in store for him." After this vivid evocation of Ambrose, Sebald, through Abramsky's point of view, describes the practice itself.

Despite the level of generality, the description is very powerful because of the selection and arrangement of a few observational details. Sebald, through Abramsky, contrasts what he then considered the "humane" practice of electroshock with still more primitive practices. In the various off-hand observations by Abramsky the reader understands that the practice that Uncle Ambrose was subjected to was anything but humane. Abramsky further observes that, especially where the shock treatments were so frequent, there was the necessity of proper documentation and assessment. He reconnects the observations about past practices to the disrepair of the building and its current occupants: the case histories and medical records have probably "long since been eaten by the mice." Finally, there is a powerful evocation of the "dried-out shell of the building" that is "creaking, and in places already caving in," overrun by the scurrying mice that will eventually "bring about its collapse." And on nights "when a full moon rises beyond the trees," Abramsky imagines hearing the "pathetic song of a thousand tiny upraised throats." These voices may belong to the mice who have overrun the building or are, perhaps, echoes of the desperate cries from the throats of the long-ago patients, including Uncle Ambrose.

Sebald's initial description of the setting and environment is compelling in part because of the details *omitted*. What is left out—and therefore left to the imagination of the reader—is more important than what is put in. This is not simply a parade of horribles. There is purposeful yet subtle use of indirection and ambiguity in the description.

Two pages later, Sebald revisits the same place with Abramsky. This time Abramsky describes Uncle Ambrose as a more fully developed character in the scene. Abramsky recalls Uncle Ambrose receiving shock treatment from the villainous Fahnstock on the day that Uncle Ambrose died:

> It was almost evening. Dr. Abramsky led me back through the arboretum to the drive. He was holding the white goose wing, and from time to time pointed the way ahead with it. Towards the end, he said as we walked, your great-uncle suffered progressive paralysis of the joints and limbs, probably caused by the shock therapy. After a while

he had the greatest difficulty with everyday tasks. He took almost the whole day to get dressed. Simply to fasten his cufflinks and his bow tie took him hours. And he was hardly finished dressing but it was time to undress again. What was more, he was having constant trouble with his eyesight, and suffered from bad headaches, and so he often wore a green eyeshade—like someone who works in a gambling saloon. When I went to see him in his room on the last day of his life, because he had failed to appear for treatment for the first time, he was standing at the window, wearing the eyeshade, gazing out at the marshlands beyond the park. Oddly, he had put on armlets made of some satin-like material, such as he might have worn when he used to polish the silver. When I asked why he had not appeared at the appointed time, he replied (I remember his words exactly): It must have slipped my mind whilst I was waiting for the butterfly man. After he had made this enigmatic remark, Ambrose accompanied me without delay, down to the treatment room where Fahnstock was waiting, and submitted to all the preparations without the least resistance, as he always did. I see him lying before me, said Dr. Abramsky, the electrodes on his temples, the rubber bit between his teeth, buckled into the canvas wraps that were riveted to the treatment table like a man shrouded for burial at sea. The session proceeded without incident. Fahnstock's prognosis was distinctly optimistic. But I could see from Ambrose's face that he was now destroyed, all but a vestige of him. When he came round from the anesthetic, his eyes, which were now strangely glassy and fixed, clouded over, and a sigh that I can hear to this day rose from his breast. An orderly took him back to his room, and when I went there early the following morning, troubled by my conscience, I found him lying on his bed, in patent-leather boots, wearing full uniform, so to speak. Dr. Abramsky walked the rest of the way beside me in silence. Nor did he say a word in farewell, but described a gentle arc with the goose wing in the darkening air.[11]

What might the legal storyteller make of this paragraph? Let us walk through the paragraph, focus on the settings and descriptions in this scene, and observe how this paragraph fits with the previous excerpt depicting this place. First, observe that Abramsky is holding a white goose wing: a prop that Sebald employs to signal to the reader the beginning and ending of the brief scene, and to direct the reader's attention. Next, as Abramsky recalls the shock treatment practices at the sanatorium, he revives Uncle Ambrose vividly with description and brings him onstage. Again, the scene does not focus on describing the practice of electroshock therapy directly; instead, the reader, from Abramsky's perspective, watches the sympathetic and dignified Ambrose dressing *after* receiving shock therapy. The description becomes visually specific here, as if a cinematic camera lens stops to focus in a close-up on a description of Ambrose: "He took almost the whole day to get dressed. Simply to fasten his cufflinks and his bow tie took him hours." Observations about Ambrose's physical symptoms from the shock therapy, including bad headaches and deteriorating eyesight, are translated from abstractions into vivid visual images that interact with Ambrose's old world meticulous nature. The reader witnesses Uncle Ambrose, the displaced emigrant, a former man-servant to European royalty, standing at the window, wearing a green eye-shade, gazing out across the marshland. It is difficult for the reader not to empathize with the character displaced in this setting and grasp his longing, his nostalgia for an eternal return; the setting matches the theme of the book itself—the emigrant severed from his past and adrift in a new world.

Ambrose then makes his "enigmatic remark" about "waiting for the butterfly man" and the scene shifts as Ambrose accompanies Abramsky to the treatment room. Fanhnstock, who is not described, but presented merely as a name, awaits Ambrose's arrival. The preparations for the electroshock are then described in clinical terms but also with a poetical description at the end of the sentence, from Abramsky's perspective or point of view: "the electrodes on his temples, the rubber bit between his teeth, buckled into the canvas wraps that were riveted to the treatment table like a man shrouded for burial at sea."

The procedure itself is not described. Here too, the emotional power of the scene, and the reader's response to the brutality of the regimen of electroshock therapy, are captured by the description of Ambrose after the events are over. What is left out of the description is as important as what is put in it. And then the scene cuts to the next day, when Abramsky goes to the room and describes Ambrose. The aftereffects of the electroshock practice, its reverberations, are captured in the way Abramsky is affected by having to recall and describe Ambrose's last days, even so many years later. Sebald closes off the scene employing the prop introduced at its start, describing Abramsky defining "a gentle arc with the goose wing in the darkening air."

Akin to Sebald's depiction of place and the practice of elctroshock therapy at a sanitarium in upstate New York, petitioners' briefs in coerced confession cases often focus on the places where bad things happen and the practices that occur within them. Like the story about Uncle Ambrose, these cases are generally set in dark environments where nefarious practices occurred long ago, often followed by complex official cover stories. It is up to the legal story-teller to piece together what actually occurred or, in some cases, to determine that what happened can never be known.

In some briefs, the environment is reconstructed through the accretion of descriptive detail. For example, in the petitioner's brief in *Reck v. Ragen*,[12] the depiction of the circumstances of the petitioner's forced confession in the "Statement of Facts" stretches over thirty pages, and the time frame extends long before and after the actual custodial interrogation. Here are several pages from this not atypical coerced confession story:

> By Friday evening, the four boys had become the focus of a major police effort. A "big show-up" was underway. A "big crowd" of people ("a hundred or more") congregated in the [North Avenue Police] Station. Reck [the defendant] was being exhibited on the second floor. Shortly after 7:00 P. M. Reck fainted.
>
> Unidentified persons assisted Reck to a bench. Reck "was placed on a stretcher on the second floor and carried downstairs." By 7:20 P. M. Reck was on his way to the Cook County Hospital "in the customary district patrol wagon."
>
> At 7:45 P. M. Reck was brought into the receiving room of County Hospital in a wheel chair. The police officers who delivered Reck told the interne on duty that Reck had experienced an "attack and felt kind of dizzy" and had suffered "one or two fainting spells." The interne examined Reck and found no marks or bruises on his body. He then concluded that Reck "was not fit for the hospital" and "rejected" him.
>
> Reck was taken directly back to the North Avenue Police Station arriving there at 8:15 P. M. He was placed on exhibition in a show-up. Quite a number of police officers were in the room, together with the latest batch of civilian viewers.
>
> After a short period, Reck became sick and Officer Reilly took him out of the show-up room and into an unfurnished handball court in the rear of the Station's second floor.
>
> Reilly said that he "did not want to have [Reck] annoyed" and thus Reilly "did not care to show him up to…anybody" because he was "…feeling careful of [Reck's] feelings.…" Therefore, Reilly saw to it that the civilians were kept out of the room. Reilly said he wanted Reck to rest.

But Emil Reck got no rest. Almost immediately, Sergeant Andrew Aitken, assigned to the Peacock murder investigation, entered the handball court. With him were Sergeant Patrick McShane and Patrolman Timothy Donovan. Besides Reck and the three police officers, no one else was in the room, nor did anyone else enter for some minutes.

Aitken and the other officers stayed with Reck "rather uninterruptedly, almost constantly" for the next half-hour. After 15 minutes, Reck was standing near a bench which had been placed in an otherwise bare handball court for the purpose of letting Reck "rest" on it. According to Sergeant Aitken, he then asked Reck the following question: "Emil, have you seen any motion pictures or read any magazines relative to ballistics? That is the reason why you disposed of your revolver for fear it may be traced back to the Doctor Peacock murder?" Aitken's version of what happened then is as follows:

"With that he sat down and slumped on the bench and became very pale. And I said, 'Are you sick?' A few moments later he answered, 'I am sick.' I says, 'What is wrong?' He says, 'I got some blood sickness while in the C. C. Camp.'"

When Reck "slumped" to the bench, he doubled up forward from the waist.

A Dr. Abraham was called into the handball court. When Dr. Abraham entered the handball court, Reck was "extremely nervous." Reck was also "exposed." His pants were undone. His shirt was unbuttoned and hanging outside of his pants. He was rubbing his abdomen. Dr. Abraham didn't know why Reck was "exposed," and no one told him. Reck told the doctor that he had a pain, pointing to his abdomen. Dr. Abraham "examined" Reck for 30 to 60 seconds.

After Dr. Abraham's 60-second check-up, Reck lay down on the bench. But the police who were present throughout did not allow Reck to rest. When still more people entered the room to question Reck, he was told to get on his feet, and "the color went away from him again." After a while, civilians were brought into the handball court to identify Reck. He was told to get up from the bench when anyone walked in.

By 9:15 P. M. civilians were again being excluded from the handball court. Although there were about fifty other people who were "anxious" to see Reck at this time, Reilly was keeping all of them out of the room. One such person got the impression that he was being given "a run around" when, after he "pushed through the crowd," the police told him that Reck "was injured." "They told me he was hurt."

Between 9:30 and 9:45 P. M. Reck became ill for the fourth time in three hours. He "bent over and said he felt sick to his stomach" and vomited on the floor. "He was bleeding from the mouth, in short gushes of blood...." "The blood seemed to come out of the corner of his mouth...." He bled for "two or three minutes." Officer Youhn was present. Officer Larke was also present but was never called to testify despite Reck's testimony of being beaten at this time. Aitken was or was not present, depending upon whether one believes his testimony at the trial or his testimony at the post-conviction hearing.

Dr. Abraham was called to examine Reck again. When Dr. Abraham entered the handball court, he saw Reck lying on a stretcher. Nearby was a pool of Reck's blood on the floor. The blood was "a bright red." It covered an area a "foot square." But Dr. Abraham did not even give Reck a 60-second examination this time.

Minutes later, at about 9:45 P. M., Reck was carried on a stretcher from the handball court to a waiting patrol wagon. Captain O'Connell gave orders to return Reck to the hospital as fast as possible. At this time, according to the official Police Department "History of Sick or Injured Person," Emil Reck had been sick for three hours and was unable to walk without aid. He had been in police custody for 59 hours.[13]

The petitioner's brief in *Reck* tells a story that can only occur in a particular type of world. Like Sebald, the petitioner merely purports to describe, depicting an environment fitting the actions taking place within it and the characters inhabiting it. Unlike Sebald, and perhaps more akin to the dissenting judge in *Rusk*, the petitioner depicts a flat and bare world. In accord with the conventions of legal storytelling, the settings are not fully developed, implicitly discounting the importance of environmental factors in determining outcomes. Furthermore, the story of Reck's journey is not freestanding; it serves as a complement to the legal argument. Nevertheless, the petitioner's functional and not atypical brief reflects compositional choices about constructing his environment in re-creating his dark journey (based on the record). Let's briefly revisit some of these choices:

1. *Sentences and Settings.* Reck's story turns on the narrative inevitability of his confession. Consequently, there is logic and linearity in Reck's world.

Reck is transported down an approximately thirty-page conveyor belt; it is an exhausting journey for Reck and, perhaps, for the reader as well. Unlike Sebald, who revisits Ambrose's treatments in a sequence of interlocking descriptive pieces, the petitioner provides a single elongated and chronological re-creation of his journey.

Reck's story is told in short sentences, mostly employing simple subject-verb-object structure, avoiding complex subordinate clauses. Reck is a passive character—an automaton or object without a clear physical description. Whenever Reck is acted upon, passive words are used. (For example: "Reck was being exhibited," "Reck was placed on a stretcher," "[Reck] was placed on exhibition in a show-up"). Whenever possible, sentences knit together direct quotations from the trial record. The paragraphs are equally short and compressed. The sentences and paragraphs are stacked neatly, one atop the next, depicting a linear and strictly chronological sequence of events. The structure and sequence of language match the setting; they are rigid and confining.

2. *Description and Detailing*. Like Sebald, the petitioner captures the reader's attention and establishes Reck's world with carefully chosen descriptive details. These details are arranged to emphasize Reck's dislocation, passivity, and deteriorating physical condition. Unlike Sebald's description, the adjectives and adverbs convey exclusively visual impressions, rather than other sensory impressions (smell, taste, or sounds). And there is the intentional selection of particularly disconcerting and tough-sounding words that further distance the reader from Reck's travails.

For example, the excerpt begins with the "big show-up" under way and a "big crowd" at the police station where Reck is "being exhibited" like an animal at the circus. Reck is in constant motion, transported from place to place; at the center of the excerpt is the recurring image of the bare bench that offers Reck the possibility of rest. There are the vivid images of Reck's deteriorating physical condition (e.g., "bleeding from the mouth, in short gushes of blood"; the blood was "a bright red" and covering "an area a 'foot square'"). These descriptive images stand out against the bleak and surreal setting.

3. *Perspective*. Sebald subtly shifts the perspective in shaping Uncle Ambrose's environment: he shifts from the perspective of the narrator to that of Dr. Abramsky to a vantage point embracing the perspective of Uncle Ambrose himself; he then backs away. The perspective in the petitioner's brief in *Reck*, however, is fixed; it is a "close" or limited third-person perspective that tracks Reck's journey.

The environment in Reck's story is well tailored to fit the theme; it is not, primarily, about the brutality of villainous police actors. Instead, it focuses on how "Emil Reck got no rest" on his long journey. The crucial prop in the setting is the bare wooden bench that suggests an invitation or a promise of rest. But despite his progressively deteriorating condition, Reck is not permitted to rest. This not so subtle psychological coercion has as much to do with the narrative outcome as does the implied suspicion of physical abuse by the three police officers on the handball court. When Reck is finally permitted to rest, it is on a stretcher, as he is being rushed from the handball court back to the hospital. At this time, the brief observes, he has been in police custody for fifty-nine hours.

Contrast the thirty-page description of Reck's journey with the brief in another forced confession case, the famous U.S. Supreme Court case *Miranda v. Arizona*.[14] The "Statement of the Case" in petitioner Ernesto Miranda's successful brief initially presents a story that is bland and generic: Miranda, accused of rape and robbery, is taken into custody where he is identified in a lineup. The arresting officers do not inform him that anything he says will be used against him, nor do they tell him of his right to consult an attorney.

Then the brief makes an interesting strategic move; it does not attempt to describe Miranda's environment. The description of what happened to Miranda is omitted altogether. Miranda simply disappears into a place repeatedly referred to in the brief as "Interrogation Room 2." When Miranda emerges, the police have his written confession in hand. The confession is admitted into evidence over Miranda's objection and he is convicted of the charges against him. The gap in the facts—what happens to Miranda when he disappears—becomes the focus of the legal argument that follows.

Here is the opening paragraph of Miranda's argument:

When Miranda walked out of Interrogation Room Number 2 on March 13, 1963, his life for all practical purposes was over. Whatever happened later was inevitable; the die had been cast in that room at the time. There was no duress, no brutality. Yet when Miranda finished his conversation with Officers Cooley and Young, only the ceremonies of the law remained; in any realistic sense, his case was done. We have here the clearest possible example of Justice Douglas' observation, "what takes place in the secret confines of the police station may be more critical than what takes place at the trial."[15]

What is going on here? The brief calls the reader's attention to what is not there rather than what is. Akin, in some ways, to Didion's attempt to suggest an ineffable quality of Los Angeles in the time of Manson, the Miranda brief is equally poetical in its language, inviting the reader to fill in what is left undescribed. The reader is compelled to speculate on what occurred in Interrogation Room 2. The legal argument is not just about precedent and *stare decisis*; it evokes more literary themes. It shows that what goes unseen may have devastating and far-reaching consequences that can never be erased, controlled, altered, or corrected. It is about the power of the forces of fate, chance, and secrecy. In the language of the petitioner's brief, once the "die had been cast," "whatever happened later was inevitable"; when "Miranda walked out of Interrogation Room Number 2...his life for all practical purposes was over."

In both literary and legal storytelling, the setting itself dictates how the audience interprets the story. Whether the place is left shrouded in mystery, as in Miranda's brief, or is developed through the accretion of carefully selected physical details, as in Reck's brief, the strategic choice of place as depicted implicates or determines the outcome of the story.

IV. Settings and Environment as Villains and Villainy in the Mitigation Stories of Kathryn Harrison's While They Slept *and the Petitioner's* Brief in Eddings v. Oklahoma

In some stories, the forces of opposition aligned against the protagonist are part of an environment that shapes the behavior of the characters. The setting matches the story, suggests crucial themes, and develops as the story progresses. For example, in Gerry Spence's *Silkwood* argument the depictions of rural and innocent townspeople and the invading big city corporate outlaws are set on the mythic and bucolic western landscape. There are intimations of plutonium from the Kerr-McGee plant's fuel rods escaping into the environment and poisoning it; the greedy big city interlopers despoil the land and contaminate the rural and innocent young workers with cancer. In Donovan's argument on behalf of Louie Failla there is a different type of environment. Mobsters compete over valuable suburban Connecticut turf in the 1990s, when new laws legalizing gambling made the land invaluable to competing factions of the Patriarca crime family. But what makes the environment of the story immediately recognizable to the jury, and Donovan's narrative persuasive, is not its literal landscape. It is how Donovan locates the telling within the context of popular and familiar mob stories. Some of these are "old school" mob stories about tenderhearted tough guys, about mob dolls and outlaws willing to sacrifice themselves to preserve their families.[16] These environments are wedded to more contemporary narrative environments, filled with double-talking wise guys and popular cultural references of the day that could have been borrowed from David Mamet[17] and Quentin Tarantino.[18]

In some legal stories, the setting or environment also shapes the narrative. In other stories, the setting and environment is itself the force of antagonism or villainy that initiates the plot and ultimately determines the narrative outcome. In postconviction relief practice and death penalty work, we find mitigation stories, where the defendant's claim is based on his childhood environment or some later traumatic events in his life story.

Here are several illustrations of stories told primarily about place; the theme of the story is typically about the power of the environment and how it overwhelms or directs the will of the protagonist. The first is taken from Kathryn Harrison's real-life crime story *While They Slept*.[19] In this story, Billy Frank Gilley murdered his two sleeping parents. When he was surprised by his younger sister, he murdered her too. In the book, Harrison acts as a crime investigator, retelling the mitigation story, focusing on the physical and psychological abuse suffered by Billy and his surviving sister Jody at the hands of their parents. The evil of the environment depicted by Harrison is pervasive, and envelops the young Billy so that seemingly there is no way out for him, other than retreating into fantasy and then striking back at his parents violently. How does Harrison tell this story to evoke sympathy for Billy and transform environment into a villain? She moves from place to place. The first stop on Billy's dark journey is the barn of the house on Ross Lane in Medford, Oregon. In these paragraphs, the violence escalates as Billy is abused physically by his father, Bill, and psychologically by his mother, Linda:

> Whether or not Bill drank surreptitiously in the barn, the structure's relative privacy and its distance from the house made it an ideal place for him to beat his son. The house on Dyer Road [where the family lived previously] was small, sometimes claustrophobic, but on Ross Lane Linda could make her decision that a punishment was required from inside the house while Bill carried it out remotely, allowing Linda to blind herself to the viciousness of what Bill could claim she demanded. This wasn't an original means of enabling cruelty, of course. Few despots bear witness to the tortures by which they maintain

control, and even though what Jody would later call "atrocities" were those of a single troubled family rather than a corrupt social order, it was a college course on literature of the Holocaust that gave Jody the language she needed to speak about what her parents had done to her and her brother, abuse that went beyond corporal punishment and that she believes was meant to break their spirits and cripple them emotionally so that they would never be able to escape.

In contrast to the incidental cuffs and slaps across the face that both Linda and Bill applied reflexively whenever their children talked back or annoyed them in some way, a real whipping was, Jody says, "threatened, then announced, and only after a period of intensifying dread, administered." But first came "hours and hours of lecturing," marathon harangues during which Billy rarely spoke. Only once does Jody remember her brother breaking his silence, by putting his hands over his ears and emitting a long, awful, and unnerving squeal, like a trapped animal that had abruptly arrived at consciousness to find itself facing immediate slaughter, a noise that perhaps surprised Billy as much as it did the rest of the family. As Billy knew, nothing he could say would prevent or lessen what was to come; defending himself might even provoke an extra lick or two. In the barn, whippings evolved from what they had been inside the house—fifteen to thirty lashes with a leather belt on bared skin—to a more formal procedure, for which *flogging* seems the more accurate term.

"My father whipped me at least once a month," Billy says in his affidavit. "I would get a whipping for not cleaning my room, or for doing my chores wrong, or getting in trouble at school, running in the house, or forgetting to feed the chickens. He almost always tied my wrists to a wall pole or a tractor tire to keep me from moving around."

It hadn't taken many beatings for Billy to figure out that a glancing blow did less damage than a direct one. Earlier punishments, back on Dyer Road, had taught him that if he flinched or writhed inadvertently, the belt didn't make solid contact when it hit his moving legs or buttocks and hurt him less. With the benefit of this experience, Billy no longer remained in place, bent over his bed with his pants off. Instead, he tells me, he'd drop to the ground and "roll around the way you're supposed to do if your clothes are on fire." Predictably, this further enraged his father and made him that much more vindictive. When the whippings were removed to the barn, Bill welcomed this new privacy as an opportunity to tie his son, standing, to a stationary object, so that he could be sure his target stayed put.

"How did he do that?" I ask Billy, remembering a conversation with Jody in which she wondered aloud if her brother submitted to their father meekly, if he offered his wrists to be tied. But Billy misconstrues my meaning.

"With a tree line," he says. "You know, the nylon ropes we used for climbing."

"No, I mean, did you..." I leave the question unfinished, feeling that to insist on an answer would be to participate in a past punishment by reawakening the humiliation of it. Besides, if Billy walked out to the barn where his father was waiting for him, why wouldn't he stand still when tied? Jody's question, I decide, isn't literal so much as a mark of her inability to imagine offering her body up for abuse. Her essence remained unbroken and defended, hidden deep within herself, one of the coping mechanisms that would allow her to navigate the night of the murders.[20]

The sense of place Harrison artfully constructs is a place of no escape, just as Reck's handball court is a place of no rest and Miranda's Interrogation Room 2 is a place where the forces of mystery, chance, and fate intersect dangerously.

First, there is an ominous recognition of one specific place and the focus on what occurs there. That is, this set piece does not begin with the practices of the villainous and brutal father but rather focuses on "the barn" in the Gilleys' new house on Ross Lane. The privacy and distance from the house make it "an ideal place for him [Billy's father] to beat his son." There is the meticulous use of selected detail, rather than the layering and accretion of factual physical detail.

The themes in a mitigation story are typically the inevitability of the events, and the progression of terror that unfolds in the dark place depicted in the story. Here, the theme is about constraint on movement and the impossibility of escape (just as we find in the defendants' briefs typically submitted in battered women syndrome, spousal abuse, and self-defense cases). Harrison moves from the events themselves (and the description of the setting) to comment on the events, articulating the theme that undergirds and interconnects the pieces of her story. Just as Miranda uses Justice Douglas's comments to shed light on his predicament, Harrison employs the comments and the perspective of a third person, the surviving sister Jody, to attempt to understand what is happening to her brother.

As in the depiction of Reck's coerced confession or Uncle Ambrose's electroshock treatments, there is a sense of a journey from place to place, rather than merely depictions of a sequence of brutal beatings. The second paragraph begins with description of the "cuffs and slaps across the face" that both Linda and Bill apply "reflexively" whenever their children talk back or annoy them. But this is merely prelude; there is the unfolding terror of "a real whipping" that awaits. Here, narrative movement slows down. First, Jody observes abstractly that, "a real whipping" is "threatened, then announced, and only after a period of intensifying dread, administered." Harrison provides a vivid image, from Jody's testimony, of Billy with his hands over his ears squealing like a trapped animal at what is about to occur. Jody then observes the escalation of the beatings, from fifteen to thirty lashes with a leather belt inside the house to "a more formal procedure, for which *flogging* seems the more accurate term."

And then it is time to move inside the barn and to shift perspectives, from Jody back to Billy, the victim of the beatings. Billy, although less articulate than Jody, describes the beatings and adds details that makes the descriptions vivid and reconnects to the theme of constraint on movement and the impossibility of escape. But it is Harrison who is in control of what happens in this place: she edits the testimony, and shapes the environment to suit her narrative purposes. Compelling details and images come from Billy's own words, but it is Harrison who chooses to include them where they affirm her narrative theme; they are the product of Harrison's editing and aesthetic judgment describing Billy's experiences.

This detailing serves as a segue, several pages later, to a description of violence in another place. The narrative strategy is similar to the previous set piece: this segment is constructed by Harrison with quotes from an affidavit taken by Billy's appellate attorney from a tree surgeon named Henry Linebaugh, who worked with Bill and Billy. The segment is supplemented with Billy's own commentary on Linebaugh's observations:

> The affidavit describes summer days so hot, Linebaugh said, "you couldn't even breathe up on the trees," with Billy left literally out on a limb, without water, for hours. Linebaugh's memory was that he found the teenage Billy alone and injured on a number of occasions, bleeding enough to require bandaging, with no first aid kit on the site, no other worker to administer it.
>
> "If my dad actually saw whatever it was," Billy says when I ask about his getting hurt, "he'd sorta sneer and ask, 'You don't need a

Band-Aid, do you?' in this real sarcastic way." Billy leans forward over the table between us to show me a scar on his wrist. "It's from a chain saw," he explains, and he tells me he got it when working alongside an untrained hire who cut a branch improperly so that it broke and hit the still-running saw, which in turn hit Billy's wrist. "It was bleeding enough to, you know, spurt a little, and the guy, he says I should maybe go to the hospital for stitches, but my dad takes a look, and, you know, it's the same thing, 'You don't *need* to go to the hospital, do you?' So I say no." Billy shrugs. "I took a break, kept the hand up over my head for ten minutes, and tied a rag around my wrist. Then it was back to work."

Hot weather was bad enough; winter posed worse dangers. "A bully," to use Linebaugh's word, Bill forced his son to climb high into the "dense, cold, freezing fog," on limbs that Billy says "were iced over, so I couldn't get even one cleat into it, couldn't get any purchase at all." One very cold day, Linebaugh found Billy stuck "forty feet up in a tree without any protective equipment...not even a hard hat...his rope snagged fifteen feet below him, in what was an egregious violation of OSHA guidelines."...Linebaugh said that the sixteen-year-old Billy "was terrified in the tree with his knees knocking in the freezing fog where his hands were blue." He freed the rope and allowed Billy to descend. The rope was badly worn, "exhibiting signs of being cut by chainsaws."

Linebaugh asked Billy where his father was, but Billy, he said, "was so cold that he couldn't talk because his teeth were chattering so fast." When he warmed up enough to say something, he told Linebaugh his dad had been gone for "two or three hours."

"Where was he?" I ask Billy.

"I dunno. Sometimes he'd of been inside, having a cup of coffee, gabbing with the client. Or if he was hungover he might of been parked somewhere, sleeping in the cab of his truck."

"Bill seemed to resent and despise his son," Linebaugh said. "Bill constantly put down his son as slow-witted and stupid. I remember when Bill would call to Billy and Billy didn't respond [because he hadn't heard his father over the noise of the chipper], Bill would punch his son in the head and yell, 'Hey Stupid!' to get his attention. The force in [*sic*] which Bill hit Billy seemed hard enough to knock him unconscious, but Billy acted like it was just a normal part of his job. It appeared to me that in his father's mind it was.

"I kept expecting to hear one day that Billy got killed while working for his father," Linebaugh concluded his affidavit. "When I heard that Billy had killed his father, it didn't surprise me at all. I remember thinking it was self-defense."[21]

Billy is trapped in another dangerous place. Again, the underlying theme is that Billy cannot escape the cruelty of his environment; the outcome is all but inevitable. The reader understands that in this irrational and terrifying environment, Billy's own violence is a way out. The outcome for Billy if he does not act seems as inevitable as what befalls Uncle Ambrose in *The Emigrants* after therapy or as what happens to Ernesto Miranda after he leaves Interrogation Room 2. Although Bill is clearly a villainous character, this is not a simple melodrama. Billy's enemy is an environment that consumes him, terrorizes him; we understand that he perceives that his only possibility for escape from the terror is parricide.

An environment does not come into existence on its own; it is constructed through a composition of quotations and descriptions of selected details in an overall composition of scenes pointing toward a seemingly inevitable narrative outcome. Here is an excerpt from the petitioner's brief in *Eddings v. Oklahoma*.[22] In many ways this is a legal version of the mitigation story told by Kathryn Harrison about Billy Gilley in *While They Slept*. In *Eddings*, the Oklahoma courts refused to consider Monty Eddings's childhood history in mitigation of his murder sentence for the shooting death of a police officer who had approached the car in which the sixteen-year-old Eddings and his fourteen-year-old sister were running away from home. The narrative strategy in the petitioner's brief is akin to Harrison's; Eddings commits murder while trying to escape from his abusive environment with his sister, whom he is attempting to protect. Further, the murder committed by Eddings is, in part, a product of his dark childhood history that the court has refused to consider: a history that may suggest Eddings's punishment should be mitigated, and he should avoid a death sentence. The excerpt is from the "Statement of the Case" in the petitioner's brief, presenting a portion of Monty Eddings's story about his childhood history that the court has refused to consider at sentencing:

> In mitigation, Eddings produced the testimony of four expert witnesses. Stephen Dorn, petitioner's Missouri probation officer, testified that he had met Monty Eddings when Eddings was fourteen and was referred to the juvenile authorities for four break-ins and for tampering with a motor vehicle. In investigating Eddings' past, Officer Dorn

learned that, when Eddings was five years old, his natural parents were divorced. From the time he was five until he was fourteen, Eddings remained with his mother, Mary Kinney, in Jasper County, Missouri. During this period, Ms. Kinney used alcohol excessively, and, according to Jasper County authorities, may have been involved in prostitution. The report which Probation Officer Dorn "received from the Jasper County Juvenile Court was...that...Monty could pretty much—in their own language—do his own thing. He could come and go when he wanted to...starting at the age of five." Observing that a childhood without rules or discipline often "leads [to] a chaotic adolescence," Officer Dorn testified that when Monty Eddings turned fourteen, Ms. Kinney sent him to his natural father, Ronald Eddings, "because she couldn't control the child."

Ronald Eddings proved a marked contrast to Ms. Kinney in his child-rearing methods. Officer Dorn described him as "quite an authoritarian," noting that "Monty was always fearful of his father, because his father tended to overreact; or rather than discuss things with him, would take it out in more physical means...[b]eatings, slapped, that sort." According to Officer Dorn, Eddings's step mother was unable to "cope with the problems of a fourteen...year old male child with serious emotional behavior"—indeed, her reports to juvenile authorities on Monty Eddings "indicated some sort of schism of thought." In Officer Dorn's view,

> Monty was very scared, I think, of his home situation with his father. He was very hostile. Monty didn't have anyone he could turn to and discuss his problems; and I think Monty was holding a lot of these things within him, and what happened was just a combination of Monty holding everything in and just releasing it all at one time. Towards the end, he became very hostile and bitter.

Officer Dorn summarized that Monty Eddings's actions derived from "a mother who didn't have time for him in Jasper County...a stormy history of divorce; a...step-mother up in Camdenton who he finally goes to live with who has no idea how to raise a child, and who, herself, had problems with children; a father who didn't have time for anything but doing his job." ...

...Eddings's final witness in mitigation was Dr. Anthony C. Gagliano, a licensed psychiatrist in private practice in Tulsa, Oklahoma.

Dr. Gagliano interviewed Eddings in the Sapula County Jail. He indicated that Eddings "was very upset about [his parents'] divorce" when he was five, "[a]nd he had always maintained the fantasy that they would remarry." His natural mother instead remarried a policeman from Joplin, Missouri, when Eddings was seven, and Eddings responded with "anger, hatred, rebellion, rejection, loss." Dr. Gagliano told of one incident when Eddings

> …wanted to impress his mother or father. I don't know why he did it, but he washed down the walls, and he thought it would be nice if the walls were clean. And his [step-]father walked in, and I think removed his shoe and hit him quite severely with his shoe for dirtying the walls.

Dr. Gagliano stated that the incident engendered "Anger. Hatred."

Dr. Gagliano diagnosed Eddings as suffering from "an antisocial or a dissocial disorder," characterized by an "arrested emotional development at age seven" and an inability to display his emotions. He stated that at the time Officer Crabtree was shot, Eddings "acted as a seven year old seeking revenge…[against] the original cause of his anger…the Policeman who married his mother, and who stole his mother away." Eddings' disorder could be treated, Dr. Gagliano thought, though the treatment might take "many years—fifteen or twenty years of real intensive therapy." [23]

When we compare this mitigation story and the environments depicted within it with the two excerpts from *While They Slept* we find they both employ quotations, witness testimony, and affidavits. Both provide generalizations about the impact of the environment on the defendant to crystallize these abstractions. Both shift perspectives strategically, enabling the reader to understand various aspects of the story.

In Eddings's brief, however, the detailing is not nearly as vivid and there is none of the movement characteristic of Billy Gilley's dark journey. Stylistically, the simple declarative sentences depict slices from Monty Eddings's past spliced together with the testimony of various expert witnesses. There are some assertions about how Eddings's childhood history affects his conduct, but the incidents supporting these assertions (whether the precise circumstances of Monty Eddings's childhood or incidents such as when the stepfather hits Eddings with his shoe) are not as compelling or as dramatic as the accounts of abuse in Harrison's storytelling.

The differences in Eddings's brief and Harrison's Billy Gilley story can be accounted for in various ways: they may arise from the material available in the record, the abilities of the storyteller, different aesthetic conventions of drafting a "Statement of the Case" in a brief to the U. S. Supreme Court, or the creation of an environment that is appropriate to the purposes of the argument, rather than constructing the most powerful and compelling mitigation story possible.

In *Eddings*, the narrative is left undercooked or undeveloped. The particular quality of the environment depicted in *Eddings* is both intentional and purposeful. The straightforward presentational style of Eddings's brief, likewise, chooses not to overdramatize the facts. Eddings's environment is appropriate to this brief and fits the legal purposes of the argument. Unlike Harrison's narrative, the story is not designed to depict evil or terror. Instead, it takes slices of Eddings's past from the perspective of two of these witnesses (a policeman and a psychiatrist). The story is simply designed to meet a lower threshold and to demonstrate that the evidence of Eddings's past and social history were legitimate mitigating factors that should have been taken into account in determining Eddings's punishment. The legal argument in this brief is left to do the heavy lifting and the narrative is made subservient to it, whereas Harrison's depiction of Billy Gilley's past was designed to persuade the reader that parricide was all but inevitable and that Billy Gilley took the only possible escape route that he believed was available to him.

V. Concluding Observations

All stories require a place for the events of the story to unfold. The skillful writer can determine the way in which the reader or listener interprets and understands the events of the story through strategic choices about how the setting is developed and described. Some stories will require the setting to be described in poetically presented sensate fragments, pulling the reader into the setting. Others will require that the place be only minimally described or not described at all, purposefully requiring the reader to supplement the setting with his own imagination or leaving the place a mystery. As we have seen from the legal and nonlegal examples, setting, place, detail, and environment can be implemented in countless ways. What is clear is that the legal writer who thinks strategically about how to describe the setting, how to set the stage, can evoke the power of environments to strongly affect the reader and possibly determine the story's ending.

8

Narrative Time

A BRIEF EXPLORATION

Listen:
Billy Pilgrim has come unstuck in time.
*Billy has gone to sleep a senile widower and awakened
on his wedding day. He has walked through that door in
1955 and come out another one in 1941. He has gone back
through that door to find himself in 1963. He has seen his
birth and death many times, he says, and pays random visits to all the events in between.*
He says.
*Billy is spastic in time, he has no control over where he is
going next, and the trips aren't necessarily fun. He is in
a constant state of stage fright, he says, because he never
knows what part of his life he is going to have to act next.*

—KURT VONNEGUT JR., SLAUGHTERHOUSE FIVE
OR THE CHILDREN'S CRUSADE: A DUTY-DANCE
WITH DEATH

I. Introduction

In legal writing and clinical skills courses, young lawyers and law students are
typically instructed to organize their presentation of facts simply and "chron-
ologically." They are told to keep the presentation straightforward and candid,
and to be wary of overly shaping the facts of the story. But this instruction is,
at best, naïve, and, more accurately, deceptive and self-deluding. First, chronology is not an all-encompassing or a preferential strategy for organizing

events in narrative time but merely one modality (perhaps the default mode) for ordering events into story. In chronology, story time appears to mimic how time unfolds in "real life" and seems to order events onto a shared "one-size-fits-all" narrative spine. Many stories are unlike the events that occur in our daily lives, which are measured against the clock. In complex stories there is seldom a strict or pure linear chronology available. Language, almost by its nature, does not allow it; we seemingly move back and forth effortlessly in story time, and do so in extremely subtle and complex ways. Intuitively, we make selective choices from events as we shape them into stories, and we bend malleable story time to fit the demands of narrative. The depiction of time in all but the simplest of stories is, on close inspection, extremely complex, far more complex than a strict and literal chronology contemplates or allows.

Understanding this complexity is at the core of this chapter: it is embodied in the principle that there are at least two sequential progressions of time inherent in the telling of any story. The events depicted in the story follow one another in a temporal sequence, which we can call story time. But there is a second order of narrative time; that is, the recounting itself typically proceeds differently. This second temporal sequence, a separate discourse time, may or may not parallel the first sequence. The two sequences must be purposefully constructed and coordinated.

Fortunately, we are all intuitively gifted and well-practiced storytellers. We have been telling stories all our lives—whether we are aware of our practice or not. Further, it is our professional work as lawyers. Consequently, we are adept at coordinating these components of narrative time; although we seldom separate analytically discrete dimensions of narrative time. Nevertheless, it is extremely helpful for all professional storytellers, including legal storytellers, to develop a conceptual understanding of this important distinction. Although legal storytellers are not narratologists and do not need to have, at their fingertips, the esoteric vocabulary and definitions of aspects of narrative time, it is helpful to move beyond "chronology" and understand the other techniques that enable us to move about in time within a story.

It is also important to explore the malleability of the narrative time frame of any story, including legal stories. All stories are artificially constructed structures set in a narrative time meant to appear to convey "real" time. But there are innumerable possibilities for how to construct the temporal framework of a story. These choices about the time framing are crucial to all that transpires within the plot of the story, and how events unfold within it. That is, the subject of narrative time is not just about ordering events within a story; it is also about the architecture of the story itself. Crucial points in time include when (and where) to begin the story and when (and where) to end it; these choices compel the unfolding of the events of the story itself. Furthermore, legal stories, especially those litigation stories presented by advocates to judges or juries, are typically unfinished stories. Although an implicit "right" ending is proposed or suggested, it is typically left to the decision maker to provide the ending, completing the story and inscribing final meaning on the tale. It is, consequently, especially important for legal storytellers to choose the beginnings of their stories carefully, because that choice implicitly signals the ending of the story.

In this chapter, we look at several features of this complex and compelling subject. In addition to revisiting examples from this book, and providing terminology from narratology, it is helpful to draw further guidance from the masterful novelist and writing teacher Kurt Vonnegut, including paragraphs from Vonnegut's famous time-travel novel *Slaughterhouse Five*. In addition to providing an absorbing and still highly relevant reading experience, Vonnegut's novel is a memorable meditation on the subjects of temporality and narrative time, rich in its comic-yet-profound observations. Perhaps because of his mocking playfulness, Vonnegut's depiction of Billy Pilgrim's journey across time provides a bridge between the difficult concepts of formal narratology and the more pragmatic work of all storytellers, especially legal storytellers. Like Vonnegut's protagonist Billy Pilgrim, legal storytellers move about purposefully in time, bending and shaping time within their stories to accommodate their purposes.

II. *The Ordering of Discourse Time*
A. The Sequence of the Telling: Billy Pilgrim Watches the Movie Backward

> *Billy looked at the clock on the gas stove. He had an hour to kill before the saucer came. He went into the living room, swinging the bottle like a dinner bell, turned on the television. He came slightly unstuck in time, saw the late movie backwards, then forwards again. It was a movie about American bombers in the Second World War and the gallant men who flew them. Seen backwards by Billy, the story went like this:*
>
> *American planes, full of holes and wounded men and corpses took off backwards from an airfield in England.*

Over France, a few German fighter planes flew at them backwards, sucked bullets and shell fragments from some of the planes and the crewmen. They did the same for wrecked American bombers on the ground, and those planes flew up backwards to join the formation.

The formation flew backwards over a German city that was in flames. The bombers opened their bomb bay doors, exerted a miraculous magnetism which shrunk the fires, gathered them into cylindrical steel containers, and lifted the containers into the bellies of the planes. The containers were stored neatly in racks. The Germans below had miraculous devices of their own, which were long steel tubes. They used them to suck more fragments from the crewmen and planes. But there were still a few wounded Americans, though, and some of the bombers were in bad repair. Over France, though, the German fighters came up again, made everything and everybody as good as new.
When the bombers got back to their base, the steel cylinders were taken from the racks and shipped back to the United States of America, where factories were operating night and day, dismantling the cylinders, separating the dangerous contents into minerals. Touchingly, it was mainly women who did this work. The minerals were then shipped to specialists in remote areas. It was their business to put them into the ground, to hide them cleverly, so they would never hurt anybody ever again.

The American fliers turned in their uniforms, became high school kids. And Hitler turned into a baby, and all humanity, without exception, conspired biologically to produce two perfect people named Adam and Eve, he supposed.

Billy saw the movie backwards then forwards—and then it was time to go out . . . and meet the flying saucer.[1]

B. Chronology

Chronology describes the dominant principle purportedly employed by legal storytellers to organize the telling of their stories in time. But what, exactly, is chronology? A dictionary of narratology defines "chronological order" as "[t]he arrangement of situations and events in the order of their occurrence. 'Harry washed, then he slept' observes a chronological order, whereas, 'Harry slept after he worked' does not. Chronological order is very much privileged by positivist historiography."[2] Likewise, chronology is "privileged" in positivist legal storytelling and, in many ways, serves as the default mode for organizing events in time. By using chronology, legal storytellers attempt to signal to listeners and readers that they are not attempting to manipulate the events of a story, and are subordinating narrative to legal argumentation and principles. There are other reasons to employ chronology as a primary mode of organizing and presenting events in story time. As David Lodge observes, "The simplest way to tell a story, equally favored by tribal bards and parents at bedtime, is to begin at the beginning, and go on until you reach the end, or your audience falls asleep."[3]

Chronology, in some form and to some degree, is apparent in the telling of all the legal stories I have analyzed thus far in this book. Sometimes, employing a strict and linear chronology is a purposeful choice. But more often, an effective legal story is designed to *appear* as if it is being presented in a strict and linear chronology, controlled by the events unfolding in time rather than by the imagination of the storyteller. But upon closer inspection and analysis, this is seldom the case; narrative presentation of a story in discourse time is typically far more complex.

Why then is there such an apparent emphasis on chronology in legal storytelling? There are several possible reasons. Perhaps there is a strong presumption that chronology embodies how events transpire in real time, and it certainly arouses the least suspicion, especially from highly skeptical judicial readers and listeners. The legal storyteller must not lose credibility and must signal to her audience that she is depicting events candidly and "objectively." The legal storyteller typically employs simple chronology to persuade the listener or reader that she is subordinating narrative to legal argumentation, merely presenting rather than manipulating the facts to suit her purposes.

Beneath all these reasons is a narrative conceit, a shared misconception about the relationship between causality and chronology. That is, storytellers often rely on strict chronology based on the presumption that chronological and causal connections are always interrelated; that earlier events presented in a narrative sequence cause the later events. This fallacy is defined by Gerald Prince in his dictionary of narratology:

Post hoc ergo propter hoc fallacy: A confusion, denounced by scholasticism, between consecutiveness and consequence. According to

Barthes (following Aristotle), the mainspring of *narrativity* is related to an exploitation of this confusion, what-comes-after-X in a narrative being processed as what-is-caused-by-X: given "It started to rain, and Mary became nostalgic," for example, Mary's nostalgia tends to be understood as caused by the weather conditions.[4]

Nevertheless, even the most seemingly linear, straightforward, and chronological stories, when examined closely, are seldom presented in a strict chronology. Stories are inevitably filled with departures from a literal chronology, taking off at one point in time, landing at another. Like Billy Pilgrim in his spaceship time travels, storytellers frequently move about in time within narrative, although seldom with the obvious extremity of Vonnegut's reverse causality as presented in the excerpt from *Slaughterhouse Five*. Nevertheless, there is seldom a standardized one-size-fits-all, strict and truly linear chronology available for telling legal stories. Unlike Billy Pilgrim, who is involuntarily committed to a mental hospital for attempting to explain to his listeners how he has become unstuck in time, the legal storyteller typically does not want to emphasize her departures from chronology. But there are techniques that all storytellers inevitably employ to move about in time, departing from chronology, either purposefully, intuitively, or inadvertently. This chapter identifies and foregrounds some of these narrative techniques.

C. Variations on Chronology

Billy couldn't read Tralfamadorian, of course, but he could see how the books were laid out in brief clumps of symbols separated by stars. Billy commented that the clumps might be telegrams.

"Exactly," said the voice.

"They are telegrams?"

"There are no telegrams on Tralfamadore. But you're right: each clump of symbols is a brief, urgent message— describing a situation, a scene. We Tralfamadorians read them all at once, not one after the other. There isn't any particular relationship between the messages, except that the author has chosen carefully, so that, when seen all at once, they produce an image of life that is beautiful, surprising

and deep. There is no beginning, no middle, no end, no sus-
pense, no moral, no causes, no effects. What we love in our
books are the depths of the many marvelous moments seen
at one time."[3]

Unlike Tralfamadorians, we do not read all of our moments at one time, together. We move in sequence from one moment in discourse time to the next in understanding the events within the story. In a story, however, these moments in time seldom proceed in rigid lockstep with the ticking of a clock. There are, of course, a few notable exceptions. For example, in the film *High Noon*, one minute of screen time for the audience equals approximately one minute of "real time" replicating the two hours before the arrival of Frank Miller on the noon train. The film proceeds to provide a purportedly strict chronology of events occurring during this time. This is an effect, however, that can only be achieved in film. Unlike movies (and perhaps this is one of the reasons films seem so "real" to us and are a dominant mode of storytelling in our time), other forms of storytelling cannot effectively capture and embody "real" time. Nevertheless, the arrangement of moments must appear to present a natural and sequential unfolding of the events in story. However, a pure and rigid chronology is seldom the most effective way to capture narrative time in story; indeed, the grammar of sentences often departs from chronology even when the storyteller attempts to sequence events into a linear and chronological discourse time that mirrors the unfolding of events within the story itself. A storyteller can seldom match the depiction and unfolding of events with the ticking of a clock; the narrative presentation of a story distorts the shape of the events depicted within it.

There are techniques and narrative devices that storytellers employ intuitively to depart from chronology, to tell stories effectively in a discourse time that intentionally rearranges the sequencing of events, establishing a different order than the sequence in which these events purportedly occur within the story itself ("story time"). In narratology, there is a specific name for this departure or separation: *anachrony*. Prince's dictionary of narratology provides this definition:

Anachrony: A discordance between the order in which events (are said to) occur and the order in which they are recounted: a beginning *in media res* followed by a return to earlier events constitutes a typical anachrony. In relation to the "present" moment, the moment when chronological recounting of a sequence of events is interrupted to make room for them, anachronies can go back into the past (*ret-rospection, analepsis, flashback*) or forward to the future (*anticipation, prolepsis, flashforward*). They have a certain *extent* or *amplitude* (they cover a certain amount of *story time*) as well as a certain *reach* (the story time they cover is at a certain temporal distance from the "present" moment): in "Mary sat down. Four years later she would have the very same impression and her excitement would last for a whole month," the anachrony has the extent of one month and a reach of four years.[6]

Let's now return, briefly, to several law stories analyzed in the first three chapters of this book and to several supplemental literary examples illustrating various departures from or variations on a linear chronology. These illustrations will show the techniques storytellers employ to structure discourse time within a narrative framework, separating the order in which events are said to occur in the story from the order in which they are actually recounted. The storyteller uses these techniques to present the story in the most effective and compelling way.

D. "Analepsis" or "Flashback"

Prince defines analepsis as "[a]n anachrony going back to the past with respect to the 'present' moment; an evocation of one or more events that occurred before the 'present' moment (or moment when the chronological recounting of a sequence of events is interrupted to make room for the analepsis) a *retrospection; a flashback*."[7] Analepsis can be, characteristically, of two types: "Completing analepses, or *returns*, fill in earlier gaps resulting from *ellipses* in the narrative. Repeating analepses, or *recalls*, tell anew already mentioned past events."[8]

The analysis of the opening paragraphs of *Emma* in chapter 3 provided a brief illustration from literature, when in the second paragraph the story shifts and returns in time to provide the backstory of Emma's past. In Hollywood films and television "flashbacks" are a staple of the cinematic storytelling vocabulary: for example, the story cuts dramatically to a scene from the character's past that reveals crucial backstory explaining pieces of the plot or some crucial aspect of a particular character's motivations. Other complex characters may reveal pieces of their crucial backstories presented in summary as the action slows down, momentarily making room for dialogue. For example, in *High Noon* we learn of the death of Amy's father and brother in a gunfight in a brief summary when she explains the origins of her Quaker and pacifist beliefs; likewise, crucial backstory about Helen Ramirez's relationship with Frank Miller and Kane is also revealed in summary form within careful snippets of dialogue.

Analepses are also used, and often used extensively, in legal storytelling practices. For example, the petitioner's brief in *Eddings* responds to the Oklahoma courts' refusal to consider Eddings's childhood history in mitigation of his murder sentence. The brief relies extensively on flashbacks to incidents from Eddings's childhood that were not considered at sentencing.

Another legal example employing strategic disjunctions in narrative time is Jeremiah Donovan's clever, darkly comedic, and meticulously constructed closing argument on behalf of Louie Failla. Recall, for example, how Donovan starts off the argument theatrically "in media res" within the present tense of the trial itself. The newspaper reporters covering the trial specifically emphasize the appearance of the seemingly already-defeated Donovan as he initially approaches the jury "his head bowed, his voice exhausted" after listening to other closing arguments of the other defendants attacking the credibility of his client Failla, since it was Failla's voice on the surveillance tapes that was the crucial linchpin in the prosecutor's case against them for the murder of Billy Grasso. He begins with references to the trial and to the complexity of the judge's charge. Then Donovan sets these present-tense events aside as if he can go no farther and tells his story of "the legendary O'Toole" presented in an Irish barroom brogue. This initial story sets the comedic tone of the narrative that follows and establishes his baseline depiction of Failla's character. After the story within a story Donovan cuts intertextually like a movie director, providing a flashback that moves back into the past, where the jury is reintroduced to Louis Failla who is living in a "rented duplex out in East Hartford" that "hasn't been painted for eighteen years.... He is living essentially in poverty.... Why is he living in poverty?"[9] Donovan then answers his own rhetorical question by moving even further back into the past, inserting a visual scene developing the backstory of the relationship between Failla and the murderous mobster William Grasso.

Donovan continues: "A made member of the Patriarca crime family, how could he be living in poverty? Because something has happened, and William Grasso has essentially shunned Louie Failla.... They keep him out of all activities. Grasso has done that.... [He] wouldn't let Louie be involved in anything."[10]

Donovan, in other important places, doesn't merely rely on snippets or quotations from dialogue as interlineations to provide backstory in summary form. Instead, he often fills in spaces, what narratologists define as "ellipses" or omissions in time, by slowing down the storytelling and inserting fully developed and "time-consuming" scenes.

Donovan's argument on behalf of Failla, like the examples from literature and movies, and like the petitioner's brief in *Eddings*, departs effortlessly and intentionally from the rigid and linear chronology typically suggested in legal writing texts and clinical literature. In doing so, Donovan matches discourse time to the coherent and purposeful depiction of the events within the story. The narrative logic shapes the order and sequence of the events; Donovan does not need to point out exactly when these events are taking place in real time, or emphasize the disjunctions or departures from a strict chronology, as long as the sequence in discourse time is well coordinated with the story time. Indeed, in his closing argument, Donovan as storyteller has the confidence *not* to identify precisely the timing of the various occurrences depicted in his story. Donovan avoids breaking the "spell" of the story by revealing the strategic default codes underlying the timing of the events depicted in the narrative.

E. "Prolepsis" or "Flash-forward"

In legal storytelling, the use of *prolepsis* (flash-forward) is less common, but it is still employed, especially in trial storytelling. Prince defines *prolepsis* as "[a]n anachrony going forward with respect to the 'present' moment; an evocation of one or more events that will occur after the 'present' moment (or moment when the chronological recounting of a sequence of events is interrupted to make room for a prolepsis); an *anticipation*, a *flashforward,* a *prospection*."[11] As with analapses, there are technically two types of prolepses, completing and repeating prolepses.[12]

Here, from Gerry Spence's closing argument on behalf of Karen Silkwood, is an illustration of a "completing" prolepsis or flash-forward. Spence moves rapidly across time and anticipates the future twenty years after the completion of the trial. He visualizes what will happen to the community and workers at the Kerr-McGee plant if the jury fails to fulfill its heroic oath by stopping Kerr-McGee through speaking the only language the Beast understands, the language of money, and awarding compensatory and punitive damages for Silkwood's death:

> Now I have a vision. It is not a dream—it's a nightmare. It came to me in the middle of the night, and I got up and wrote it down, and I want you to hear it.... Twenty years from now—the men are not old, some

say they're just in their prime, they're looking forward to some good things. The men that worked at that plant are good men with families who love them. They are good men, but they are dying—not all of them, but they are dying like men in a plague. Cancer they say, probably from the plutonium plant.[13]

Then he moves backward in time:

He worked there as a young man. They didn't know much about it in those days.... Nobody in top management seemed to care. Those were the days when nobody in management in the plutonium plant could be found, even by the AEC, who knew or cared. They worked the men in respirators. The pipes leaked. The paint dropped from the walls. The stuff was everywhere.[14]

Use of prolepses (and analapses) is not limited to oral storytelling. There are numerous examples in legal briefs. In legal briefs these time shifts are often marked by the formalities of captions or headers that signal to the reader the shift in time that is taking place. In written legal briefs, the direction of time can and often does turn on a dime; there are subtle movements and adjustments from sentence to sentence, and often even within sentences. That is, temporal moves are made on a "micro" or grammatical level as well as on the "macro" level in the strategic shifting and placement of scenes and summaries within the arrangement of a carefully structured plot.

Prince illustrates this quick movement (a prolepsis) in time in a sequence of two sentences: "John became furious. A few days later, he would come to regret this attitude, but now, he did not think of the consequences and he began to scream."[15] Similarly, legal storytellers are constantly marking and adjusting time within their stories; although we purport to emphasize chronology as the primary mode of legal storytelling, it is inevitable that stories depart from a chronology, calibrating and coordinating "discourse time" with the most effective presentation of the events of the plot in story time.

F. "Ellipsis"

"When there is no part of the narrative (no words or sentences, for example) corresponding to (representing) narratively pertinent situations and events that took time, ellipsis pertain."[16] Simply put, an ellipse is an open space in story time not yet filled in by events. It is an "omission of an element within a series" of events set in story time. The ellipse can either be explicit and identified by the narrator or it can be implicit, "inferable from a break in the sequence of events recounted."[17] It is the story time that remains to be filled in; the removed and typically unstated past after a flashback returns to the present moment. There is, for example, an ellipse when Jeremiah Donovan moves from the present tense of the trial and returns into the past:

> First of all let's talk about chronology here. With respect to Louie Failla, this case begins in about February of 1989. What do we know about Louis Failla at that point? Well, he's living in a rented…[a rented duplex] out in East Hartford. Hasn't been painted in eighteen years…. He is living in poverty.[18]

Then Donovan asks rhetorically, "Why is he living in poverty? A made member of the Patriarca crime family, how could he be living in poverty? Because something has happened."[19]

The flashback (analepsis) creates a gap in the story events, and Donovan goes about filling in the space (an ellipse) with other events set in time. Likewise, there are structured ellipses breaking the chronology in the presentation of story events in the various legal stories and briefs that I have analyzed. For example, in his *Silkwood* argument Gerry Spence jumps from the present to imagine a time twenty years in the future and, likewise, jumps forward over time from his initial statement of the law of strict liability set in old England, anticipating the jury charge on strict liability for Kerr-McGee.

Mieke Bal, a respected narrative theorist on the subject of narrative time, identifies the popular movie *Back to the Future* as a movie that, just as its title suggests, is built on the clever device of gradually filling in "ellipses" in the present by vacillating between the past and the future to retrieve events and information crucial to completing the story. Just as Billy Pilgrim does in *Slaughterhouse Five*, the protagonist of *Back to the Future* becomes unstuck in time and fills in the ellipsis in the present by alternative time travels into past and future. The vehicle for his journey is a Delorean automobile modified for time travel by a mad scientist (alternative to the flying saucer outfitted on Tralfamadore for Pilgrim).

An "ellipse" in narrative time in a story is equivalent to the grammatical marking "…." An ellipse may be filled in implicitly by the imagination of the reader-listener. Alternatively, it may be completed explicitly and purposefully by the narrator. Often the purpose of the ellipse is to powerfully emphasize, rather than to deemphasize, the omitted event as the reader is left to wonder what happened next, until the reader's anticipation and expectation are fulfilled later in the discourse time of the story.

G. Pacing and Rhythm

As previously observed, discourse time seldom, if ever, moves ineluctably forward matching the movements of the hands of the clock. There are constant variations on chronology within the architecture of time in any narrative. This is so even in the formal legal storytelling in written briefs, where it is conventional and often the best narrative strategy to appear to make the discourse time look like it is presenting a simple and straightforward linear chronology, attempting to avoid the appearance that the author is manipulating the events within his presentation. But narrative time in any story is a fabrication, inevitably reshaping and transforming the events depicted within it. This manipulation or creative reconstruction is apparent when analyzing the pacing or rhythm of a story.

Simply put, unlike the ticking of the clock, discourse time does not move at a constant pace with events given the same amount of time and narrative importance measured exclusively by their duration. There are, of course, rare exceptions, especially in film, where it is possible to match the discourse time to story time, as is attempted in presenting the story in *High Noon*. But this is a rare exception. It is the storyteller who determines the emphasis to place on particular events, what to include and what to omit (ellipsis), and how to position events in the story (by employing ellipsis, flashbacks, flash-forwards).

One factor that establishes the pacing of the plot is whether a particular passage is—employing terminology presented in chapter 6, on style—presented as *scene* or *summary* or even, occasionally, in a *stretch*. In a scene the discourse time is roughly equivalent to story time. The style chapter presents illustrations of scenes from nonfiction and legal stories. For example, Norman Mailer's depiction of Gary Gilmore's murder of Max Jensen is a scene. Likewise, Jeremiah Donovan's recounting of the dialogue between Louie Failla and Tito Morales in Failla's car is another. In the Petitioner's brief in *Atkins* the pacing deliberatively slows down as Atkins attempts to visualize images and recounts in twisted dialogue the voices of the various participants in a murder.

In summary, however, the passage of time is compressed; story time significantly exceeds discourse time and events are often glossed over. That is, summary unfolds quickly, diminishing the importance of events within the narrative. For example, the initial paragraphs of the "Statement of the Case" in the petitioner's brief in *Atkins* provides a summary of the robbery of and murder of Eric Nesbitt by Atkins and Jones: "He was robbed of the money in his wallet, driven in his own truck to an ATM and required to withdraw more money, then driven eighteen miles to York County, where he was shot eight times and killed with a semi-automatic handgun." The particularities of the events in time are swallowed in a quick gulp of time, although the story later returns to alternative versions of these events revisited in scenes.

Likewise, in Donovan's closing argument on behalf of Louie Failla, Donovan speeds up narrative time in summaries that gloss over many months of time, while at other points he slows down time to meticulously reconstruct specific dialogue between Failla and various mobsters plotting the murder of Tito Morales in fully developed scenes.

Finally, in stretch the storytelling is slowed down in time further so that discourse time significantly exceeds story time. Again, Donovan makes good use of stretch when depicting crucial conversations between Failla and the mobsters plotting the murder of Tito Morales. He employs visual cartoons to detail the dialogue and then provides a second set of cartoons that reveal and explore Failla's internal thought processes and complex unspoken motivations; translating Failla's thoughts, and the subtext of the scenes, into supplementary dialogue.

Often the line between stretch, scene, and summary is not entirely clear. For example, in the excerpt from Capote's *In Cold Blood,* Hendricks, the schoolteacher-witness, slows down his recounting of scenes so that he, and the reader, can begin to more fully experience the emotional complexity of his own reactions to the images that are uncovered as he moves room to room in his memory. Thus the pacing of interconnected scenes is gradually slowed from summary to scene and into stretch as Hendricks moves through the rooms of the Clutter farm, and discovers the victims in this Gothic horror story. The important point here is to understand that there is a clear distinction between scene, summary, and stretch, and establishing a purposeful rhythm between these three discrete modes is a concern of narrative time, just as it is a concern of style.

A closely related concept from narratology is rhythm. The concept, according to Bal, is as striking as it is elusive. There can be stylistic rhythms created in the construction of sentences in writing, or in the use of recurring patterns in speech. Likewise, there can be more encompassing structural rhythms suggested by intentional patterns in the construction and placement of scenes, summaries, and ellipses in narrative time. Filmmakers, for example, often refer to rhythm or tempo, analyzing the cinematic beats of images, which are built into scenes, and then into sequences of scenes. Rhythm is equally relevant for creating underlying patterns in written and spoken stories. Prince defines rhythm as "[a] recurrent pattern in narrative *speed* and, more generally, any pattern, of repetition with variations. The most common rhythm in classical narrative results from the alteration of scene and summary." In legal storytelling, the classical rhythm is also between the alteration of scene and summary; unlike literary storytelling the emphasis typically is not on the presentation of scenes, but rather on the use of summaries. This does not diminish the importance of scenes employed. Indeed, as we have explored in my analysis of legal examples in previous chapters, the reverse is typically true: because there are fewer scenes employed in legal storytelling practices, they are often of crucial importance.

H. Establishing the Time Frame—Beginnings and Implied Endings to Unfinished Stories

People aren't supposed to look back. I'm certainly not going to do it anymore.

I've finished my war book now. The next one I write is going to be fun.

This one is a failure, and had to be, since it was written by a pillar of salt. It begins like this:

Listen:
Billy Pilgrim has come unstuck in time.
It ends like this:
Poo-tee-weet?[20]

The first chapter on plotting identified two crucial points set "in time" establishing the narrative framework of the story—the beginning and the ending. Beginnings and endings are interconnected. The choice of the opening typically anticipates the ending of the story. So much so that the novelist and writing teacher John Gardner, as noted there, advises aspiring novelists and creative writers to construct their stories backward from their endings to determine what their beginnings should be. Likewise, the clinician's admonition to the legal storyteller is to always know where the narrative is headed before the journey of the story begins, always keeping in mind the point and purpose of the story in addition to the narrative destination that is desired as the outcome of the tale. This goal, however, is difficult for many legal storytellers to achieve because the story is typically incomplete. While the creative writer or popular storyteller is in control of the story, and writes her ending, the legal storyteller typically does not. It is up to another, a jury or a judge in litigation, to write the ending of the tale. Nevertheless, legal storytellers, such as Jeremiah Donovan or Gerry Spence, or the authors of the various briefs identified in this book, all tell their stories in ways that strongly anticipate, even when not explicitly providing, proposed endings. Further, these endings are implicit from the beginning.

For example, in Donovan's closing argument on behalf of Louie Failla, the proposed resolution is a return to the anterior steady state where Failla's motives are finally understood and he is reunited with his real family (his wife, daughter, grandchild, and even Tito Morales, who now awaits Louie in prison) and, perhaps, with his adopted mob family as well (who now understand the reason for his storytelling, to avoid the commands of the mob boss Billy Grasso). Spence's closing argument in *Silkwood* anticipates a transformed steady state—the ending foresees a moment when the jury punishes the Beast Kerr-McGee and compels it to rectify its corporate behavior and heed the warning of the prophet Karen Silkwood. By imposing this ending onto the tale the jury prevents an impending environmental disaster that looms ahead.

III. Concluding Observations

Simply put, in legal storytelling just as in literary and popular storytelling, it is important to find a way to tell stories in an order that will make the story most persuasive and effective. As Anthony Amsterdam observes when teaching capital defenders the art of narrative persuasion, the story must develop narrative "clout" often without regard to chronology of the events depicted within the story. But unlike Vonnegut's Billy Pilgrim in *Slaughterhouse Five*, the story and the storyteller cannot draw attention to these intentional departures from chronology. Recall that Billy Pilgrim was institutionalized for calling direct attention to what he was doing in his departures from chronology and travels in time. Likewise, in legal storytelling, there are grave dangers in obvious manipulations of time as it is twisted into story. Artfulness and effectiveness is typically in understatement, in employing time-travel devices that conceal, rather than reveal, the underlying movements made within time, the intentionality of the storyteller, and the purpose of the narrative. All decision makers, especially skeptical judges, may well perceive any obvious departures from the supposed realism implicit in a pure linear chronology as subterfuge, as covering holes in the plot of the story, or as simply the gimmicks of a narrative trickster who cannot be trusted.

Nevertheless, it is also true that *all* stories depart from chronology, and reshape narrative time in service of the plot regardless of whether the storyteller is aware of these maneuverings. Occasionally movies, such as *High Noon*, may attempt to employ real time as an explicit time framework for narrative. This is, of course, the exception to the rule. And, even here, there are backstories, and ministories, and artful time shifts embedded in the narrative. Legal stories, whether written or oral, can never match against, or be truly set in, real time. The stories that lawyers tell are told within the artifice of story time. And so it is vital to propel intentional narrative time travel, although such flights may often seem dangerous and unconventional. Why do effective legal storytellers so often risk the departure from linearity and simple and rigid chronology? Here is a partial preflight checklist of strategic reasons for time travel in legal storytelling practice:[21]

- to create the kind of world in which your plot action will seem plausible, *before* you relate any pieces of the plot action that may be received skeptically;
- to depict features of that world that will drive your plot action or mold one of your characters, *before* you show their effects;
- to provide whatever framing your story needs before it gets going;
- to provide whatever foreshadowing your story needs, at appropriate junctures;
- to create and maintain suspense;
- to implement the basic narrative structure underlying your story;
- to effectuate the particular sequence that your plot requires;
- to provide information about your players that will build up a portrait of their characters, *before* they act in ways that you want interpreted in light of their character;
- to reinforce your plot or your players' characters or the ordering principles of the world of your story with ministories at appropriate junctures;
- to keep any ministories or subparts of the story properly subordinated to the larger story; and
- to serve any other function that your particular story may require.

In this chapter, I have identified several of the narrative techniques and devices artful advocates employ to move about purposefully in time within a story, and provided illustrations of the theory in action from legal and literary examples presented in earlier chapters of this book. These brief illustrations provide merely the starting places for deeper explorations of narrative time travel in legal storytelling practice.

9

Final Observations

BEGINNINGS AND ENDINGS

To avoid all display of art itself requires consummate art.
—QUINTILIAN, INSTITUTIO ORATIO

> *The F.B.I. intercepted a mob initiation ceremony.... It was responsorial, much like the old Latin mass, "io voglio... io voglio... entrare... entrare... in questo orginazione... in questo orginazione." It sounded like a Latin prayer. When they burned the picture of the saint you could hear the crackling of the fire on tape. I mean, this ceremony had been handed down from sixteenth century Sicily so you expect it to be dramatic. However, what was equally dramatic was all the activity surrounding it. Afterwards, after all the cleaning up and goodbyes, you hear the steps of the final participant going to the door, the door squeaks open, and then, to the empty room, you hear someone say, "No one will ever know what went on here today—except for us and the fucking Holy Ghost."*
>
> —JEREMIAH P. DONOVAN, "REMARKS ABOUT LAWYERS AS STORYTELLERS,"

LET ME END this book at the beginning: more than twenty years ago, I accepted an invitation from Anthony G. Amsterdam, my former boss and then the clinical director at New York University School of Law, to attend and participate in the recently convened Lawyering Theory Colloquium. The colloquium was composed of upper-level students, clinical practitioners, law-yering skills teachers, and visiting academics. We met weekly to explore narra-tive theory, metaphor, language theory, and rhetoric, and to better understand how these often highly theoretical academic concerns might contribute to teaching the work that lawyers do. Indeed, there was a shared belief that these interdisciplinary academic subjects might enliven and transform law school pedagogy. The colloquium was presided over by Tony Amsterdam, Jerome Bruner, and Peggy Cooper Davis. Amsterdam is an inspirational teacher, the father of clinical legal education, a recipient of a MacArthur Foundation genius grant, and the almost-mythical attorney who argued *Furman* success-fully before the U.S. Supreme Court. Bruner is the pioneering educational psychologist and a towering intellectual figure of the twentieth century in several disciplines, including educational psychology and narrative stud-ies. Recently, the School of Education at Oxford University was named in his honor. And Peggy Cooper Davis is a highly regarded clinician, a former judge, a nationally recognized legal historian, and a first-rate narrative theo-rist. Of course, their respective intellectual contributions and stature cannot be reduced to a few simple sentences.

More important than their "street cred" and academic celebrity is the fact that each is a remarkable teacher, and a compelling and charismatic character: Amsterdam emits a constant white-hot intellectual intensity and analytical clarity and believes, wrongly, that everyone is as smart as he is and can be transformed and enlightened through education. Bruner is a sophisti-cated intellectual raconteur with a seemingly endless interdisciplinary range. Bruner also possesses an endearing and, at times, almost positively gleeful intellectual playfulness that is a perfect counterpoint to Amsterdam's inten-sity. Peggy Cooper Davis manifests great kindness, compassion, and a deep and pragmatic wisdom. Together they are like the embodiment of the parts of Burke's narrative Pentad, or at least Bruner's version of Burke's Pentad: parts working together seamlessly and interactively, each in service of the other.

Once a week I took the train into New York to attend the colloquium. There was an electrical buzz in the air at those sessions, especially when the topics and discussions focused on legal storytelling and narrative theory.

Some years later, Amsterdam and Bruner published their influential syn-thesis of their colloquium work in *Minding the Law*.[1] In alternating chapters, they set forth their interdisciplinary theories and then applied the theory to analysis of U.S. Supreme Court opinions in civil rights cases. The book's argu-ment confirms what every litigator knows intuitively—effective storytelling is crucial in legal argumentation; it is often outcome determinative. Beneath the purportedly objective analytical texts and legalistic arguments are the sub-texts of the stories told. We tell these stories to understand and gain control of a world constructed by and, employing Bruner's terminology, "bathed" and "swaddled" in stories.

In the colloquium, there was a shared understanding that effective storytelling skills are crucial in all areas of practice, and especially in litigation. Of course, there are many constraints on legal storytelling, and the stories told must be factually meticulous and truthful. Legal storytellers are, at least by training, highly ethical storytellers. But there was a sense that this crucial subject, and the skills of storytelling, is largely ignored in law school pedagogy and curriculum. Perhaps narrative and storytelling are systematically or intentionally devalued to emphasize the primacy of analytical positivism and Langdellian formalism that makes stories subservient to legal doctrine. In a traditional legal education, students typically study fragments of stories only insofar as the facts inform doctrinal analysis. Perhaps storytelling skills are discounted because most academics have spent careers in insular and analytical environments, observing stories primarily through top-down readings employing an often opaque lens cap of theory. Or perhaps it is because, as all storytellers have long known, the storyteller never explicitly foregrounds or makes the audience aware of the narrative principles that shape the various components of the story told—including the specific subject matters of this book—such as plot, character, style, setting, and time. The storyteller must construct a seamless world that sings with the verisimilitude of life. The dangers for the legal storyteller are obvious when the machinery of the story becomes apparent, and this is especially so where an already skeptical audience is suspicious of the truthfulness of the story and wary of manipulation.

There was another difficulty about the subject matters and theory presented at the Lawyering Theory Colloquium: academic narrative theory often seems abstract, esoteric, and difficult to parse. Narrative theorists write primarily for other academic specialists. It is difficult to cross academic boundaries and formulate the relevant "take-aways" that might be useful to generalists, law students, and practitioners. What exactly are the lessons that might be distilled as useful and that would send us forward in further exploration and navigation of this uncharted territory? There seemed little applied theory presented in academic and clinical literature employing examples drawn from popular culture, from literature and, most important, from litigation practice.

It struck me that I could attempt to fill this gap; I might even translate some of the relevant narrative theory into conceptual vocabulary useful to litigation attorneys, law students, and academic generalists. Also, I could select sample illustrations drawn from popular culture and literature and provide several close bottom-up readings of litigation stories from law practice. I thought that an engaging narrative sampler and primer, providing a simplified distillation of the academic narrative theory presented in the colloquium, would provide a useful starting point for further explorations by intrepid lawyer-storytellers. Simply put, that is what I have attempted to do in this book.

While attending the colloquium, I was simultaneously teaching a seminar, Law and Popular Storytelling, in the evening division at the University of Connecticut School of Law and, by day, directing the Legal Writing Program. One of the students in my Law and Popular Storytelling class was an undercover police detective with the Hartford Police Department, who had been assigned to help infiltrate the Connecticut faction of the Patriarca crime family. During our semester together, he shared that he would be testifying at the upcoming federal trial of eight "made" members of the Connecticut faction of the Patriarca crime family, who stood charged with various counts of racketeering, including the execution of the Connecticut "capo" of the family, an irresistibly evil gangster, Billy "The Wild Guy" Grasso. After class one evening, as was our practice, the class adjourned to the local bar. My student suggested that I consider attending the trial. He reasoned that since I taught a course about understanding the relationship between popular storytelling and legal storytelling, I might be interested in the trial as a living illustration of narrative theory in action.

That summer I scrupulously attended the entire trial, which proved to be a thirteen-week-long storytelling spectacular. In the years following the trial, I wrote four law review articles revisiting portions of the trial—especially the closing arguments—as narrative—that is, as storytelling.[2]

The stories and storytelling in that trial provided a remarkably complex interweaving of plots, counterplots, and subplots. The stories assumed forms that seemed compelled by the nature of the material itself, the characters of the various defendants and witnesses, and the invention and style of the various attorneys. The stories were part drama, part tragedy, part suspense thriller, part crime story, part melodrama, and part murder mystery. The trial was a carnival of theatricality and a showcase of artful storytelling practice. Yet it was also a deadly serious business, a storytelling in a "field of pain and death."[3] The consequences of the defendants' convictions—they stood accused of murder, conspiracy to commit murder, and a plethora of lesser racketeering offenses—were grave indeed.

Nevertheless, the storytelling at trial was often surprisingly lighthearted; the stories recounted were at times poignant and told in voices that were almost lyrical. The courtroom was often filled with the raucous humor of a comedy club, especially when FBI surveillance tapes were played, revealing the intimate details of the various mobsters' personal lives. The defendants' personal stories were interwoven with the multiple legal stories of conspiracy and crime that arose from their professional lives.

I knew several of the defense attorneys and prosecutors from practice, including Jeremiah P. Donovan, the former chief trial attorney in the United States Attorney's office in Connecticut. As my analysis in this book hopefully suggests, Donovan is an inventive and analytically self-reflective trial attorney. Donovan had been assigned by the trial judge, Alan Nevas, the former U.S. Attorney in Connecticut, to represent one of the defendants, Louis Failla.

After the court adjourned each day, I went to the courthouse library to work and then headed downhill toward a construction site that doubled as a parking lot while the courthouse was undergoing renovations. As the trial progressed, I observed that there was one other car in the parking lot at this late hour: the Jeep Cherokee belonging to Donovan. Typically, Jeremiah would be sitting in his car, talking animatedly and in a highly stylized manner. There was no one else with him in the car. Initially, I thought he might be talking on his car phone, but he was not. This scene repeated itself, especially during the final stages of the trial. Only after the trial concluded did I fully realize what Donovan had been doing in his car at the end of the trial: he was working to craft the two-hour closing argument that he would deliver at the end of the defendants' case, on behalf of his client, Failla.

Through this external storytelling process Donovan was interweaving all the emerging narrative pieces and strands of evidence. These included the damning excerpts from the FBI surveillance tapes that condemned Failla by his own words plotting the murder of Tito Morales. The evidence also included excerpts from sympathetic surveillance tapes that Donovan had introduced during the presentation of Louie's defense, tapes in which Louie spoke of the love he felt for his own family, including Tito Morales, as well as his hatred of the quintessentially evil Grasso.

The image of Donovan in his car struggling to transform argument into story, attempting to make it work both artistically and legally, fitting the evidence that had emerged at trial within the constraints of the law, stayed with me then as it does now. Donovan's struggle is the struggle of all storytellers, including legal storytellers. In so many ways it was the same artistic process of vision and revision, telling the story over and over, trying to get it all just right, so that the story can fully do its work upon the listener or reader.

This book began with close readings of two illustrative legal stories—Gerry Spence's closing argument on behalf of Karen Silkwood and Jeremiah Donovan's closing argument on behalf of Louie Failla. I chose these two stories, embedded within the larger stories of the trials, because I thought of these arguments as discrete pieces, severable from the entirety and also representative of the stories that lawyers, especially litigation attorneys, employ as persuasive instruments. I also chose these illustrations because they were highly engaging and entertaining stories.

I hope that the closing arguments and other stories presented in this book are illustrative of the lessons that this text attempts to convey: Spence's Silkwood argument provides the legal version of a good old-fashioned melodrama, featuring clearly defined heroes and villains. In its way, especially coming after the trial, it is a highly charged story with a well-paced plot. It borrows features from popular Westerns and monster movies, and blends in references to other important pop cultural sources and news events that are crucial for context.

For example, Spence's "Cimarron Syndrome" cleverly cross-references the movie *China Syndrome* and the disaster at Three Mile Island with the story of the trial itself. The parts of the story—plot, character, setting, style, and time—all fit together in a compelling and well-balanced arrangement that Kenneth Burke and Jerome Bruner would surely appreciate. At its core it is a legal melodrama, Spence's version of a genre typical in torts lawsuits. The story presents a moralistic tale about good defeating evil, embodied in the incorporeal corporate villain who comes alive. Spence tells an open and unfinished story; the proposed outcome is clearly signaled and predetermined by the selection of the genre. Silkwood is cast in the role of the fallen martyr and prophet, who comes on stage to save the community and townspeople. It is left to the heroic jury to save the community and redeem the innocent townspeople, and to give Silkwood's shortened life meaning.

Although the trial story and closing arguments are shaped into melodrama, this is neither a shallow or unfelt story. Indeed, just the opposite: it is a deeply felt story that is both truthful and factually accurate. What makes the story work upon the jury is its truthfulness: it is about corporate greed for profits, the irresponsibility of a soulless beast gone crazy on a lawless and primitive landscape, and the dangers signaled for the future if the Beast is not stopped when it finally emerges from beneath the bucolic mud springs. The story is factually meticulous yet also metaphoric; it works both levels, signaling the future while resonating in our present time.

The second example is my presentation and reading of Jeremiah Donovan's argument told on behalf of Louie Failla. In many ways it is a smaller story, about the actions of one of the eight defendants, the lowest-ranking mobster in a complex RICO case, who is accused of plotting the murder of his grandson's father. It is a story set within the context of a thirteen-week trial in which Louie Failla is merely a minor player who does not testify and seldom takes center stage in the trial itself. Yet it is a story told in purposeful counterpoint to the prosecution's much larger melodramatic mob tale of unrepentant and evil gangsters chased by heroic cops protecting the public. Donovan's retelling of the tale, primarily in his closing argument, is a character-based story that attempts to humanize Failla against the weight of the evidence and the self-incriminating tapes where Failla plots the murder of his grandson's father and ingratiates himself with his mob family. Employing a complex sequence of visual cartoons, Donovan's version looks beyond Failla's words and inside Failla's thoughts. Donovan's story explores Failla's consciousness in a way that is characteristic of literary and modernist stories, constructing a more complex yet unified version of Failla's character than the evidence seems to allow. Although Failla is convicted, Donovan's story is successful with the various audiences he seeks to reach: Failla receives leniency from the judge, who departs from the federal sentencing guidelines in sentencing Failla. Of equal importance is the way Donovan's story redeems and explains Failla's words and deeds in the eyes of both his real family and his adopted mob family.

These stories, and the other popular and law stories excerpted in this book, are not models or recipes in a storytelling cookbook. They serve as illustrations, and suggest lessons, themes, and techniques that can be borrowed or recycled for use in future cases.

The stories that lawyers tell are like, yet unlike, the stories told by other storytellers, including journalists, creative writers, and moviemakers. Lawyers' voices are different. There are often explicit constraints on form and substance. Likewise, there are procedural and evidentiary rules that shape how law stories are told. Themes are determined by legal theories and often these theories are, in turn, shaped by the underlying stories. And, of course, the stories told by attorneys must be factually meticulous and truthful; lawyers are ethical realists. A final characteristic of law stories, especially the stories told in litigation practice, is that these stories are typically open or unfinished stories—their endings are strongly implied but not ordered or prescribed. It is up to a decision maker to write the ending, provide the closure and the coda that gives the story its meaning, and determine the outcome. And so, in a book on legal storytelling by a lawyer, it seems fitting that there is no explicit ending or single conclusion, no final lesson or outcome or point of departure. My purpose in this primer is merely to provide a starting point for better understanding the art of legal storytelling practice. I hope that readers have found my initial exploration of this subject of some value, and that the theory and illustrations stimulate and encourage legal storytelling creativity and inform the highly ethical storytelling work lawyers do.

Notes

CHAPTER 1

1. Kenneth Burke, *A Grammar of Motives* (New York: Prentice-Hall, 1945).

CHAPTER 2

1. 359 Mass. 319, 268 N.E.2d 860 (1971).
2. Ibid., 320–21, 268 N.E.2d at 860–61.
3. Ibid., 323, 268 N.E.2d at 862.
4. Ibid.
5. Peter Brooks, *Reading for the Plot: Design and Intention in Narrative* (Cambridge, MA: Harvard University Press, 1992), 11–12.
6. David Lodge, *The Art of Fiction: Illustrated from Classic and Modern Texts* (New York: Penguin Books, 1992), 216.
7. Anthony G. Amsterdam and Jerome Bruner, *Minding the Law* (Cambridge, MA: Harvard University Press, 2002), 113–14.
8. Lodge, *The Art of Fiction*, 216.
9. Ibid., 217.
10. Ibid.
11. The technical term from narrative theory for such a reversal is "peripeteia." For those interested, a dictionary of narratology defines peripety as "[t]he inversion (reversal) from one state of affairs to its opposite. For example, an action seems destined for success but suddenly moves towards failure, or vice versa. According to Aristotle, peripety (peripeteia) is, along with recognition (anagnorisis), the most potent means of ensuring the tragic effect." Gerald Prince, *Dictionary of Narratology*, rev. ed. (Lincoln: University of Nebraska Press, 2003), 71.
12. Amsterdam and Bruner, *Minding the Law*, 113–14.
13. John Gardner, *The Art of Fiction: Notes on Craft for Young Writers* (New York: Vintage Books, 1985), 177.
14. *Shorter Oxford English Dictionary*, 5th ed., s.v. "theme" (New York: Oxford University Press, 1993).
15. Ibid. (emphasis added).

16. Philip N. Meyer, "Why a Jury Trial Is More Like a Movie Than a Novel," *Journal of Law and Society* 28 (2001), 133.

17. Ibid.

18. Gardner, *Art of Fiction*, 70.

19. Joel Seidemann, *In the Interest of Justice: Great Opening and Closing Arguments of the Last 100 Years* (New York: Regan Books, 2004), 56.

20. Northrop Frye, *Anatomy of Criticism: Four Essays* (Princeton, NJ: Princeton University Press, 1971), 47.

21. Michael Roemer, *Telling Stories: Postmodernism and the Invalidation of Traditional Narrative* (Lanham, MD: Rowman & Littlefield, 1995), 280–81.

22. Francois Truffaut, *Hitchcock* (New York: Simon & Schuster, 1967), 141, quoted in Roemer, *Telling Stories*, 282.

23. For examples of epic tales with battles between heroes and villains, see Ananda K. Coomaraswamy and Sister Nivedita, *Myths of the Hindus and Buddhists* (New York: Dover, 1967), 6; Kevin Crossley-Holland, *The Norse Myths* (New York: Pantheon Books, 1980); William Peter Blatty, *The Exorcist* (New York: Harper Torch, 1994); *The Exorcist*, directed by William Friedkin (1973); *Alien*, directed by Ridley Scott (1979).

24. See George Lakoff and Mark Johnson, *Metaphors We Live By* (Chicago: University of Chicago Press, 1980), 83–85; Amsterdam and Bruner, *Minding the Law*, 20–53.

25. Literary theorists and critics use the term "intertextuality" to refer to the way in which a story interacts with other stories that are familiar to the reader or audience—essentially, the resonances of other well-known tales that a story awakens and the deepening and complication of the story that results from those resonances. See Prince, *Dictionary of Narratology*, 46.

26. Roemer, *Telling Stories*, 276.

27. Ibid.

28. In narratology, the term "instantiation" captures how shared understandings of "how the world works" order events into narrative, and—like *causality, story logic,* and *genre*—serve as another constraint on a plot shaping the narrative and determining narrative outcomes. Such beliefs may include, for example, simply that "good will vanquish evil in the end" or that "no bad deed finally goes unpunished" or that "redemption is a possibility for us all in the end when we accept responsibility for what we have done and seek forgiveness with the fullness of our hearts," etc.

29. Peter Brooks observes, "an infraction of order … [is] preeminently what it takes to incite narrative into existence." Brooks, *Reading for the Plot*, 26.

CHAPTER 3

1. Michael Lief, H. Mitchell Caldwell, and Benjamin Bycel, *Ladies and Gentlemen of the Jury: Greatest Closing Arguments in Modern Law* (New York: Simon & Schuster, 1998), 127–57.

2. *Silkwood*, directed by Mike Nichols (1983).

3. This "backstory" in this section compresses and simplifies the explanation presented in Lief, Caldwell, and Bycel's *Ladies and Gentlemen of the Jury*, 119–22. Quotations from Spence's closing argument are taken from the text of the argument as presented by Lief, Caldwell, and Bycel, 127–57.

4. Ibid., 127–28.

5. Ibid., 128.

6. Anthony G. Amsterdam and Randy Hertz, "An Analysis of Closing Arguments to a Jury," *New York Law School Law Review* 37 (1992), 55, 61.

7. Gerry Spence, *Win Your Case: How to Present, Persuade, and Prevail—Every Place, Every Time* (New York: St. Martin's Griffin, 2005), 224–25.

8. See Peter C. Lagarias, *Effective Closing Argument* (Newark, NJ: Lexis, 1999), 362.

9. Lief, Caldwell, and Bycel, *Ladies and Gentlemen*, 129.

10. Ibid., 144.

11. Ibid., 130.

12. Gerry Spence, *How to Argue and Win Every Time* (New York: St. Martin's Press, 1995), 126.

13. Syd Field, *Four Screenplays: Studies in the American Screenplay* (New York: St. Martin's Press, 1995), 126.

14. Ibid., 240–41.

15. Lief, Caldwell, and Bycel, *Ladies and Gentlemen*, 140.

16. Ibid., 156.

17. Gerry Spence, remarks, NACDL Conference on "Lawyering on the Edge" (Chicago, November 3–6, 1999). See also Gerry L. Spence, "How to Make a Complex Case Come Alive for a Jury," *ABA Journal*, April 1986, 65.

18. Spence, "Lawyer on the Edge."

19. Amsterdam and Hertz, "Analysis of Closing Arguments," 64–75.

20. Lief, Caldwell, and Bycel, *Ladies and Gentlemen*, 130.

21. Ibid., 131.

22. Spence, "Lawyering on the Edge."

23. John H. Blume, Sheri L. Johnson, and Emily C. Paavola, "Every Juror Wants a Story: Narrative Relevance, Third Party Guilt and the Right to Present a Defense," *American Criminal Law Review* 44 (2007), 1090.

24. Jerome Bruner, *Beyond the Information Given: Studies in the Psychology of Knowing* (New York: Norton, 1973).

25. Lief, Caldwell, and Bycel, *Ladies and Gentlemen*, 130.

26. Ibid., 131.

27. Ibid., 138.

28. Ibid., 156.

29. Ibid.

30. Ibid., 142.

31. Ibid.

32. Truffaut, *Hitchcock*, 141.

33. Spence, *How to Argue*, 269.
34. Ibid.
35. Ibid., 271.
36. Michael Roemer, *Telling Stories: Postmodernism and the Invalidation of Traditional Narrative* (Lanham, MD: Rowman & Littlefield, 1995), 282–83.
37. Lief, Caldwell, and Bycel, *Ladies and Gentlemen*, 131.
38. Ibid., 137.
39. Letter of defense counsel William Paul to Peter Langarias in Langarias, *Effective Closing Argument*, 466.
40. Lief, Caldwell, and Bycel, *Ladies and Gentlemen*, 131–32 (bracketed term in original).
41. Ibid., 132–33 (bracketed term in original).
42. Ibid., 133, 135.
43. Ibid., 135.
44. Ibid., 135–36.
45. Ibid., 137.
46. Ibid., 138–39 (bracketed terms in original).
47. Ibid., 139.
48. Ibid., 139–40.
49. Ibid., 140.
50. Ibid.
51. Ibid. (bracketed term in original).
52. Ibid., 140–41.
53. Ibid.
54. Ibid., 141.
55. Ibid.
56. Ibid.,
57. Ibid., 141–42.
58. Ibid., 142.
59. Ibid.
60. Ibid., 143.
61. Ibid.
62. Ibid., 142.
63. Ibid., 143.
64. Ibid., 144.
65. Ibid.
66. Ibid., 145 (emphasis added).
67. Ibid. (emphasis added).
68. Ibid. (emphasis added).
69. Ibid. (emphasis added).
70. Ibid., 145–46.
71. Ibid., 146.

72. Ibid.

73. Ibid., 149.

74. Ibid., 150.

75. Ibid., 152–53.

76. Ibid., 153.

77. Ibid.

78. Ibid., 154.

79. Ibid., 154–55.

80. Ibid., 156.

81. Ibid.

82. Ibid.

83. Ibid.

84. Ibid.

85. Ibid.

86. Ibid.

87. Ibid., 156–57.

88. Quotation in section head from Roemer, *Telling Stories*, 3.

89. See Peter Brooks and Paul Gewirtz, *Law's Stories: Narrative and Rhetoric in the Law* (New Haven, CT: Yale University Press, 1996), 103; see also John Gardner, *The Art of Fiction: Notes on Craft for Young Writers* (New York: Vintage Books, 1985), 165.

90. Lief, Caldwell, and Bycel, *Ladies and Gentlemen*, 128.

91. Ibid., 156.

92. Ibid., 131.

93. Ibid., 138, 140.

94. David Lodge, *The Art of Fiction: Illustrated from Classic and Modern Texts* (New York: Penguin Books, 1992), 3–4. An immaterial portion of Lodge's quote from Austen is omitted.

95. Jane Austen, *Emma*, quoted in Lodge, *Art of Fiction*, 3–4.

96. Ford Madox Ford, *The Good Soldier*, quoted in Lodge, *Art of Fiction*, 5.

97. Lodge, *Art of Fiction*, 5.

98. See Ronald B. Tobias, *20 Master Plots and How to Build Them* (Cincinnati: F&W Publications, 2003), 161.

99. Robert McKee, *Story: Substance, Structure, Style, and the Principles of Screenwriting* (New York: Harper Collins, 1997), 81.

100. Lodge, *Art of Fiction*, 5.

101. Ibid.

102. Ibid.

103. Ibid.

104. Anthony G. Amsterdam and Philip N. Meyer, "Making Our Clients' Stories Heard: A Guide to Narrative Strategies for Appellate and Postconviction Lawyers" (Administrative Office, U.S. Courts, 2008), 3.71.

105. *Double Indemnity*, directed by Billy Wilder (1944).

106. Vladimir Propp, *Morphology of the Folktale* (Austin: University of Texas Press, 2005), 30–36.

107. Roemer, *Telling Stories*, 16.

108. Matthew Joseph Bruccoli, ed., *Conversations with Ernest Hemingway* (Jackson: University Press of Mississippi, 1986), 123.

109. Lief, Caldwell, and Bycel, *Ladies and Gentlemen*, 156.

110. McKee, *Story*, 105.

111. Ibid., 317–18.

112. Ibid., 319.

113. Ibid.

114. Ibid.

115. Ibid.

116. Lief, Caldwell, and Bycel, *Ladies and Gentlemen*, 145–46.

117. Ibid., 140.

118. Ibid., 149.

119. Ibid., 151.

120. Ibid., 154–55.

121. Ibid., 156.

122. McKee, *Story*, 209.

123. Peter Brooks, *The Melodramatic Imagination: Balzac, Henry James, Melodrama, and the Mode of Excess* (New Haven, CT: Yale University Press, 1976), 86.

CHAPTER 4

1. David Lodge, *The Art of Fiction: Illustrated from Classic and Modern Texts* (New York: Penguin Books, 1992), 26.

2. John Gardner, *The Art of Fiction: Notes on Craft for Young Writers* (New York: Vintage Books, 1985), 6.

3. E. L. Doctorow, *City of God* (New York: Random House, 2000), quoted in A. O. Scott, "A Thinking Man's Miracle," Book Review Desk, *New York Times*, March 5, 2000, sec. 7.

4. *The Maltese Falcon*, directed by John Huston (1941).

5. Heraclitus, *Heraclitus*, in *The Pre-Socratic Philosophers*, by Geoffrey Stephen Kirk, John Earle Raven, and Malcolm Schofield (Cambridge: Cambridge University Press, 1983), 210–11.

6. Edith Wharton, *The Writing of Fiction* (New York: Simon & Schuster, 1997), 36–37.

7. Lodge, *Art of Fiction*, 67.

8. F. Scott Fitzgerald, *The Last Tycoon* (New York: Scribner's, 1970), 163.

9. Bob Dylan, "It's All Over Now, Baby Blue," *Bringing It All Back Home*, Columbia Records, 1965.

10. Michael Roemer, *Telling Stories: Postmodernism and the Invalidation of Traditional Narrative* (Lanham, MD: Rowman & Littlefield, 1995), 16–17.

11. Jerome Bruner, *Making Stories: Law, Literature and Life* (New York: Farrar, Straus, Giroux, 2002), 64.

12. Irwin Shaw, interview, *Paris Review*, no. 4, Winter 1953, available at http://www.theparisreview.org/interviews/5157/the-art-of-fiction-no-4-irwin-shaw.

13. See Richard E. Nisbett and Lee Ross, *Human Inference: Strategies and Shortcomings of Social Judgment* (Englewood Cliffs, NJ: Prentice-Hall, 1980), 31.

14. See Lee Ross, "The Intuitive Psychologist and His Shortcomings: Distortions in the Attribution Process," in *Advances in Experimental Social Psychology*, vol. 10, ed. Leonard Berkowitz (New York: Academic Press, 1977), 173.

15. See Daniel T. Gilbert and Patrick S. Malone, "The Correspondence Bias," *Psychological Bulletin* 117, no. 1 (1995), 21.

16. Lodge, *Art of Fiction*, 183.

17. Ibid.

18. E. M. Forster, *Aspects of the Novel* (New York: Harcourt, Brace, 1954), 67.

19. Gerald Prince, *A Dictionary of Narratology*, rev. ed. (Lincoln: University of Nebraska Press, 2003), 31.

20. Forster, *Aspects of the Novel*, 67–68.

21. Ibid.

22. Ibid., 68–70.

23. Ibid., 67.

24. Prince, *Dictionary of Narratology*, 85.

25. Forster, *Aspects of the Novel*, 78.

26. Lodge, *Art of Fiction*, 183.

27. Ernest Hemingway, quoted in *Writers at Work: The* Paris Review *Interviews*, ed. George Plimpton (New York: Viking Press, 1963), 233.

28. Lodge, *Art of Fiction*, 183.

29. See Robert McKee, *Story: Substance, Structure, Style, and the Principles of Screenwriting* (New York: Regan Books, 1997), 104 ("The finest [screen]writing not only reveals true character, but arcs or changes [of] that [character's] inner nature, for better or worse, over the course of the telling").

30. Katherine Anne Porter, quoted in Plimpton, *Writers at Work*, 151.

31. Wharton, *The Writing of Fiction*, 94–95 (emphasis in original).

32. Roemer, *Telling Stories*, 275.

33. See *Sergeant York*, directed by Howard Hawks (1941); *Meet John Doe*, directed by Frank Capra (1941); *The Pride of the Yankees*, directed by Sam Wood (1942). For a discussion of Cooper's acting career, see Advameg, Inc., "Gary Cooper—Actors and Actresses—Films as Actor, Publications," Film Reference, http://www.film-reference.com/Actors-and-Actresses-Co-Da/Cooper-Gary.html.

34. Wharton, *The Writing of Fiction*, 94–95.

35. Margaret Mehring, *The Screenplay: A Blend of Film, Form and Content* (Boston: Focal Press, 1990), 187.

36. *High Noon*, directed by Fred Zinnemann (1952).

37. Peter Brooks, *The Melodramatic Imagination* (New Haven, CT: Yale University Press, 1976), 16–17.

38. James Wood, *How Fiction Works* (New York: Farrar, Straus & Giroux, 2009), 62.

39. Anthony G. Amsterdam and Philip N. Meyer, "Making Our Clients' Stories Heard: A Guide to Narrative Strategies for Appellate and Postconviction Lawyers" (Administrative Office, U.S. Courts, 2008), 7.34.

40. Mieke Bal, *Narratology: Introduction to the Theory of Narrative* (Toronto: University of Toronto Press, 1997), 43–66; Michael J. Toolan, *Narrative: A Critical Linguistic Introduction* (New York: Routledge, 1994), 119–37.

41. Amsterdam and Meyer, "Making Our Clients' Stories Heard," 7.34.

42. Ibid., 7.35.

43. Porter, quoted in Plimpton, *Writers at Work*, 151.

44. Ibid., 152.

45. Tobias Wolff, *This Boy's Life: A Memoir* (New York: Harper and Row, 1989), 63.

46. Ibid., 87–88.

47. Ibid., 89–91.

48. Anthony G. Amsterdam and Jerome Bruner, *Minding the Law* (Cambridge, MA: Harvard University Press, 2002), 113–14.

49. Wolff, *This Boy's Life*, 88.

CHAPTER 5

1. Nick Ravo, "Mafia Trial in Hartford Opens with Guilty Plea," *New York Times*, May 4, 1991.

2. Edmund Mahony, "Defendant Takes Hits from Both Sides," *Hartford Courant*, July 17, 1991.

3. Alix Biel, "To Wit," *Hartford Courant*, May 16, 1993.

4. Jerome Bruner, *Actual Minds, Possible Worlds* (Cambridge, MA: Harvard University Press, 1986), 37.

5. Ibid., 38.

6. The strategy of redefining the story elements in the prosecution's case is one of three primary defense strategies. According to W. Lance Bennett and Martha Feldman, the defense may "alter the interpretation of a story's central action through challenge, redefinition, or reconstruction of the story itself." W. Lance Bennett and Martha Feldman, *Reconstructing Reality in the Courtroom: Justice and Judgment in American Culture* (Piscataway, NJ: Rutgers University Press, 1989), 98.

7. Mahony, "Defendant Takes Hits."

8. Transcript of Closing Argument at 6, *United States v. Bianco*, No. H-90-18 (AHN) (D. Conn. July 16, 1991) [hereinafter Transcript] (transcript of closing

argument of Jeremiah Donovan on behalf of Louis Failla), *aff'd,* 998 F.2d 1112, 1128 (2d Cir. 1993).

9. Ibid., 7–8.

10. Ibid., 8.

11. Ibid.

12. Ibid., 8–9.

13. Ibid., 9.

14. Ibid.

15. Ibid., 9–10.

16. Syd Field, *Screenplay: The Foundations of Screenwriting* (New York: Dellacorte Press, 1982), 9.

17. Ibid., 66.

18. Transcript, 10–11.

19. Ibid., 11.

20. Ibid.

21. Mahony, "Defendant Takes Hits."

22. Transcript, 12.

23. *Butch Cassidy and the Sundance Kid,* directed by George Roy Hill (1969).

24. Transcript, 13.

25. Ibid., 14.

26. Ibid., 19–20.

27. Ibid., 22–23.

28. Ibid., 24–25.

29. Ibid., 25.

30. Ibid., 26.

31. Ibid., 41–43.

32. Mahony, "Defendant Takes Hits."

33. Transcript, 47.

34. Ibid.

35. Ibid., 47–48.

36. Ibid., 49.

37. Ibid.

38. Ibid., 55.

39. Ibid., 56.

40. Ibid.

41. Ibid.

42. Ibid., 57.

43. Ibid., 57–58.

44. Ibid., 59.

45. Ibid.

46. Ibid.

47. Ibid.

48. Ibid., 60–61.
49. Ibid., 61.
50. Ibid., 61–62.
51. Ibid., 64.
52. Ibid., 64–65.
53. Ibid.
54. Syd Field, *The Screenwriter's Workbook* (New York: Dell, 1984), 86.
55. As pointed out earlier, according to Bennett and Feldman, the defense may "alter the interpretation of a story's central action through challenge, redefinition, or reconstruction of the story itself." Bennett and Feldman, *Reconstructing Reality*, 98. The success of this strategy "depends on the defense's ability to find a story element that is ambiguous enough to support another definition and, at the same time, central enough to the story to effect the meaning of the central action." Ibid., 102. Here, the defense attempted to provide a counterstory with "an internally consistent interpretation of the defendant's motives." Ibid., 103.
56. Transcript, 75–76.
57. Ibid., 74–75. Donovan tells the jury:

   You have a tougher job. In trying to determine intention, the person's intention is necessarily very largely a matter of inference. No witness, you know, can be expected to come in here and testify that he looked into another person's mind and saw therein a certain purpose or intention. I tried to do it with cartoons. I can't do it. No FBI agent or expert can come in and testify what Louie's intention was. Now how do we do it? One way in which a jury can determine what a person's purpose and intention was at any given time is by determining what that person's conduct was and what the circumstances were surrounding that conduct, and from these, from the conduct, to infer what his purpose or intention was. To draw such inferences is not only the privilege, but it's the duty of the jury, provided, of course, the inference you draw is a reasonable one. Ibid.

58. Ibid., 76. Donovan says, "we don't send people to jail, we don't take people away from their wives, their children, their grandchildren, unless we are persuaded that he has done what the Government said and persuaded beyond a reasonable doubt." Ibid.
59. Margaret Mehring, *The Screenplay: A Blend of Film, Form and Content* (Boston: Focal Press, 1990), 195.
60. Ibid.
61. Ibid., 54.
62. Ibid.
63. Robert McKee, lecture, Story Structure Workshop, March 11–12, (New York, 1990) (notes on file with the author).
64. Mehring, *The Screenplay*, 54.
65. Ibid., 55 (emphasis added).

CHAPTER 6

1. James Ellroy, *My Dark Places* (New York: Vintage Books, 1997).

2. Norman Mailer, *The Executioner's Song* (New York: Vintage, 1998), 223–24.

3. Truman Capote, *In Cold Blood* (New York: Vintage, 1994), 58–60, 62–65.

4. Frank McCourt, *Angela's Ashes* (New York: Simon & Schuster, Touchstone, 1996).

5. David Lodge, *The Art of Fiction:Illustrated from Classic and Modern Texts* (New York: Penguin Books, 1992): 117–19.

6. Ibid., 118.

7. Ibid., 119.

8. Anthony G. Amsterdam and Philip N. Meyer, "Making Our Clients' Stories Heard: A Guide to Narrative Strategies for Appellate and Postconviction Lawyers" (Administrative Office, U.S. Courts, 2008).

9. Jerome Bruner, *Beyond the Information Given: Studies in the Psychology of Knowing* (London: Allen and Unwin, 1974).

10. Ellroy, *My Dark Places*, 1.

11. Ibid., 2

12. Ibid.

13. Ibid., 3–6.

14. Lodge, *The Art of Fiction*, 117.

15. Ibid., 119.

16. Ibid.

17. Brief for Petitioner, *Riggins v. Nevada*, 504 U.S. 127 (1992).

18. Ibid., 2.

19. Ibid.

20. Ibid., 6–7.

21. Ibid., 8.

22. Ibid.

23. Ibid.

24. Ibid., 21.

25. David Lodge observes that the "purest form of showing" is "quoted speech of characters in which language exactly mirrors the event." Lodge, *The Art of Fiction*, 121.

26. Lodge observes that "the purest form of telling is authorial summary, in which the conciseness and abstraction of the narrator's language effaces the particularity of the characters and their actions." Ibid., 122.

27. Ty Alper, Anthony G. Amsterdam, Todd E. Edelman, Randy Hertz, Rachel Shapiro Janger, Sonya Rudenstine, and Robin Walker-Sterling, "Stories Told and Untold: Lawyering Theory Analyses of the First Rodney King Assault Trial," *Clinical Law Review* 12 (2005), 1.

28. Lodge, *The Art of Fiction*, 122.

29. Ibid.

30. Mailer, *The Executioner's Song*, 223–24.

31. Ibid.
32. Capote, *In Cold Blood*, 16.
33. Ibid., 60, 62.
34. Ibid., 61–62.
35. Ibid., 61–62.
36. Ibid., 64–66.
37. Ibid., 65–66.
38. Atkins v. Virginia, 536 U.S. 304 (2002), 2001 WL 1663817.
39. Gerald Prince, *A Dictionary of Narratology*, rev. ed. (Lincoln: University of Nebraska Press, 2003), 19. Prince defines "dialogic narrative" as "characterized by the interaction of several voices, consciousnesses, or world views, none of which unifies or is superior to (has more authority than) the others." In dialogic as opposed to monologic narrative, the narrator's views, judgments, and even knowledge do not constitute the ultimate authority with respect to the world represented but only one contribution among several—a contribution that is in dialogue with, and frequently less significant and perceptive than that of (some of), the characters.
40. Brief for Petitioner at 1, *Atkins v. Virginia*, 536 U.S. 304 (2002), 2001 WL 1663817.
41. Ibid., 2.
42. Ibid.
43. Ibid.
44. Ibid.
45. Ibid.
46. Ibid., 3.
47. Ibid.
48. Ibid.
49. Ibid., 4.
50. Ibid., 4–5.
51. Ibid., 6.
52. Ibid. (citations omitted).
53. Ibid., 6–7 (citations omitted).
54. John Gardner, *The Art of Fiction* (New York: Vintage Books, 1985), 155.
55. Ibid., 155–59.
56. Ibid., 155.
57. Ibid., 156.
58. Ibid., 157.
59. Ibid.
60. Lodge, *The Art of Fiction*, 26.
61. Brief for Petitioner at 38–39, *Atkins v. Virginia*, 536 U.S. 304 (2002), 2001 WL 1663817.
62. McCourt, *Angela's Ashes*, 11.

63. Ibid.

64. *Williams v. Taylor*, 529 U.S. 362 (2000), 1999 WL 459574.

65. Ibid., 3.

66. Ibid.

67. Ibid.

68. Ibid., 3–4

69. Ibid., 4–5.

70. Mailer, *The Executioner's Song*, 305–6, cited in Joshua Dressler, *Cases and Materials on Criminal Law* (St. Paul, MN: West, 2009), 46.

71. Wayne Booth, *The Rhetoric of Fiction*, 2d ed. (Chicago: University of Chicago Press, 1983), 274–81.

72. Transcript of the Morning Session of Closing Argument of Robert F. Devlin, Assistant United States Attorney, at 12, *United States v. Bianco*, No. H-90-18 (AHN) (D. Conn. Argued July 15, 1991) (D. Conn. 1990, *affirmed* 998 F.2d 1112 (2d Cir. 1993).

73. Ibid. at 22.

74. Transcript of Government's Rebuttal Closing Argument by John Durham, Assistant United States Attorney, at 50–51, *United States v. Bianco*, No. H-90-18 (AHN) (D. Conn. Argued July 18, 1991) (emphasis added).

75. Janet Malcolm, "Iphigenia in Forest Hills: Anatomy of a Murder Trial," *New Yorker*, May 3, 2010, 36.

76. Ibid., 36.

77. Ibid.

78. Ibid.

CHAPTER 7

1. Joan Didion, *The White Album* (New York: Farrar, Straus, Giroux, 1979), 42.

2. According to former "Family" member Brooks Poston, Manson told the group on New Year's Eve 1968: "Are you hep to what the Beatles are saying? Helter Skelter is coming down. The Beatles are telling it like it is." "The Influence of The Beatles on Charles Manson," last accessed March 25, 2012, at http://law2.umkc.edu/faculty/projects/ftrials/manson/mansonbeatles.html.

3. Bob Dylan, *Nashville Skyline,* Columbia Records,1969.

4. Leonard Cohen, *Songs of Leonard Cohen*, Columbia Records, 1967.

5. John Gardner, *The Art of Fiction* (New York: Vintage Books, 1985), 45.

6. *Rusk v. State*, 43 Md. App. 476, 406 A. 2d 624 (1979). The Maryland Supreme Court reversed the decision of the Court of Special Appeals in *State v. Rusk*, 289 Md. 230, 424 A.2d 720 (1981).

7. *Rusk v. State*, 43 Md. App. at 484, 406 A.2d at 628.

8. Ibid.

9. Ibid., 488–492, 406 A.2d at 631–32.

10. W.G. Sebald. *The Emigrants* (Frankfurt: Eichborn; London: Harvill Press, 1996), 112.

11. Ibid., 115–16.

12. Brief for Petitioner, *Reck v. Ragen* [decided *sub nom.* Reck v. Pate], 1961 WL 101763.

13. Ibid., 14–21 (footnotes containing transcript references and additional detail omitted). This is only a portion of a much longer narrative of Reck's interrogation. The full narrative runs from page 10 through page 40. For another example of this kind of detailed narration of police interrogation in intimidating settings, see Brief for the Petitioner, *Clewis v. Texas*, 1966 WL 100419, at 12–25.

14. *Miranda v. Arizona*, 384 U.S. 436 (1966).

15. Brief for Petitioner, *Miranda v. Arizona*, 384 U.S. 436 (1966) (transcript references and footnotes omitted), at 10.

16. Donovan's notes, for example, call one of Failla's friends "a character right out of Damon Runyon," noting that Runyon was "a journalist, author, and film writer and producer whose slick and racy Broadway characters provided the inspiration for Frank Loesser's musical *Guys and Dolls*." Jeremiah Donovan, "Some Off-the-Cuff Remarks about Lawyers as Storytellers," *Vermont Law Review* 18 (1994), 751, 752, citing *Encyclopedia Americana* (international ed., 1986), 870.

17. *House of Games*, written and directed by David Mamet (1987); *Heist*, written and directed by David Mamet (2001).

18. *Pulp Fiction*, cowritten and directed by Quentin Tarantino (1994).

19. Kathryn Harrison, *While They Slept: An Inquiry into the Murder of a Family* (New York: Random House, 2008).

20. Ibid., 128–30.

21. Ibid., 134–36.

22. Brief for Petitioner, *Eddings v. Oklahoma*, 455 U.S. 104 (1982), 1981 WL 389845.

23. Ibid., 12–14 (transcript references and footnotes omitted).

CHAPTER 8

1. Kurt Vonnegut Jr., *Slaughterhouse Five or The Children's Crusade: A Duty-Dance with Death* (New York: Delacorte Press/Seymour Lawrence, 1994), 70–72.

2. Gerald Prince, *A Dictionary of Narratology*, rev. ed. (Lincoln: University of Nebraska Press, 2003), 13.

3. David Lodge, *The Art of Fiction: Illustrated from Classic and Modern Texts* (New York: Penguin Books, 1992), 74

4. Prince, *A Dictionary of Narratology*, 76.

5. Vonnegut, *Slaughterhouse Five*, 84.

6. Prince, *A Dictionary of Narratology*, 5.

7. Ibid., 82.

8. Ibid., 5.

9. Transcript of Closing Argument at 10–11, *United States v. Bianco*, No. H-90-18 (AHN) (D. Conn. July 16, 1991) [hereinafter Transcript] (transcript of closing argument of Jeremiah Donovan on behalf of Louis Failla), *aff'd*, 998 F.2d 1112, 1128 (2d Cir. 1993).

10. Ibid.

11. Prince, *A Dictionary of Narratology*, 78.

12. "Completing prolepses fill in later gaps from ellipses in the narrative. Repeating prolepses, or advance notices, recount ahead of time events that will be recounted again." Ibid., 77.

13. Michael S. Lief, H. Mitchell Caldwell, and Ben Bycel, *Ladies and Gentlemen of the Jury: Greatest Closing Arguments in Modern Law* (New York: Simon & Schuster, 1998), 154–55.

14. Ibid.

15. Prince, *A Dictionary of Narratology*, 77.

16. Ibid., 25.

17. Ibid.

18. Transcript, at 10–11.

19. Ibid.

20. Vonnegut, *Slaughterhouse Five*, 20–21.

21. Anthony G. Amsterdam and Philip N. Meyer, "Making Our Clients' Stories Heard: A Guide to Narrative Strategies for Appellate and Postconviction Lawyers" (Administrative Office, U.S. Courts, 2008) 10.13–10.15.

CHAPTER 9

1. Anthony G. Amsterdam and Jerome Bruner, *Minding the Law* (Cambridge, MA: Harvard University Press, 2000).

2. Narrative and story are, most simply put and for our immediate purposes, synonymous. Narrative is the more highbrow and academic term, more sophisticated perhaps; while story is more down-to-earth and commonplace. Some academics make fine high cultural distinctions between these two words. See, for example, Gerald Prince's definitions of and distinctions between narrative and story in *A Dictionary of Narratology*, rev. ed. (Lincoln: University of Nebraska Press, 2003).

3. Robert Cover, "Violence and the Word," *Yale Law Journal* 95 (1986), 1601.

Index

Failla and, 101–3
of *The Hand*, 14–16
in *High Noon*, 20–27
in *Jaws*, 20–27
in movies, 70
narrative logic of, 12–13, 18
narrative profluence in, 11–12, 64
pacing of, 197–99
sequence of, 11, 12, 13
setting for, 156
themes and, 16
voice and, 118
plot goals, 112–13
struggle toward, 113
plot trajectory
constraints on, 12–13
in melodrama, 65, 66
of novels, 8
opening and, 8
point of view. *See* perspective
Poo-tee-wee, 199
popular culture, 6
Porter, Katherine Anne, 84
post hoc ergo propter hoc fallacy, 189–90
premature ending, in melodrama, 24
present-tense voice, 6
in *The Estate of Karen Silkwood v.
Kerr-McGee*, 29, 38–39, 52
Prince, Gerald, 189–90, 195, 198–99
proem, 32
in *The Estate of Karen Silkwood v.
Kerr-McGee*, 58–59
profluence. *See* narrative profluence
progressive complications
of antagonist, 24
by Donovan, 92, 111
in *The Estate of Karen Silkwood v.
Kerr-McGee*, 41–43
in *High Noon*, 25–26
prolepsis, 194–95
Propp, Vladimir, 63
protagonist. *See also* hero

characters as, 74–75
Failla as, 92, 96–97
as hero, 78–80
inner contradiction of, 112
scene and, 78
screenwriters on, 112, 113
steady state and, 24
punitive damages, 19
in *The Estate of Karen Silkwood v.
Kerr-McGee*, 31, 35
purposeful motion, toward ending, 64

Quintilian, 202

Racketeer Influenced and Corrupt
Organizations Act (RICO), 91, 95,
97, 100, 208
Ramirez, Helen (fictional character), in
High Noon, 77, 80–81
rape, 160–64
rebuttal
in *The Estate of Karen Silkwood v.
Kerr-McGee*, 29, 38, 40, 52–55
hero and, 40
steady state and, 38
Reck, Emil, 170–75
Reck v. Ragen, 170–75
Reich, Charles, 41–42
"Remarks About Lawyers as Storytellers"
(Donovan), 202
reverse causality, 190
rhetorical questions, 51
by Donovan, 104
rhythm
chronology and, 197–99
Lodge on, 119
in movies, 198–99
voice and, 119–26
rhythms of language, 5
RICO. *See* Racketeer Influenced and
Corrupt Organizations Act
Ricoeur, Paul, 8